Training Compassion

The Official Guide to CBCT®

Lobsang Tenzin Negi, PhD

with Timothy Harrison, MArch and Michelle Liberman, MSc

Foreword by His Holiness the **Dalai Lama**

Center for Contemplative
Science and Compassion-Based Ethics
Emory University

Find out more at *compassion.emory.edu*

ISBN: 978-1-962972-00-0 (Hardback edition)
ISBN: 978-1-962972-01-7 (Paperback edition)
ISBN: 978-1-962972-02-4 (Ebook edition)

Developmental editing by Michael Rohani
Book design by DesignForBooks.com

Photo credits: Background textures on pages i–ix, xi–xiii, xvi–1, 24–25, 38–41, 58–61, 76–79, 98–101, 126–129, 150–153, 178–181, 202–205, 228–229, 236–237, 240–241, 246–247, 250–251, 263, 269, 271; White Snow/Shutterstock.com, page x; Liudmila Kotvitckaia/Shutterstock.com, page x; Dalai Lama Trust page xi; Studio Barcelona/Shutterstock.com, page xvi; Hung Chung Chih/Shutterstock.com, page 3; Scomputer Photo/Shutterstock.com, page 5; Muskoka Stock Photos/Shutterstock.com, page 24; Africa Studio/Shutterstock.com, page 29; Monkey Business Images/Shutterstock.com; page 33; Fizkes/Shutterstock.com, page 36; Fizkes/Shutterstock.com, page 38; Vvvita/Shutterstock.com, page 42; Eldar Nurkovic/Shutterstock.com, page 42; M Agency/Shutterstock.com, page 42; Michaelvbg/Shutterstock.com, page 42; Anatta_tan/Shutterstock.com, page 42; Wavebreakmedia/Shutterstock.com, page 45; Elizaveta Galitckaia/Shutterstock.com, page 47; Ju999/Shutterstock, page 47; Leolintang/Shutterstock.com, page 58; Lolostock/Shutterstock.com, page 64; Africa Studio/Shutterstock.com, page 67; B-D-S Piotr Marcinski/Shutterstock.com, page 67; Korneeva Kristina/Shutterstock.com, page 67; Vvoe/Shutterstock.com, page 76; Wosunan/Shutterstock.com, page 82; Teerasan Phutthigorn/Shutterstock.com, page 84; Taniascamera/Shutterstock.com, page 89; Andrejs Polivanovs/Shutterstock.com, page 89; Krakenimages/Shutterstock.com, page 98, Keith Klosterman/Shutterstock.com, page 103; Photo of mural in the Nava Jetavana temple, Shravasti, Uttar Pradesh, taken by Anandajoti, page 106; Marek Poplawski/Shutterstock.com, page 109; Eakrin Rasadonyindee/Shutterstock.com, page 114; Twinsterphoto/Shutterstock.com, page 117; Avanna Photography/Shutterstock.com, page 124; Patcharanan/Shutterstock.com, page 126; Southbank Centre (https://www.flickr.com/photos/southbankcentre/13008430294/), page 132; Vixit/Shutterstock.com, page 134; Basson Van Zyl/Shutterstock.com, page 139; Harbucks/Shutterstock.com, page 143; Arthimedes/Shutterstock.com, page 150; Ramon Martinez/Shutterstock.com, page 159; Macrovector/Shutterstock.com, page 162; Ground Picture/Shutterstock.com, page 164; Kangsar/Shutterstock.com, page 169; SergeyIT/Shutterstock.com, page 177; Fizkes/Shutterstock.com, page 178; Katrina Brown/Shutterstock.com, page 182; Munawer Munawer/Shutterstock.com, page 183; Rawpixel.Com/Shutterstock.com, page 185; Aleksandr Finch/Shutterstock.com, page 187; BearFotos/Shutterstock.com, page 187; Dgdimension/Shutterstock.com, page 187; Drazen Zigic/Shutterstock.com, page 217; Dusan Petkovic/Shutterstock.com, page 187; Jesus-Keller/Shutterstock.com, page 187; Karkas/Shutterstock.com, page 187; Maya Lab/Shutterstock.com, page 187; Rawpixel.com/Shutterstock.com, page 187; Seventyfour/Shutterstock.com, page 187; Yuttana Contributor Studio/Shutterstock.com, page 187; Thinnapob Proongsak/Shutterstock.com, page 202; Veja/Shutterstock.com, page 207; Michael Zysman/Shutterstock.com, page 208; Simone Hogan/Shutterstock.com, page 212; Regissercom/Shutterstock.com, page 215; Maqe/Shutterstock.com, page 217; Fizkes/Shutterstock.com, page 218; Children in Crossfire/Richard Moore page 210; Itx Ismail/Shutterstock.com, page 228; Emory University/advisory council, page 241; Emory University/Dalai Lama, page 245; Cover photo, (background texture) White Snow/Shutterstock.com, cover illustrations by Michael Rohani.

Printed in the U.S.A.

Contents

Module 5 Cultivating Self-Compassion: Part 2 127

Module 6 Expanding Our Circle of Concern 151

To humanity

Foreword

For more than two decades now, I have been leading and encouraging discussions with scientists and educators on ways to incorporate the values of compassion and ethics into our everyday life, including in the education system. My reason for doing so is not to promote Buddhism. Rather, through my own personal experience, I have seen the benefit of the Nalanda Tradition of Buddhism, specifically the mind-training teachings, in preserving my peace of mind. It has also enabled me to sharpen my mind through analysis.

Emory University President Gregory L. Fenves and Provost Ravi V. Bellamkonda meeting with His Holiness the Dalai Lama in Dharmsala, India, in December 2022.

All human beings want happiness and don't want suffering, but both relate to our mental state. Therefore, having peace of mind and being less subject to destructive emotions are very useful, and so this ancient Indian knowledge can be of benefit to the whole of humanity. This education should be conducted in a strictly secular context so that everyone can benefit from it irrespective of one's religious status.

I remain grateful to Emory University in being one of the partners in implementing this idea. Its Cognitively Based Compassion-Training (CBCT®) as well as Social, Emotional and Ethical Learning (SEE Learning®) have the objective of bringing secular ethics and compassion training to educators and students in schools and universities as widely as possible.

CBCT in particular is based on the mind-training tradition. Emory has developed a systematic protocol for cultivating compassion through analytical meditation. For almost two decades, such a system has been the subject of scientific research that has demonstrated the tangible benefits of compassion training. The hope is now to extend the program so that it can benefit as many people around the world as possible, and this is the intention behind

Emory's Compassion Shift® initiative. This guide comprehensively explains the practices for cultivating compassion, and I feel it will be useful to everyone.

My partnership with Emory University goes back to the founding of the Emory–Tibet Partnership in 1998. I am encouraged by the University's continued efforts to research and promote the basic human value of compassion, and I commend Emory and Dr. Lobsang Tenzin Negi's long-standing contribution to them.

Tenzin Gyatso
His Holiness the 14th Dalai Lama
29 September 2023

Preface

Lobsang Tenzin Negi was born in the Himalayas and trained in Tibetan Buddhist monasteries under the tutelage of His Holiness the Dalai Lama. Upon completing the Geshe Lharampa degree, the highest-level degree in Tibetan monastic education, he came to Atlanta, Georgia, in 1991. He had been advised by the Dalai Lama to pursue studies in modern psychology and cognitive science in order to explore how an interdisciplinary bridging of Western scientific and Buddhist perspectives on the mind and emotions could contribute to a deeper understanding of the human condition and address the ailments of modern society. He thus enrolled in a PhD program at Emory University's Institute of Liberal Arts, a department focused on interdisciplinary study and research. His dissertation focused on the impact of emotions on wellbeing from both scientific and Tibetan Buddhist perspectives. Upon completing his doctorate, he began teaching in Emory's Department of Religion in 2000.

It was in 2003, while he was teaching "Tibetan Buddhism: The Psychology of Enlightenment," that the seeds of a compassion training protocol were planted. One student in the class, Molly Harrington, was engaged in efforts to raise awareness of mental health on campus. She saw that many students were struggling with anxiety and depression—often in isolation. Moreover, she recognized that stigma around mental health issues was depriving many students of the very thing that might help them most: connection and belonging. Ms. Harrington was convinced that the same contemplative practices covered in the class, if put in the form of a program, could be healing for students across campus. She encouraged Prof. Negi to develop such a program.

"We need a revolution of compassion based on warm-heartedness that will contribute to a more compassionate world with a sense of oneness of humanity."

— HIS HOLINESS THE DALAI LAMA, *OUR ONLY HOME: A CLIMATE APPEAL TO THE WORLD*

For Prof. Negi, Ms. Harrington's request brought to mind the Dalai Lama's 1998 Emory commencement address, in which he emphasized the indispensable role of compassion in contributing to our flourishing at an individual and societal level. His Holiness had already written extensively on the benefits of expanding compassion and the specific methods for its achievement, in *The Art of Happiness* (co-authored with Howard C. Cutler) and *Ethics for the New Millennium*. Drawing from these seminal works, as well as his own interdisciplinary research in the science of mind and emotions and his deep familiarity with the extensive Tibetan Buddhist *lojong* ("mind-training") tradition, Prof. Negi developed the rationale and method for a secular compassion training program that could be practiced by people of any, or no, religious faith.

This program, known as CBCT® (Cognitively Based Compassion Training), is a set of contemplative practices that helps participants establish and cultivate safety, mindfulness, self-compassion, and compassion for others. CBCT was created with the goal of contributing to greater human flourishing.

Since its development in 2004, CBCT has been offered to countless Emory students through the counseling center, and in 2020, it became an accredited class for undergraduates. Further, CBCT has been introduced and taught in medical schools, hospital systems, and chaplaincy trainings. It has been practiced by teachers, nurses, veterans with post-traumatic stress disorder (PTSD), men with AIDS, incarcerated peoples, and so many others. The CBCT teacher certification program has yielded hundreds of Emory-certified CBCT instructors practicing around the world, including India, Israel, England, Germany, Brazil, Mexico, Spain, Korea, Taiwan, Mongolia, and New Zealand. The training materials have been translated into Portuguese, Spanish, and German.

Emory's Center for Contemplative Science and Compassion-Based Ethics (informally known as the Compassion Center) is dedicated to refining this technique in compassion training that has been tested over millennia in order to bring healing at an individual, social, and systems level. For over two decades, the Compassion Center has invited neuroscientists and psychologists to study the positive effects of practicing CBCT on wellbeing, and the results have been promising. These studies have shown that it is possible to cultivate compassion, and we further believe it is possible for it to become an enduring trait, our second nature, even while we care for ourselves and become stronger individuals.

Today, CBCT holds the distinction of being one of the longest-running and most studied compassion protocols of its kind. It has formed the cornerstone of a global initiative, the Compassion Shift, which aims to advance a global culture of compassion through two educational programs—CBCT for adults and SEE Learning® (Social, Emotional and Ethical Learning) for children. The Compassion Shift owes much to the generosity of its founding benefactors: the Gaden Phodrang Foundation of the Dalai Lama and the Rob and Melani Walton Foundation, as well as the major contributions of Pierre and Pamela Omidyar and Alessia Bulgari. As part of this initiative, CBCT is being custom-tailored to assist professionals in four important fields: healthcare, business, education, and mental health. This will go a long way in supporting the Compassion Center's long-term vision of a compassionate and ethical world for all.

A NOTE ON SEE LEARNING®
(SOCIAL, EMOTIONAL AND ETHICAL LEARNING)

In 2015, Prof. Negi was asked by the Dalai Lama to develop a framework and curricula for secular ethics to be implemented in schools around the world. This program came to be known as SEE Learning. Prof. Negi led a team of trained CBCT instructors to design the framework. The team drew heavily on their CBCT training, as well as prior experience in adapting the meditative protocol for elementary school children and foster children. Again, the writings of the Dalai Lama proved foundational to the development of SEE Learning.

Like CBCT, SEE Learning uses contemplative and reflective exercises to establish and support the practices of cultivating safety, mindfulness, self-compassion, and compassion for others, moving from received knowledge to personalized insight to embodied understanding. In this way, CBCT and SEE Learning share the same underlying principles and many of the same practices, although the latter is specifically adapted to the needs and contexts of educators, schools, and students. Since its development, SEE Learning has reached more than seven million children and has been adopted in school systems in more than 40 countries, from India to Ukraine, from Brazil to Mongolia. Learn more at seelearning.emory.edu

Overview of CBCT

"The ultimate source of a happy life is warm-heartedness. Even animals display some sense of compassion. When it comes to human beings, compassion can be combined with intelligence. Through the application of reason, compassion can be extended to all seven billion human beings."

— THE DALAI LAMA,
WITH RASMUS HOUGAARD, *HARVARD BUSINESS REVIEW*, 2021

Part 1: Why Train Compassion?

What Is Compassion?

Compassion has been explored for centuries by philosophers, religious leaders, writers, and poets, and more recently by scientists, and there are many different understandings of what it means. Many associate it with sympathy, empathy, or love. Some view compassion as an emotion or a motivation, while others believe it requires action. Some see it as weak or even dangerous, others, as strong and energizing. Some view compassion as a luxury, others, as essential for humanity's survival.

Pause and consider: What is your view of compassion?

For now, as you begin this CBCT journey, see if you can stay open to exploring compassion with fresh eyes.

Compassion, and specifically the training of compassion, has been a primary focus of the *lojong* or "mind-training" tradition of Indo-Tibetan Buddhism for over a thousand years. More recently, compassion has captured the interest of scientists in the fields of evolutionary biology, psychology, and neuroscience, leading to research and discoveries that support these ancient practices.

CBCT reflects the coming together of the rich *lojong* tradition and recent scientific understanding. The protocol relies on perspectives from both worlds to provide a program accessible to people of diverse backgrounds, including those with a strong faith tradition and those with none at all. CBCT understands compassion as follows:

Compassion is the warm-hearted concern that unfolds when we witness the suffering of others and feel motivated to relieve it.

WHAT ABOUT LOVE?

Love is the warm-hearted wish to see others happy and well. Like compassion, love also springs from feelings of endearment and from a genuine concern for others' wellbeing. In the *lojong* tradition, love and compassion are described as deeply interconnected. When we have this warm-hearted concern for others, we naturally want them to be happy, and we don't want them to suffer. In this way, love and compassion always go together.

The warm-hearted urge to relieve suffering is a natural capacity of the human heart. Based on over 40 years of research as a primatologist and ethologist, Frans de Waal explains that all human beings share a common foundation for compassion rooted in biology. While this biologically based compassion is innate, it is also limited, in that we mostly feel it for those closest to us. However, despite the biased nature of innate compassion, de Waal points out that human beings also have a natural capacity to extend compassion more broadly to larger and more diverse groups.[1]

CBCT is designed to do just this: to expand our compassion and make it more inclusive. In this way, compassion is understood as a capacity or a skill that can be trained like any other. Much like learning to speak a language or to play a sport or musical instrument, compassion can become effortless and spontaneous through practice. And notably, it is never too late to start cultivating this capacity. In recent decades, neuroscientists have used advanced brain imaging to discover that our brains can grow new neurons (brain cells) and regenerate damaged ones throughout our lives. In fact, intentional efforts to train our minds produces measurable and lasting impacts on the structure of our brains.[2] This supports the notion that we always have the capacity to change and, more specifically, that we can train compassion.

Personal Reflection[3]

"CBCT has given me a chance to reevaluate the purpose and current trajectory of my life. It has pointed my nose in a direction allowing me to become who I might hope to be—or at least give it my best shot! It has allowed me to acquire a strong and confident backbone, while simultaneously being able to exhibit an open heart. Let me proclaim that this opening back up to the world, with a compassionate stance, was no small feat."

— **CBCT** INSTRUCTOR AND PRACTITIONER

Connecting to Compassion

1. Consider the CBCT definition of compassion: *the warm-hearted concern that unfolds when we witness the suffering of others and feel motivated to relieve it.*

2. Look around and find an object that represents either a memory or quality of compassion.

   ❀ Examples: a photo of a loved one, a blanket given by a grandparent, a symbol or image from your faith tradition, a vase of flowers, a stone that connects you with nature, a warm cup of tea, a work of art, a piece of jewelry or clothing, an instrument, a note from a friend.

3. Once you've found your object, take a few moments to write about or reflect on why you chose it.

   ❀ If your object represents a memory of compassion, describe how it felt to experience warm-hearted concern and the motivation to relieve suffering, or how it felt to be on the receiving end of compassion.

   ❀ If your object represents a quality of compassion, describe the characteristics of the object that fit with the definition.

4. Take a few moments to reflect on what it was like to connect to compassion through this object. What types of feelings or sensations do you notice right now as you reflect on compassion in this way? What have you learned through this activity? Write down 5–10 words or a few phrases that come to mind.

▶ Takeaway

Compassion is something we can tap into, wherever we are. Even ordinary objects carry meaning and associations that remind us of supportive moments and memories. They can serve as comfort when we feel upset or sick and bring joy or warm-heartedness to a difficult or average day. As we connect to compassion in this way, we can uncover its meaning, presence, and value in our everyday lives.

Anchoring Story

Fundamental Need for Compassion: A True Story

When victorious soldiers entered a detention camp at the end of World War II, they were met by hundreds of children who had survived unspeakable horrors. As a first task, the soldiers set up a soup station to slowly reintroduce food and nutrients to the starving kids. The children formed two lines as the soldiers did their best to ensure that what they had lasted long enough to feed each child. It was not enough; the soup ran out in one of the lines. As the next child approached in that line, the soldier serving soup froze, holding his empty ladle. He stared at the young boy, hungry and weak, and was overcome with a deep desire to help. Not knowing what else to do, the soldier knelt and embraced him.

After what felt like a long time, the soldier looked up and noticed that some of the children who had been standing in the other soup line had abandoned it. They formed a new line in front of him, each of them waiting their turn to receive a hug. While they still needed nutritious food, what was even more pressing for them in that moment was their need to feel safe and nurtured. In other words, they needed compassion.

Where would we be without compassion? Each of us enters this world helpless and vulnerable; from birth, we depend on others to attune to our needs and care for us. When we really think about it, our need for compassion is as basic as our need for nourishing food or clean water. This is true not just for individuals, but, as the Dalai Lama has urgently stated, for the survival of humanity as a whole.

Of course, this is not to suggest that compassion could stand in for basic material needs, but rather that emotional needs are equally essential for wellbeing. Neither material needs nor emotional needs are enough in and of themselves; we all need both to thrive.

"Love and compassion are necessities, not luxuries. Without them, humanity cannot survive."

— THE DALAI LAMA, ART OF HAPPINESS, 1998

Compassion Training Supports Wellbeing

Does compassion training contribute to wellbeing? Does it have measurable benefits on our health? These are the questions that the initial studies of CBCT set out to answer in 2005. To examine the impact of compassion training on stress, first-year college students at Emory University were put through a carefully monitored test designed to induce psychological stress. The test allowed researchers to examine the students' stress responses through blood samples, measuring the stress hormone, cortisol, and the inflammation marker, interleukin-6, or IL-6.

Our body's response to a psychological stressor can be measured in a lab with remarkable consistency. The adrenal glands raise cortisol hormone levels in the blood, getting us ready for what researchers term the fight-or-flight state. Meanwhile, the immune system activates inflammation, as marked by the presence of IL-6 in the blood, getting us ready to fight off infection. Taken together, these two phenomena show that the human body tends to respond to psychological stress in much the same way that it responds to physical pain.

After administering the stress tests, researchers then looked at the participants' rate of recovery. They found that participants recovered faster from a stress test after having taken CBCT, but only those who practiced for 90 minutes or more per week (an average of 13 minutes per day). Their cortisol returned more quickly to baseline, in what psychologists consider a measure of resilience. Their levels of IL-6 in blood tests were significantly lower as well, showing less inflammation after the training.[4]

A little stress can be a good thing. It can help us feel sharp and vibrant and ready to learn. But chronic stress, that feeling of being intensely or constantly on alert, is associated with heart disease, cancer, diabetes, and other inflammatory diseases. Chronic stress can impact the daily quality of life, causing fatigue, brain fog, and a feeling of edginess. It can lead to anxiety and depression, as well as make us feel irritable, withdrawn, and disconnected when, in fact, connection is what we may need most as social beings.[5]

These initial studies began to demonstrate how CBCT, if practiced regularly, can help mitigate chronic stress by strengthening resilience. Over time, more research has suggested a number of other promising outcomes:

CBCT RESEARCH OUTCOMES

Significant decrease in:

- ᕼ stress biomarkers and inflammatory response[6]
- ᕼ depression[7]
- ᕼ loneliness[8]
- ᕼ PTSD symptoms[9]

Significant increase in:

- ᕼ hopefulness[10]
- ᕼ compassion and related neural activity[11]
- ᕼ empathy and related neural activity[12]
- ᕼ self-compassion[13]

For a full list of published CBCT studies, visit compassion.emory.edu.

The early CBCT studies suggested a clear link between cultivating compassion and improved *resilience*—our ability to bounce back emotionally from stressful experiences. The field of compassion science has since grown, and numerous studies also suggest that compassion training is linked to improved emotion regulation and wellbeing—decreasing rumination, activating pleasure circuits in the brain, increasing self-reported happiness, creating more optimistic and supportive communication styles, and serving as an antidote to burnout.[14]

Science, history, and common sense all point to the reality that compassion is essential for survival. One could say that humans evolved to favor compassion! Without cooperation, trust, gratitude, and reciprocity—as well as the many other qualities associated with compassion—humans would not have survived, let alone flourished.[15] These attributes have protected and supported all social groups of humans and other mammals, as well as a number of more simple organisms, such as ants and bees.

Personal Reflection

"As a 35-year-old veteran with a history of trauma, depression, and traumatic brain injury, I have found tremendous relief from the CBCT program. I have registered three times now, so for 30 weeks, I have been studying and practicing, and I can now say that I can meditate anywhere, and no longer struggle with attentional or interpersonal tasks at work. At home, I no longer engage interpersonally in ways that increase or cause me anger, and my relatives and friends have even commented on my lack of reactivity. I have become a daily meditator, and I use CBCT principles to be a practitioner in everyday life."

— PARTICIPANT IN A **CBCT** STUDY WITH MILITARY VETERANS

Part 2: A Cognitive Approach

Why Is CBCT Cognitively Based?

While it is true that compassion is primarily an emotion, emotions are inextricably linked with cognition. For example, if a child sees their favorite teacher walk into the room, they may feel joy. But this response would not be the same for every child—a student who does not know this teacher may feel fear when they walk in. Same teacher, different emotions. The difference is due to the students' *cognitive appraisal*—how they view the teacher. Cognitive appraisals typically unfold unintentionally and below the level of awareness. However, we can make conscious cognitive shifts that lead to corresponding shifts in our emotions. So while compassion is an emotion, it is also deeply linked to and dependent on cognition.

Cognitive Strategies for Regulating Emotions

The primary goal of compassion training is to expand and deepen warm-hearted feelings for others, and CBCT applies various cognitive strategies to regulate our emotions and foster this warm-heartedness. In 2020, scientists at Stanford University identified three emotion regulation strategies that correlate to three distinct areas of activation in the brain:[16]

- **Attention deployment:** The ability to shift the attention away from something that causes an unwanted emotional response and hold it on something else.

- **Self-distancing:** The ability to step back from one's own emotions and thoughts and to witness them without becoming overly entangled.

- **Cognitive reappraisal**: The ability to shift one's perspective on a situation as a means of transforming harmful habits and reinforcing healthier emotional and behavioral responses.

The word for meditation is bhavana in Sanskrit, which literally translates as to cultivate. In Tibetan, it's called gom, which translates as to familiarize. CBCT trains the mind in order to cultivate compassion and to familiarize ourselves with the skills and perspectives that generate and sustain it.

To expand compassion, CBCT draws on ancient meditation practices that tap into all three of these powerful strategies.

These three strategies are strengthened in CBCT through two modes of meditation, stabilizing and analytical. *Stabilizing meditation* is the more common mode in contemporary practice. Stabilizing meditation helps us strengthen attention deployment and self-distancing. This, in turn, gives us greater control over our attention and impulses, as well as greater insight into our mental patterns. After some practice with these skills, we shift to *analytical meditation*. In analytical meditation we practice the strategy of cognitive reappraisal. This means that we explore broader and more realistic perspectives that can promote healthier and more compassionate responses to the situations we encounter.

Personal Reflection

"I feel I know myself better after this training. I feel like I have better control of my emotions, and/or am able to control my reactions or judgments in situations I don't have any control over. I have gotten to learn about my 'faulty thought patterns' and to accept them, which is not an easy task. Now, it is a question of continuing to work with what I have learned about myself and continue applying what I have learned. In some cases, I am able to even show compassion, but if the feelings toward the person who has hurt me are too strong, at least I am able to not let them consume me. This training and the group of people who attended it with me have helped me immensely in dealing with my happiness and helping others with theirs, when possible."

— CANCER SURVIVOR AND CBCT PRACTITIONER

The CBCT Model of Change

One of the things that helps us cultivate compassion is integrating new views into our ways of thinking. However, taking on new views—even when we want to—does not always happen easily or right away, especially when the views are different from the ones we currently hold. The CBCT Model of Change presents a process by which we can deepen perspectives to foster lasting and meaningful shifts over time. This model draws on a comprehensive approach from the *lojong* tradition called *ta-gom-cho-sum* in Tibetan, which translates to "view-familiarization-behavior."

View here refers to us gaining a more accurate perspective on things, or arriving at a deeper or broader understanding of a situation, which in turn can help us have a healthier response to that situation. *Familiarization* is the process of deepening these perspectives so that they become gradually embodied. Once embodied, these views naturally lead to an enduring shift in *behavior*. Here, "behavior" includes both the emotional responses and the subsequent actions on account of these emotions. The more we embody these accurate views through deliberately engaging the familiarization process, the more spontaneous our healthier responses become.

This approach can be powerful for changing an unwanted habitual reaction—a harmful behavior, an emotional hang-up, a prejudice, a cycle of frustration with a family member, a tendency to excessively self-criticize—and for cultivating a healthier reaction that contributes to our wellbeing or to the wellbeing of others. Such changes take time and practice. To fully take on a new or broader view, the model offers a step-by-step approach to move through three levels of understanding, as explained below:

Contemporary science tells us that our perspectives influence how we feel, and how we feel then influences how we act. The "view-familiarization-behavior" approach from the ancient *lojong* tradition aligns with this scientific understanding. Foundational to this approach—and to the CBCT Model of Change—is using cognitive reappraisal to reshape emotional and behavioral responses. This technique is also central to several leading evidence-based therapies, including Cognitive Behavioral Therapy, Dialectical Behavioral Therapy, and Mindfulness-Based Cognitive Therapy. Paul Ekman, a psychologist and pioneer of emotion science, emphasizes the importance of reappraisal in his emotion timeline model as well. We will refer to Ekman's work in the later modules of CBCT, beginning in Module 4.

Level 1—Content Knowledge: To reshape our views, we first need to understand them at an intellectual level. This first level of understanding comes from receiving content knowledge—hearing or reading about a new or broader view on a given topic. We gain this knowledge through activities such as reading informative books, listening to podcasts, or attending classes or talks. This level of understanding is reached when the information we receive makes logical sense to us and we are able to recall it in detail. While this is an important first step, this is insufficient to bring about changes to deeper, ingrained habits of thinking and behaving.

Level 2—Personalized Insight: Personalized insight is the second level of understanding where we resonate with the knowledge and connect it to our lived experience. This is developed through critical thinking and reflective practices, including insight activities and formal analytical meditations, along with informal practices where we bring the insights into our daily lives. (We'll explore more about formal and informal practices in the next chapter, "Getting Started"). These practices are designed to inspire "aha" moments, connecting the content knowledge to our lived reality, and moving our understanding from the head to the heart. At this level, we experience increased meaning, motivation, and conviction, and for this reason, personalized insight has much more impact than content knowledge alone. But even so, these insights can be fleeting and in themselves may not lead to lasting changes.

Level 3—Embodied Understanding: Embodied understanding is the third and final level of understanding. Here, the insights have fully soaked in and become second nature. We move toward this level by continuing the process of familiarization—examining the personalized insights from new or different angles, applying them to diverse situations, and then deliberately sustaining these insights in our awareness. This is done through formal practices that combine stabilizing and analytical meditation, along with informal practices that bring the insights into our daily lives. Embodying more realistic and helpful views leads to spontaneous, healthier emotional and behavioral responses. Through this process, desired habits become our new disposition, and unwanted habits are left behind.

This model can apply to many areas of life. For example, let's imagine we want to learn how to swim. We might start off by reading instructional books to inform us on technique—how to tread water, how to kick our legs and move our arms through the water. This learning is the first level of understanding—*content knowledge.* While this helps us gain an understanding of how to swim, it would be challenging to fully grasp the concepts until we are in the water and trying for ourselves. Moving our legs about in the shallow end of the pool, practicing the backstroke, we gain a personal and felt understanding of the content. This experience, and the associated "aha" moments, is the second level of understanding—*personalized insight.* But even still, going in the water once or twice won't be enough to become a natural swimmer. It will take many times getting into the water and practicing the techniques for them to become second nature. This process of familiarization leads us to the final level of understanding—*embodied understanding.*

The CBCT Model of Change, illustrated in the diagram below, incorporates both the view-familiarization-behavior approach and the learning model of the three levels of understanding. This method—drawn from the *lojong* tradition and supported by contemporary science—is the basis by which we cultivate the key insights that give rise to compassion in CBCT.

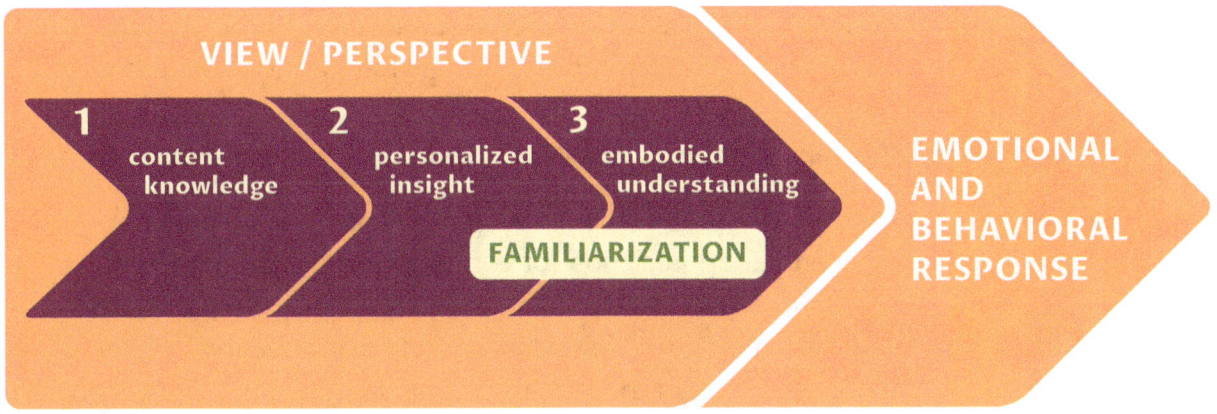

CBCT Model of Change Diagram

Part 3: The Conditions That Lead to Compassion

The Modules of CBCT

The practices of CBCT are presented in eight modules. These practices strengthen skills and insights that can be understood as a complete set of conditions that lead to compassion. As we strengthen inner capacities through carefully designed exercises, compassion deepens and expands naturally. In his book *The Neurobiology of We,* psychiatrist Daniel Siegel notes that "though the

"What can prevent the result from arising when all the necessary conditions are complete?"

— DHARMAKIRTI, INDIAN LOGICIAN, C. 600 CE

13

ability to navigate the inner sea of our minds is our birthright, it does not come automatically, any more than being born with muscles makes us athletes. The scientific reality is that we need certain experiences to develop this essential human capacity."[17] In other words, if we want to develop compassion, we need certain experiences to support that development.

The exercises of CBCT provide these experiences in a way that is easy to follow and that is accessible to people from diverse cultures and backgrounds. The modules of CBCT move in a sequence, and each one sets the stage for the modules to come. That said, their themes and outcomes overlap, and many find that they influence each other in surprising and supportive ways that are not obvious from the linear presentation. The following gives a brief introduction to each module and its role in the overall sequence.

Module 1: Connecting to a Moment of Nurturance

To start, we connect to nurturing moments to elicit feelings of safety, deepen our appreciation for compassion, and strengthen our motivation to expand it. This is done by recalling a time (or times) from our past in which we felt safe, comforted, or cared for. We then spend time immersed in the nurturing and warm feelings associated with the moment and reflecting on the benefits of that moment in our lives. This practice is considered foundational to CBCT, as it supports both the resilience and the motivation to train compassion.

Module 2: Developing Stable and Clear Attention

In this module, we train attentional stability to improve focus, mental clarity, and resilience. Typically, this is done by placing and retaining our attention on a chosen set of physical sensations, such as feelings associated with the breath, then noticing when the mind wanders and gently bringing it back to the point of focus. This is where we most deliberately train the emotion regulation strategy of *attention deployment,* as we strengthen the ability to redirect our attention and keep it where we want it to be.

Module 3: Enhancing Self-Awareness

In this module, we train the skill of non-judgmental awareness to cultivate greater insight into our mental and emotional habits. We also gain greater flexibility in how we respond to these habits. This training takes the form of turning our attention inward, witnessing unfolding thoughts, emotions, impulses, and other inner experiences while neither pushing them away nor becoming overly entangled in them. This practice trains the emotion regulation strategy of *self-distancing,* as we create space for greater self-awareness and choice.

Module 4: Cultivating Self-Compassion Part 1: Accepting Our Vulnerabilities with Kindness

In this module, we deepen our understanding and acceptance of the shared human condition to soften harmful responses of excessive self-criticism, self-blame, and shame. We deepen the understandings that we are not alone in experiencing setbacks or having limitations, none of us are in full control, and we all have strengths. This is done through the process of analytical meditation, which involves engaging in the third emotion regulation strategy, *cognitive reappraisal.* Analytical meditation, which relies on cognitive reappraisal, will be central to all the remaining modules.

Module 5: Cultivating Self-Compassion Part 2: Finding Meaning in Our Vulnerabilities

In this module, we strengthen our ability to find meaning in our challenges and vulnerabilities, to relieve feelings of helplessness and despair, and to tap into empowerment and self-agency. Through analytical meditation, we familiarize ourselves with the understanding that we can grow from our setbacks, that they can help us to connect to our values, and that they can inspire us to seek ways to help others. In this module, we shift our attention toward what we can do rather than fixating on what we cannot.

Module 6: Expanding Our Circle of Concern

In this module, we turn our attention from ourselves to others. We take steps to identify with others in order to promote a sense of connection with a widening group of people and to soften the hard line between ingroup and outgroup. Taking the analytical approach, we broaden our awareness to see our shared aspirations to be well and avoid harm and to recognize our shared human condition. Making our common humanity more visible strengthens our identification with others and deepens our felt sense of being connected.

Module 7: Deepening Gratitude and Tenderness

In this module, we attune to and appreciate the benefits we receive from others. This fosters feelings of warmth and affection for a widening group of people and moves us away from a narrow self-focus that can feed disconnection. This is done by making visible the extraordinary interconnectedness and interdependence of today's world. This analytical approach promotes our understanding that, as social beings, we benefit from and depend on many individuals within and beyond our inner circle. Reflecting on this reality naturally extends a felt sense of gratitude and tenderness toward a wider range of individuals.

Module 8: Harnessing the Power of Compassion

In this module, we make visible what others are up against, remain mindful of the tenderness we feel for them, and apply discernment. In doing so, we elicit genuine compassion and promote effective compassionate action. This is done through the analytical approach of examining others' struggles from a systems lens. By uncovering the many causes and conditions that contribute to their predicaments, we gain a better understanding of what people are going through. Combining this awareness with a tender connection, we tap into compassion and commit to discovering what we can do to make a difference.

CBCT Integrative Model

Compassion training is traditionally compared to growing a lush and flourishing garden of flowers. In the end, we get to harvest the flowers, but a garden will grow only when we have taken all the steps to create the necessary conditions. This is also true for compassion: Just wishing for compassion won't allow it to arise any more than simply wishing for flowers will lead to a beautiful garden. Each module of CBCT is like the tending, watering, and weeding of a garden—essential conditions for the widespread flowering of compassion.

The garden metaphor can help make sense of the following diagram of the CBCT Integrative Model. Originally published in the scholarly journal *Social Theory and Health*,[18] this model was developed to aid researchers in understanding and studying the causes and conditions that lead to compassion.

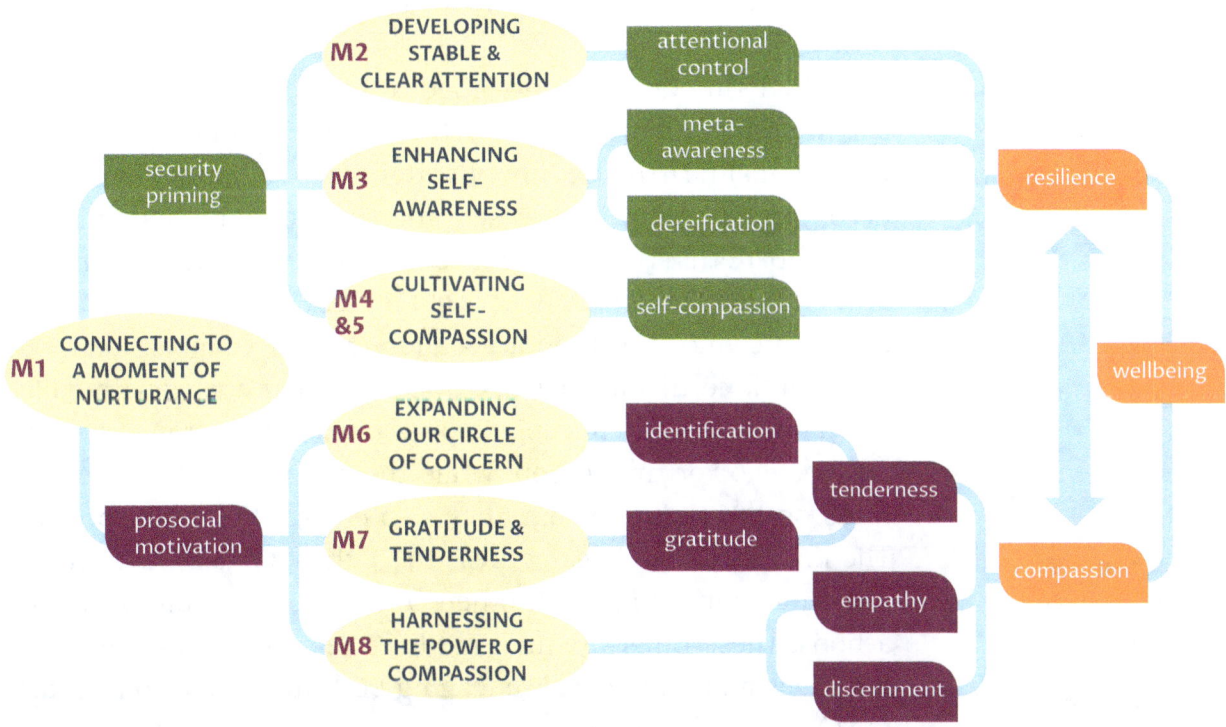

This diagram illustrates the theoretical underpinnings and learning sequence of CBCT and proposes a distinct outcome for the practice taught in each module. Taken together, the practices are hypothesized to lead to greater wellbeing, which is the primary outcome of cultivating a healthy balance of resilience and compassion. This diagram can serve as our map for navigating the territory ahead.

Personal, Social, and Systems Domains

The modules of CBCT can be understood as falling under the three domains described by Daniel Goleman and Peter Senge in their book *The Triple Focus*.[19] They argue that, for meaningful change and both individual and group flourishing, we need to focus equally on three domains: inner focus, other focus, and outer focus. *Inner focus* refers to the personal domain, our own emotions, skills, and capacities. *Other focus* refers to social domain, our relationships and how we engage with others in our lives and communities. *Outer focus* refers to the systems domain, the ability to look at the bigger picture and understand the many causes and conditions that lead to any outcome.

CBCT's modules are designed to provide insight and expertise in each of these domains. The first five modules engage the Inner domain. There, we turn our attention to our inner landscape, becoming familiar with our sensations, emotions, thoughts, and mental patterns. We strengthen our resilience as we gain greater awareness and understanding of our minds and increase our ability to regulate emotions. Modules 4 and 5, the self-compassion modules, continue this inner work by introducing analytical meditation, and specifically, the ability to see our situation from a systems perspective. For this reason, while the self-compassion modules focus on the Inner domain, they also engage the Outer domain. The final three modules address the Other domain, focusing on fostering connections with others and discerning compassionate actions. These other-oriented modules rely on our taking a systems lens and, in this way, engaging both the Outer domain and the Other domain as well.

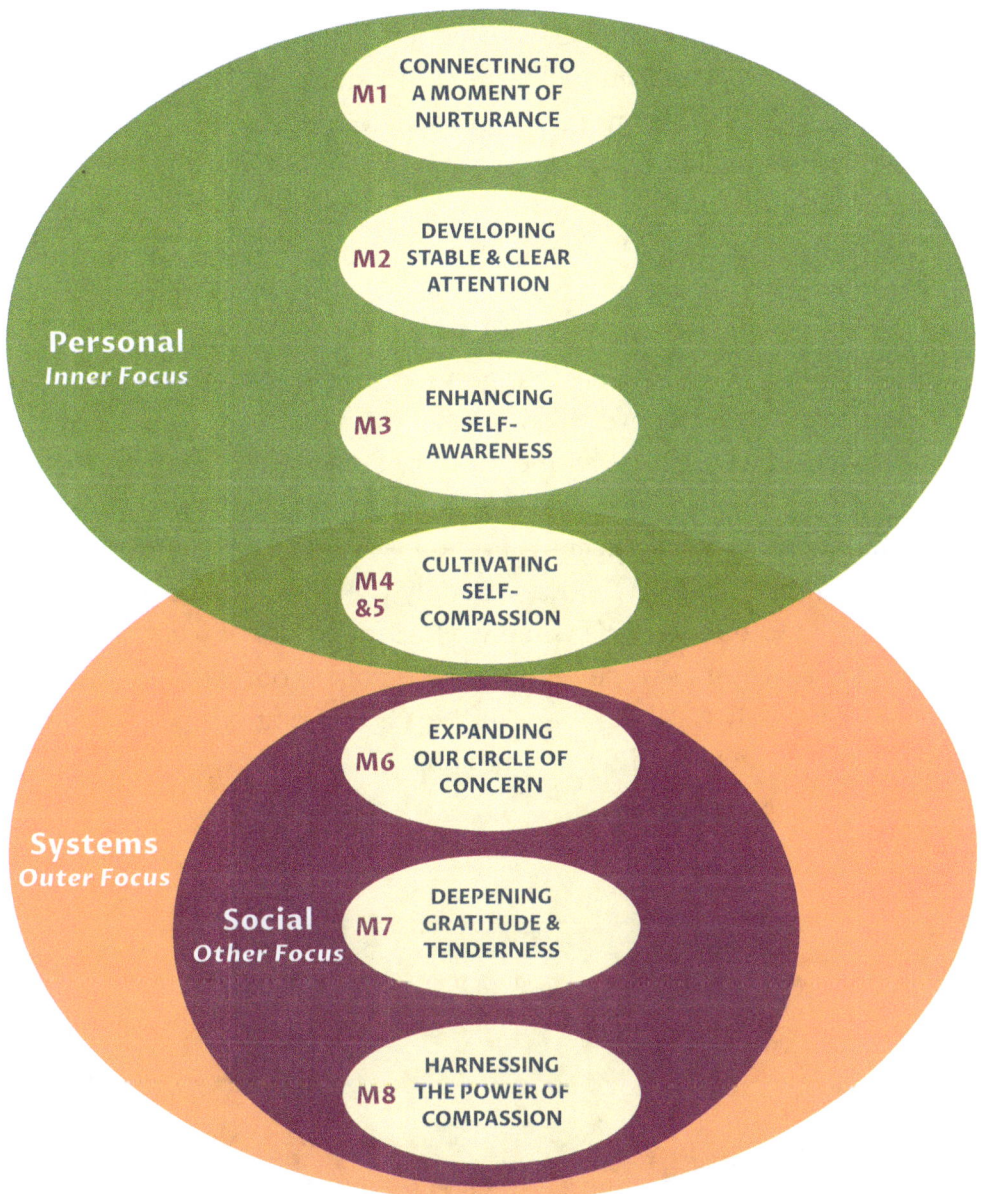

Resilience as the Foundation

The first five modules of CBCT focus on the cultivation of personal resilience. While such resilience is helpful in and of itself, it also serves as the foundation for expanding compassion to others.

To better understand resilience and its role in compassion training, let's explore a concept we will call the Zone of Wellbeing

(ZOW). This approach was developed by Elaine Miller-Karas, the director of the Trauma Resource Institute in California and developer of the Community Resiliency Model (CRM). The ZOW is sometimes called the zone of resilience, the "OK zone," or the window of tolerance.

Being in the ZOW means being in a state of psychological and physical balance, or homeostasis. It is when both branches of the autonomic nervous system (ANS), the sympathetic and para-sympathetic, are communicating smoothly with all parts of the body, and neither is overly dominant. In the same way the body has systems to regulate temperature to stay around 98.6 degrees Fahrenheit (37 degrees Celsius), our sympathetic and parasympa-thetic systems work to keep us in the ZOW.

Being in the ZOW is our naturally preferred state because it feels good to be there. It's when we feel in control of what we say and do, allowing us to be better able to make good decisions and be our best selves. When we're in the ZOW, we are flexible in our responses to new or difficult situations.

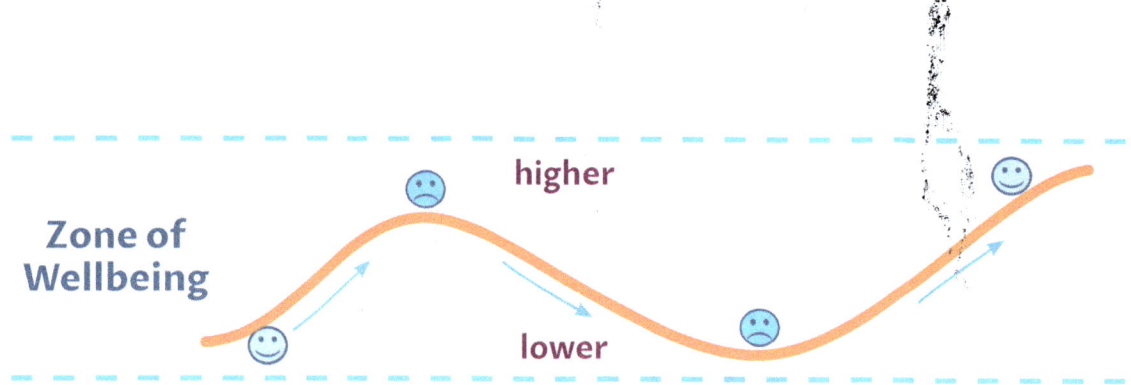

In the ZOW, we can still experience a wide range of emo-tions. Depending on the situation, we can become more excited, more activated, calmer, or sleepy. We can have stronger emotions, such as joy, sadness, wonder, even anger or grief. But in the ZOW, we experience these emotions without being completely over-whelmed by any of them. Our ANS is keeping us in balance.

The ZOW diagram is helpful to understand what is happening with our inner experience. "Higher" refers to higher energy, where we often experience emotions such as excitement, anticipation, or anger. "Lower" refers to lower energy, where we are more likely to have emotions such as contentment, disappointment, or sadness. Whether higher or lower, in the ZOW we can experience any of these emotions while not feeling unsafe or out of control.

At times, though, as we all know from experience, we can get bumped out of the ZOW. This can happen because we experience a stressful life event, or a series of them. When this happens, our ANS will do its best to get back to the ZOW, but as shown in this diagram, sometimes it gets stuck outside the zone.

HIGH ZONE:

hyper-arousal (i.e., distress in the form of panic, rage, edginess, mania, etc.)

LOW ZONE:

hypo-arousal (i.e., distress in the form of numbness, exhaustion, depression, etc.)

The *high zone* is described in scientific terms as "over-arousal" or "hyper-arousal." When we get stuck in this state, we may describe it as feeling anxious, enraged, agitated, afraid, manic, scattered, or "on high alert." While we can sometimes experience these emotions and remain in our ZOW, the high zone refers to an experience of being out of control or in greater distress. Physiologically, we may even experience trembling or shaking, rapid and shallow breathing, headaches, nausea, muscle tightness, indigestion, or changes in our vision and hearing.

It is also possible to get stuck in a *low zone*, called "under-arousal" or "hypo-arousal." When in this zone, we may describe this as feeling lethargic, exhausted, or without energy. We may not even want to get out of bed. In the low zone, we describe ourselves with words like feeling isolated or lonely, numb, checked out, depressed, unmotivated, or without optimism or hope. We may become uninterested in activities that we usually enjoy.

Remember that all types of emotional states can be experienced to some degree within the ZOW. When we are "out of the zone," whether on the high or the low side, emotions have added intensity to the point that we no longer feel in control of our thoughts or actions. We have a hard time taking in new information or seeing things from a fresh perspective. We become stuck, and we don't want to be there. It just doesn't feel good.

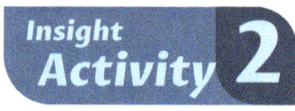

What Keeps Us in Our ZOW?

1. Recall a time you were in your ZOW. Describe the feelings, sensations, and actions that you experienced. If helpful, write these out or illustrate them in the ZOW diagram below.

2. If it feels safe, recall a time you were able to get back into your ZOW after being in the high or low zone. Describe what it felt like to bounce back from more difficult emotional states. If helpful, draw this shift in the ZOW diagram below.

If you have the sense that you are currently out of your ZOW, we recommend reviewing strategies for staying in or returning to the ZOW in the next chapter, "Getting Started," on page 31.

HIGH ZONE:

- -

**Zone of
Wellbeing**

- -

LOW ZONE:

▶ **Takeaway**

Why is resilience important for compassion? Think for a moment about the definition of compassion: the warm-hearted concern that unfolds when we witness the suffering of others and feel motivated to relieve it.

If we are outside of our ZOW, our attention naturally focuses on our own distress, making it difficult to notice what others are up against, and to attune to and respond to their needs. When we are outside of the ZOW, we are less able to see clearly and take steps that will serve the situation well. We are more likely to respond impulsively, and we are more likely to act in ways that cause harm to ourselves or to those around us.

Compassion is a response to suffering that requires strength and resilience. Being in the face of suffering is not always easy. Staying in the ZOW puts us in a position to be there for others. It gives us the courage and capacity to face their suffering without becoming overwhelmed.

Personal Reflection

"The work I've been doing with CBCT has been life-changing. I see and walk in the world differently. I like to think I am less likely to contribute to systems of oppression. I find myself revitalized and ready to stay in the classroom when I thought I was about to quit."

— ELEMENTARY SCHOOL EDUCATOR

Conclusion

As you finish this chapter, **pause and consider:** What new perspectives, if any, do you have on compassion? What stands out to you? What insights do you want to hold onto? What questions do you have?

Getting Started

"The ultimate reason for meditating is to transform ourselves in order to be better able to transform the world."

— MATTHIEU RICARD,
WHY MEDITATE?: WORKING WITH THOUGHTS AND EMOTIONS

Practices for Training Compassion: Formal and Informal

Over time and with practice, compassion can become increasingly embodied as we engage each module's practices and build key capabilities. Each of CBCT's modules offers two types of practices, *formal* and *informal*, to support this process.

Formal practices, commonly referred to as meditations, are deliberate mental exercises aimed at strengthening a particular skill or insight. These practices involve turning the attention to the inner life of thoughts and emotions and, in the later modules, engaging in analytical reflection. Formal practices are typically done sitting in a quiet place, but can be done laying down, standing, or even walking. By strengthening the skills and perspectives in the formal practices, we are better able to bring them into our daily lives, sometimes spontaneously and sometimes by deliberately engaging in informal practices. *Informal practices* are ways in which we deliberately engage these skills and insights in our daily lives.

The more we apply a skill or insight, using both formal and informal approaches, the stronger it gets. And the easier it is to call on when we need it. For example, if our goal was to deepen gratitude, as we do in Module 7, we could begin to strengthen this skill by engaging in the formal practice. We deepen gratitude in Module 7 through a formal practice that systematically brings our awareness to the many ways we benefit from others. Through this reflection, we naturally unleash responses of gratitude. We can then continue to strengthen our gratitude in our daily lives through informal practices. For example, as a way of building our capacity for gratitude, we might plan to journal at a certain time each day, listing all the people or things that have benefited us that day. Or we may choose to increase feelings of gratitude in the moment, perhaps while we are in conversation with a friend, by recalling all that they have contributed to our wellbeing.

Both formal and informal practices are essential for compassion training and are described toward the end of each module's chapter. You will find the formal practices under the heading "Instructions for Self-Guided Practice" and the informal practices under the heading "Bringing the Skills to Life."

Setting Up a Formal Practice

"It was a time in my life when I was an emotional mess," said Cassy. "I was explosive at work, and when I came home alone to my apartment, I couldn't stop replaying the events of the day. I couldn't stop imagining scenarios of conflict that I predicted would happen. It was torture. I tried things like practicing the flute, which I loved as a child, but it was hard to concentrate. A therapist I worked with had been a meditation practitioner for 30 years. He spent a year trying to get me to just sit and count each breath up to 10. I wouldn't do it for the longest time. The first time I tried it, the internal storm was so strong I thought the attempt to meditate was making matters worse. But getting quiet just showed me what was happening. It just felt worse because I was looking at it for the first time. And then I realized that this internal storm was what was creating the stormy relationships and work interactions in my life. So I decided to try meditation for real. I started with the 10 breaths. Then, I set a timer and did one minute. I worked my way up to two minutes. It was hard to remain still and open when my mind, and emotions were so roiled. But after a couple of months, things started to settle a bit more, and I got stronger. I started to be able to play the flute again. I started to find some relief."

TIPS FOR MAKING THE PRACTICE A HABIT:

- It can help to have a **designated place to meditate.** Consider keeping a meditation chair or cushion in this space, as well as some tools like a timer with a chime or bell, objects that bring you joy, such as flowers or a candle, photos of beloved or inspiring people, or other items that bring comfort. If you can create this designated meditation spot, just entering such a space signals the brain that it is time to settle and focus.

- It helps to have a **regular time set aside for meditation**. Many people like to meditate in the morning when the mind is rested and open. While it may mean having to get up a little earlier, this routine can set you up well for the day. Other people meditate before sleep at night. Either way, try to make a plan and stick to it. As with any new habit, saying, "I'll do it when I have time or when I feel like it," makes the routine less likely to take root.

- To get yourself jumpstarted, you might want to try **connecting the new meditation routine to an old habit.** For example, if you already go for a walk every morning, add to the ritual to sit down to meditate as soon as you get back.

Like Cassy, when we are emotionally dysregulated, agitated, or exhausted, we will not even be able to start a formal practice of meditation. That's why it is important to create the right conditions for the practice, conditions that are more conducive to a settled body and mind.

Where and When to Practice

Ancient manuals on meditation speak of finding the right time and place for meditation, and this still applies today. Though nowhere is perfect, find a place that is as safe and as quiet as possible. Consider a quiet corner in your home, a sacred space in your community, or a favorite place in nature. The time you choose should also be protected as best you can. Choose a time when there are fewer demands on your attention and a lesser chance of being interrupted. If others are around, consider letting them know you are meditating and ask that they respect your time and space.

Even in the calmest surroundings, there is no guarantee that your mind will settle down. You may still be dysregulated and agitated, like Cassy was at first. After you've created helpful external conditions, you can turn to setting up helpful internal conditions to settle your body and mind.

Finding Balance between Distracted and Sluggish

When engaging in a formal practice, you will find that you sometimes begin to slide toward one of two extremes: on the one hand, distracted and scattered; on the other, sluggish or tired. This is what minds do—it doesn't mean there is something wrong, it just means you have a mind. To keep the mind centered between these extremes, you will sometimes need to put effort into coming back into balance. If you notice a slide toward distractedness, you can intensify your attention on the focus of the practice. If you notice a slide toward sleepiness or fuzziness, you can wake yourself up by taking a few deeper breaths and opening the eyes wide to let in more light, then returning to the focus of the practice with more energy.

Settling Practice Steps

All the formal CBCT practices begin with three simple steps. With practice, it will get easier to move intentionally toward a balanced state of being alert and calm. This state will serve as a home base for engaging the various formal practices that follow.

Step 1: Finding a Supportive Posture

Ask yourself: What position best supports not only stillness, but also a balance of relaxation and alertness?

In the long history of contemplative traditions, maintaining this balance—both energized and calm—is most often helped by placing the body in a seated position. Many people sit comfortably on a chair or on a cushion on the floor. If seated in a chair, place the feet solidly on the floor, with some space between them. If seated on the floor, use a cushion so that the hips are above the knees and sit cross-legged, or kneel with a supportive cushion between the legs, whichever is more stable and allows greater comfort over time. If sitting is not comfortable, standing or lying down are also options. Meditation is a practice of the mind, so any body position can work. Experiment over time with what works for you.

When settling into a posture, it can help to roll the shoulders around or gently stretch the neck to allow these areas to soften and relax. If you notice other places in the body where you feel tightness—arms or hands, or in the muscles around the eyes and jaw—you can deliberately soften those areas as well. If you find that you are especially agitated, a few minutes of gentle stretching, yoga, or similar exercise can help before transitioning to stillness.

There are several optional approaches to the posture that you may find helpful for maintaining a still and balanced body. If seated or standing, you can gently stretch the head upward to create a little more height or space between the vertebrae. Then, allow the spine to settle a little, as if your vertebrae were stacked like beads on a string. The shoulders are not slouching forward; rather, the

Note:

Please take care of yourself and respect what your mind and body tell you that you need at any given time. You are your best guide to what you need in each moment.

If at any point during the settling practice you find that you are very uncomfortable, whether physically or emotionally, please feel free to stop altogether. Open the eyes wide, stand up, walk around, get a drink of water, go outside for some fresh air, or reach out to connect with a friend. It can be counterproductive to power through discomfort. It may not be a good day to practice, or you may decide that this practice is simply not for you. Stopping is always okay. You may skip ahead to a later practice that feels safer, and you can always come back anytime if you feel like trying again.

chest is wide and open. The lower back is not rounding backward; rather, the hips are slightly rotated forward, creating a gentle curve in the spine. It is often helpful to keep your eyes slightly open, allowing in enough light so that you don't space out or get sleepy. Your eyes may be closed if that is more comfortable or familiar.

Step 2: Attuning to Grounding Sensations

While settling in, it helps to check in with the body's various sensations, noticing how the body is feeling in the present moment. Start, perhaps, by noticing the feelings that come from the force of gravity as it holds us to the earth, focusing on where you are supported by the chair or cushion, or noticing the feelings in your feet. You may also note feelings where your body is up against a surface, like your hands resting against one another, or your clothing or hair draping against your skin. These are grounding sensations, and dwelling on them for a few moments can help you calm and settle into the present moment.

Step 3: Settling Breaths

Next, you may begin a few rounds of gentle, elongated breaths—typically at least three—to help energize the mind and release lingering tension or agitation. Using the nostrils if that is comfortable for you, breathe with strength and steadiness, so that you may even hear the breath quietly moving in and out. On each in-breath, you notice the energizing feeling of fresh oxygen brought into the lungs and distributed throughout, enlivening and nourishing every cell of your body. On the out-breath, you can feel the release of this old air, and allow this elongated exhalation to clear away remaining tensions or sluggishness.

If it feels helpful, pause briefly between the in-breath and out-breath, and then exhale with more intensity, emptying the lungs completely, clearing out the old to make room for the new.

Each round of these initial breaths will help you come into balance and sustain the calm, alert state that supports meditation. If this feels helpful, you may want to extend this breath practice for a minute or more. Also, these deeper, intentional breaths may be returned to at any time, even in the middle of a formal practice. If a sense of being unsettled or distressed arises as you engage in the later CBCT practices, you can return to these intentional breaths, or noticing grounding sensations in the body, to settle once again. If you are struggling, don't worry. We will explore more options for settling the body and mind in the next two chapters.

Staying in or Returning to the Zone of Wellbeing

The following helpful practices are offered in the Community Resiliency Model developed by Elaine Miller-Karas.[20] These practices are trauma-informed, which means that they are helpful when strong emotions or difficult memories are present, and we will return to them for support and insight as we move through the CBCT protocol.

Grounding

Grounding is a practice in which we notice how it feels to make physical contact with an object or surface. This can include things we touch with our hands, feet, or other parts of the body in contact with something solid and supportive, like the back against a chair. Grounding can be a very helpful tool for calming the body and mind. Most of us have already unconsciously developed many grounding techniques that help us feel relaxed, secure, safe, and more comfortable. These may include things like leaning against a wall or on a table, sitting in a certain way, folding our arms in a certain way, holding objects we like, lying a certain way on a couch or in bed, and so on. However, we may not be aware that we use these intentionally to calm our bodies and return to our ZOW.

Tracking

Tracking refers to the practice of noticing sensations in the body. During a grounding practice—and for any of the practices of CBCT—we will be checking in from time to time to notice what sensations our bodies are experiencing. For example, if we are grounding ourselves by sitting in a chair with our feet flat on the floor, we would also attend to the sensations that our feet are experiencing, that our bodies are experiencing as our weight is supported by the chair, as well as the feeling of our hands resting on our laps, etc. Tracking sensations can help to bring us into the present moment and can sustain us in (or help return us to) our ZOW.

Shift and Stay

As we track our sensations in any practice, we may notice that a sensation is pleasant, unpleasant, or neutral. If we find pleasant sensations, resting our attention on that part of the body can sometimes allow the feeling to deepen and the body to relax and return to the ZOW. If we find neutral sensations, focusing attention on these can also help us come back to the ZOW. However, if instead we become aware of an unpleasant sensation, we can "shift and stay." In other words, we can scan the body to find an area that feels more comfortable (either neutral or pleasant) and then rest our attention on that new location instead. Our ability to "shift and stay" will become enhanced in Modules 2 and 3 as we cultivate skills of attention and awareness.

Help Now! Strategies

These strategies can be used to help us quickly return to our ZOW when we find ourselves in the high or low zone. They all involve engaging in a task and tracking our sensations during that experience. While these strategies are designed to activate calming sensations and feelings, every person will have their own responses to each strategy. We strongly recommend trying each of these out and discovering the ones you find the most calming and helpful for you. You can then return to those strategies whenever you need additional support.

- **Walk:** Notice the sensations of your body moving and feet touching the ground as you walk.

- **Listen:** Name all the sounds that you can hear around you.

- **Look:** Name five or more colors or shapes you can see.

- **Drink:** Drink a glass of water slowly, paying close attention to the sensations you feel (in your mouth, throat, and stomach) as you drink.

- **Count Backward:** Count backward from 20 as you walk around.

- **Push:** Notice the sensations of your muscles pushing against a wall or a table.

- **Touch:** Feel different textures of objects around you and attune to those sensations.[21]

Special Considerations for Mental Health Conditions

There is one group of experiences with formal practices that requires special care and caution. These are experiences that can happen when practitioners have an ongoing mental health problem.

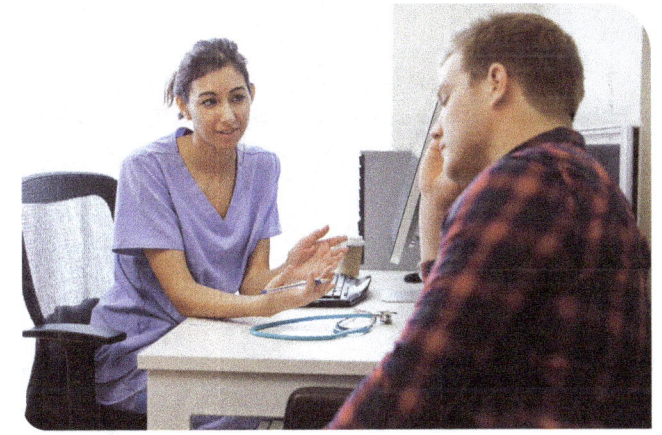

For example, people with bipolar disorder or other severe mental illness may have increased experiences of symptoms such as agitation, mania, delusions, and even hallucinations.

Another area of caution concerns symptoms of traumatic stress or PTSD due to interpersonal violence, a catastrophic illness, or a loss. During meditation, it is possible to re-experience memories that lead to intense fear, flashbacks, or other difficult experiences. Several research studies have shown that CBCT can help people who have difficult issues like PTSD from combat or assault,[22] depression,[23] suicide attempts,[24] and breast cancer.[25] However, just because CBCT is helpful for some does not mean it will be for all.

Please keep in mind that CBCT is not therapy and should not be used as a replacement for professional mental health services. If you have any concerns, it is important to discuss whether meditation is safe for you with your physician or mental health professional before beginning a CBCT program. In addition, if enrolled in a class, you should feel free to mention these concerns to your CBCT teacher.

Be honest with yourself about your needs and seek counsel if you have any doubts. In CBCT, we believe that a beneficial meditation program (or teacher) will not try to insist on certain progress or manipulate you into doing things that you do not want to do. In the end, the decision of what and how to practice is yours; be careful if you ever feel that your decisions are being dictated or imposed on you by others.

Personal Reflection

"I just want to say thank you for the course. I was the one in the first class who said that meditation was something that never worked for me. Now, I have to revise that statement. I have benefitted a lot, and I am really grateful to you and the others who put this together. I have been dealing with a lot in life and at work, and this is really giving me the tools to better cope and be a little more resilient and kind to others. I know I have years to grow, and I look forward to the journey. This was time well spent and I will certainly recommend to others."

— MEDICAL SCHOOL FACULTY MEMBER
AND CBCT PRACTITIONER

Frequently Asked Questions

Along with choosing a regular time and place, what are other tips for making the practice a habit?

Keeping a simple meditation log or a journal is helpful for many who meditate. Log the time spent, record your observations and experiences during meditation, or make a note of how the insights you gain from meditation are finding their way into your daily life.

Sharing meditation times with others or discussing your experiences can also be helpful to inspire and reinforce your habit. Doing so can also magnify what you learn through discussion with like-minded others. You may find ongoing support through places where meditation is taught, such as a meditation class, yoga studio, or your place of worship. In fact, many therapists now incorporate meditation into their practice. Community can also be found through interactive video calls, websites, and blogs. We welcome you to visit us at compassionshift.emory.edu and learn about the compassion community we are building at the Compassion Center.

How much should I be practicing?

Ten minutes per day is plenty at first, which can be broken into two five-minute sessions, morning and evening, if that's easier. During a typical training over a couple of months, you may build up to 15 or 20 minutes a day, but even that will be difficult at times. But quickly, the mind will gain skills and, before you know it, you'll be comfortable with, and taking real joy in, longer meditations. Also, remember that the CBCT approach provides much more than sitting meditation, so you'll have many other opportunities to practice and bring the core skills and insights to your life.

Is it better to listen to recordings to guide my practice or to guide myself in silence?

For most people, it's helpful to have a recording at first. After some time, or if you are already experienced with other styles of meditation, you may want to try on your own. This will allow you to go at your own pace and be more flexible in what you focus on. Even when you get comfortable with self-guiding, though, it's good to check back with the recorded source of guidance periodically. Revisiting instructions can yield new insights.

Why does it seem like my mind gets busier or even worse when I try to practice?

A significant aspect of meditation is learning to be aware of our own minds. When you start paying attention, you might discover that at first, the mind is an ongoing whirl of thoughts. The mind is always like this for most of us, but we notice it more when we

learn to pay attention. With practice, you'll quickly gain strategies to settle things down. Not every time you practice, but more frequently, you'll find a calmer, more pliable mind.

What if I feel sleepy when I try to practice?

If we are not used to relaxing the body and mind, simply engaging in the settling practice above can cue our nervous system that it's time for a nap. This drowsiness will naturally decrease as your system learns that there is much more that we can do in a relaxed state than sleeping! To get past this initial hurdle, it may help to do a little physical exercise before a session. A brisk walk around the house or 10 gentle jumping jacks can get you going. If you start to doze during a practice, deliberately intensify your mental focus or take a few full, deep breaths and open your eyes wide to cue the body to wake up. Sometimes, if the drowsiness continues, it may be time to just stop and give yourself the nap your body needs.

What if I feel strong emotions when I practice?

When a strong feeling arises during our daily lives, there are ways to distract ourselves from it. We might call a friend, grab a favorite food, watch a television program, or play a video game, all of which lessen the impact of the feeling. But when we are sitting still, we may feel the full force of an emotion in a surprising way. CBCT offers several strategies to navigate and make sense of such emotions.

What's the difference between CBCT meditations and meditations that focus on relaxing and/or reducing stress?

Relaxation and de-stressing are important, and CBCT includes a few practices to help do just that. The first three modules especially can have such effects, and being relaxed and settled provides a foundation for the practices of the later modules. CBCT is also aiming for other outcomes, such as mental clarity, self-awareness, self-compassion, inclusivity, systems awareness, and (of course) compassion itself.

Is meditation like a religion or a substitute for religious beliefs?

Not at all. Like many activities, such as singing or poetry, meditation can be supportive and enjoyable either as part of a religious practice or separately. Many who regularly practice CBCT—including Christians, Hindus, Muslims, and Jews—have reported that it enhances their religious beliefs and commitment. Some CBCT practitioners see themselves as spiritual, but not religious, and still others do not consider themselves spiritual at all but see CBCT as simply a way to support their personal wellbeing.

1

Connecting to a Moment of Nurturance

"Security is the first and foremost reason for social life . . . As is true for many mammals, every human life cycle includes stages at which we either depend on others or others depend on us. We very much rely on each other for survival."

— FRANS DE WAAL,
THE AGE OF EMPATHY, 2009

Module 1

Having learned to settle the body and mind, we can now strengthen our capacity to connect with feelings of safety in order to navigate our emotional life with more skill.

We can train the ability to access moments of safety, comfort, and nurturance and to reconnect with those nurturing feelings and sensations. Connecting with a personal experience of safety or receiving kindness calms the body and mind. As we connect to these moments, we are also reminded of the value of safety and compassion, which then helps inspire us to offer these moments to others. When we feel safe and cared for, the door to possibility opens.

ENDURING CAPABILITIES

1.1   Attuning to one's sensations and feelings

1.2   Accessing moments of nurturance to activate feelings of safety and comfort

1.3   Valuing being nurtured as a way to increase motivation to provide nurturance to others

Connecting to a Moment of Nurturance

Every single day, others are engaging in activities that help us survive and thrive. However, this truth may not always be visible to us. Regularly finding ways to re-experience the felt sense of having received love and compassion, or to keep that feeling alive and present for ourselves, provides a big opportunity to lay the foundation for making a shift toward compassion.

For this activity, we'll be referencing the Zone of Wellbeing (ZOW), or "resilient zone." This refers to the state of emotional equilibrium in which we feel both alert and calm enough to respond well to whatever is happening around us, even if those events are stressful. You may want to take a moment to review the full explanation of the ZOW in the Overview, starting on page 18.

1. Make a list of moments or circumstances in your life that help you feel more at ease, calm, protected, or centered. List moments that, when recalled, fill you with a sense of greater safety, comfort, or warmth.

    ❈ *Moments of nurturance* can take many forms. Some might recall a time we received compassion and kindness from a loved one. For others, moments might include those where we are with someone whom we trust or feel close to. With this person, we feel comforted, particularly if this person is someone who protects us, is kind to us, and cares for or helps us during times of uncertainty or difficulty. For many, it can be a moment of closeness with a spouse or child. It can be the unconditional love of a pet, a warm smile from a stranger, or support from a neighbor or teacher. It can be an imagined memory of how we were cared for as an infant or of being encouraged by a famous role model, even if we've never met them.

2. See if you can settle on just one moment. Recall as many details about it as you can. Take a few minutes, even 5 or 10,

Note:

It is very common to have trouble finding a nurturing moment, especially when first beginning this practice. If you are struggling to find a moment, please refer to the Frequently Asked Questions at the end of this chapter for some guidance and suggestions.

to bring the moment to life—picturing it, drawing it, or jotting down some notes.

❋ Consider: What did the place look like? Describe the colors, textures, environment, surrounding sounds. What time of day was it? What was the light like? What other senses are evoked—smell, touch, or taste? What emotions did you experience in that moment? What sensations did you feel in your body?

3. Now, turn your attention to the present. What emotions and sensations arise as you think of this moment? What shift, if any, do you notice in your feelings from the start of this practice to now? Consider where you are in the ZOW.

❋ If helpful, do a quick scan of your body—you can do this from the top of your head to your feet, or from

the ground up, whichever feels best for you. Where do you notice sensations in your body? What feelings are these sensations associated with? For example, tension in the neck may be associated with stress, softness in the shoulders may be associated with calm, accelerated heart rate may be associated with excitement. Compare this to where you were at the beginning of the activity.

Note:
Struggling to stay in your ZOW? Try one of the "Help Now!" Strategies on page 32!

HIGH ZONE:

- -

Zone of Wellbeing

- -

LOW ZONE:

▶ **Takeaway**

We often move through life on autopilot, unaware of the sensations and feelings we are experiencing at any given moment, until they grow and become overpowering or overwhelming. Making it a habit to check in with our body sensations and feelings allows us to have a better understanding of how we are feeling and when we might benefit from emotion regulation.

Connecting to a moment of nurturance is one strategy for regulating our bodies and minds. By simply recalling a time when we felt safe or comforted in the past, we can elicit those same feelings in the present. In this way, we can move from feelings of distress or discomfort to feelings of groundedness in our ZOW.

With practice, these moments of nurturance can be more easily recalled, bringing us more in touch with those feelings of safety, calm, and contentment.

Key Elements of the Module

"Connecting to a moment of nurturance" involves calling to mind a moment when we genuinely felt comforted and safe, and connecting to those feelings as they unfold in the present moment.

Being comforted by others is what biologists call the *social regulation of emotions*.[26] Throughout the animal world, all mammals and even birds do this for each other and for their offspring. When a child is upset, a hug, a soothing word, or a humorous distraction can bring comfort. We may have already begun to recall experiences in our own lives where others helped us feel safer or calmer. These experiences are powerful in helping to regulate emotions. They calm us in the moment and can be used as a resource to draw on throughout our lives.

Research shows that vividly imagining something can elicit the same physiological and emotional response as actually experiencing that moment.[27] By sustaining awareness on calming and nurturing moments, we activate the parasympathetic nervous system to settle both our bodies and our minds. This ability to change or induce an emotional state through a cognitive effort is a prime example of the *cognitive regulation of emotions*.[28]

Accessing nurturing moments not only provides a sense of safety and regulation, but it also allows us to appreciate the value of these moments in our lives. If we didn't have a moment of safety or care, if we didn't experience someone responding to our needs, how would our lives be impacted? By connecting to the value of nurturance, we can become more motivated to be a greater source of it for others.

THE SPIRITUAL ORIGINS OF THE NURTURING MOMENT

In the *lojong* tradition from which CBCT is drawn, each meditation begins with a practice of "taking refuge," in which the meditator spends time visualizing all the most revered people from that tradition (including Buddha). The meditator imagines being surrounded by them and receiving their support. Many other traditions have similar practices or prayers, calling to mind the support of a loving God, Mother Earth, or other sacred figures. If you have a strong faith tradition or are drawn to a figure from such a tradition, please feel free to call on that when you choose your moment of nurturance. Everyone benefits from feeling that they are supported, and the form of this support will look different to each person.

The Power of Nurturance

LaTonya's life was saved by the love and nurturance of her grandmother. After years of uncertainty and lack of proper care, LaTonya went to live full-time with her grandmother when she was nine. In this new life—in her first real home—she had a routine: breakfast, then school. She could then play with the neighborhood kids, followed by homework, and then story time before getting tucked into bed at night. As her daily life normalized, LaTonya began to excel in school. She had found refuge, calm, and safety with her grandmother, as well as new, caring teachers who recognized her brilliance.

Realizing that it was the care and stability provided by her grandmother that made the difference in her life, she decided to pursue a career in education so that she might offer the same care to other children. As LaTonya progressed in her career, there were many long and restless nights. In those moments, she thought back to her grandmother, recalling the tender memories of being tucked in as a child. She found that these memories helped her quiet her mind, get her to sleep, and generally kept her feeling safe and stable through the hectic days.

Her feelings of gratitude for the safety and care her grandmother provided continued to inspire her along her path. LaTonya went on to become a school superintendent, responsible for bringing stronger education, food programs, pre-K enrollment initiatives, and childhood development programs to some of the most troubled school systems in Texas. As much as the care she received allowed her to thrive, it also provided her the foundation

from which she could then extend care and safety to other children many times over.[29]

We all have different experiences and backgrounds. We may not have had an experience like LaTonya, but like LaTonya, we've all received care from someone in one way or another. The Module 1 practice makes those moments visible, helps us navigate the ups and downs of our lives with greater resilience, and inspires us to develop greater compassion for others.

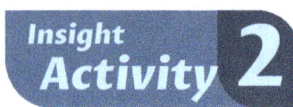

Making Visible the Value of Kindness

1. Think back to moments when you received kindness or safety from others, like LaTonya did from her grandmother. Is there one moment that stands out? This could be the same moment of nurturance you reflected on in the first insight activity or something different. It could be a moment from childhood, or a kind act from a neighbor or a stranger. Maybe it was a teacher who encouraged you?

   ❋ You might choose to reflect on a big moment or a small act of kindness that brought a smile to your face, some comfort, or feelings of warmth.

   ❋ If nothing comes to mind right away, just imagine what it would feel like to be at the receiving end of kindness.

2. Take some time to write about the positive impact(s) this moment has had (or would have had) on your life. What has this moment given you? How has it contributed to your wellbeing or led you to where you are today? What might be different, had you not had this moment?

3. Now, reflect on what it feels like to connect to the value of this moment in your life. What sensations and/or emotions surface for you? If you need some inspiration, consider some of these reflections from others who have taken CBCT:

   ❋ "I felt a warmth in my chest."

   ❋ "My stomach area felt more relaxed and open."

   ❋ "I could feel my body start to relax from my face all the way down my spine."

   ❋ "I felt a deep sense of appreciation"

   ❋ "I noticed I stopped gripping with my hands and my fingers relaxed."

   ❋ "I felt a little weepy."

❋ "It made me want to give back"

❋ "You know that wonderful happy/sad feeling? It was so poignant."

❋ "I felt a lot of grief. I miss my grandparents and my aunts and uncles."

4. In what ways, if any, does this reflection inspire you to support others?

▶ Takeaway

As we reflect on the benefits of these moments in our lives, we may feel a deepening sense of appreciation. When we make visible the value of receiving nurturance, of receiving safety and kindness, it can motivate us to be a greater source of these feelings for others because we understand how meaningful and powerful those moments can be.

Working with Negativity Bias

For many, it can be difficult to notice and attune to nurturing moments in our lives. Although we have experienced positive moments, our minds may be in the habit of letting them slip by without noticing them and without experiencing the associated positive feelings. Many of us have learned to filter the world with a *negativity bias,* meaning that we notice and recall negative events more than positive events.

Evolutionary biologists point out that we have this bias for very good reasons. It keeps us safe when there is a danger or threat to our survival. But many of us filter the world with this negativity bias even when we are not in danger, making it difficult to notice the good things that are also happening. This bias may make us more likely to feel down and, in some cases, even experience clinical depression.

This module's practice is designed to offset our negativity bias over time by practicing the ability to dwell on, and benefit emotionally from, the positive events in our lives. Importantly, this is not suggesting that we put on "rose-colored glasses," or pretend that nothing is wrong when that is not the case. Rather, this module allows us to acknowledge that we do have a bias toward the negative, so that we can deliberately balance that bias by increasing our awareness of the positive.

As we begin the practice of calling to mind nurturing moments, we may find that we start to notice more of them, and that we feel their benefits more often. The positive emotions that are often elicited from these nurturing moments are referred to as *positive affect*. Signs of this may include feeling a warm glow in our chest, smiling, or even shedding tears of appreciation.

Positive affect is understood by neuroscientists to be both flexible and plastic.[30] This means that we can get better at experiencing positive emotional states through practices such as these. As we train our attention to automatically recognize and attune to these nurturing moments, this can become our new habit of mind. In this way, the healthy emotional states that these moments elicit, can become

common and sustained. This is why the process of activating these nurturing memories or imagined moments is a technique that psychologists call security priming. The practice primes us to feel safety and comfort more naturally and more often, and studies show that security priming has a strong impact on improving mood.[31]

Take a moment to **find a comfortable posture and connect with your body** and current feelings. If you notice tension in any part of the body, feel free to stretch or move.

Allow yourself to **settle into the present experience.** Take a few deep breaths if that is comfortable. Gently inhale, and, if you like, have the sense that nourishing air is infusing your entire being. As you breathe out, see if you can release tensions and worries to some degree to allow the body and mind to settle into an unfolding sense of calm or ease.

When ready, **bring to mind a nurturing moment,** something that makes you feel better, safer, or happier. When have you experienced that? In nature? While being cared for by a friend, loved one, a mentor, or a figure from your faith tradition? If such a resource does not come to mind, see if you can just imagine a person or an environment that would support your feeling safer or better.

Choose one and **spend a few moments immersing yourself in this experience**. Bring this moment to mind as vividly as you can.

- Where is this scene happening? What do you see—what are the colors and textures; what is the light like? What about the surroundings?

- Are there sounds? Physical sensations? Are there scents in the air?

- If this is a moment of shared kindness with others, do you recall facial expressions or body language, or do you hear a comforting tone of voice?

Continue immersing yourself in this nourishing moment for a minute or so.

After connecting to your nurturing resource for a few moments, **bring your attention to your sensations and feelings in the present moment**. Has anything shifted? If you find pleasant or neutral sensations, such as a warmth in the chest, relaxation of the shoulders, or a smile on the face, you may rest with those. If, instead, you notice areas of discomfort, you can take a few breaths to settle the body and mind, or direct your attention back to the nurturing resource for a few moments, or shift your attention to a different part of the body that feels better.

Finally, reflect: How important are such moments of comfort and safety for your wellbeing? And how important are acts of kindness and compassion to create a safe and secure world where your fellow human beings can thrive? As you connect to the value of kindness and compassion, how might that impact your life and your relationships with others?

Take a moment to dedicate your practice today to those you know to be in need of health and wellbeing and, as you are able, expand this dedication to include a widening circle of beings on this earth.

And **conclude by setting an intention** to extend the skills and insights from this practice into everyday life.

Bringing the Skills to Life

↪ **Find comfort in nurturance.** Catch yourself when you are feeling anxious or stuck and shift your attention to a time when you have felt more secure, comforted, or nurtured. Sit with that moment for a minute or so and see what shifts you notice in your feelings, if any.

It may be hard to catch ourselves in those moments, so you can also consider setting designated times to deliberately check in with how you are feeling. If you then notice you are feeling at all dysregulated, you can engage in this practice.

↪ **Collect nurturing moments.** Attune to and collect nurturing moments around you. As you go through daily life, try to notice any moments that could be considered supportive or nurturing—moments large or small that brought you some comfort, joy, or warmth. Perhaps a moment that put a smile on your face. Make a list of the moments you notice and see what it feels like to have a greater awareness of them. These can then be used as possible resources to call upon in the formal meditation practice, or in times when you are in need of regulation.

↪ **Bring nurturing moments into day-to-day activities.** Recalling a moment of nurturance can be done literally anywhere and anytime. In fact, the more ordinary our location and activity, the more easily we might integrate the practice into our lives. See what happens if you try to recall a moment of nurturance:

❈ while standing in line at a grocery store

❈ while sitting as a passenger in a car

❈ while riding public transportation

❈ while waiting for a friend who is late to meet you

❈ in the waiting room at your doctor's office

❈ while sitting at the bedside of someone who isn't feeling well

Personal Reflections

"I was stressed out and in a rush to get to work. I jumped in my car and turned the key. Nothing. My car battery died, which made me more stressed and frustrated and in an increasingly bad mood. I realized I was spiraling out of my Zone of Wellbeing, like we talked about in class, so I took a moment to practice resting in a moment of nurturance. Not only did it help recenter me, but it put the entire situation in perspective. After thinking about how safe and happy I am with my wonderful girlfriend who loves me, I didn't care that much about a bad day and wouldn't let it continue to get me down. Everything else—the car battery dying, the deadlines, etc.—seemed more manageable. Even more, later in the week, when I was cuddling with my girlfriend and watching a movie, I realized how content and happy and secure I was in that moment. I took the time to experience all the little details so I could revisit the memory later when I need to rest in a moment of nurturance again."

"Working with the suffering of patients, families, and staff in the hospital setting cumulatively led me to establish the habit of internalizing harsh judgments of myself for not being able to soothe all the distress in the manner I would like. Through this training, I began to notice that I could harvest a nurturing moment at any time, even in the midst of an encounter or challenging feelings. For example, I was recently with a hospital employee who was very stressed, as they were waiting to hear from a professional committee judging the quality of their work. I empathized with that stress and was able to access a moment of nurturance for myself and then invited him to do the same, which brought relief to both of us and even allowed him the calm and space to bring about new perspectives, which seemed to be of help to him."

"I had just begun my first CBCT class and one day was walking my five-year-old son to kindergarten. My son was crying and complaining about being cold on our walk to school. I usually related to my son as my own father interacted with me and would just be annoyed and tell my son to 'toughen up.' But instead, reflecting on my recent CBCT practice, I paused, opened my own coat up, and pulled my son close to me. My son stopped crying and we walked to school, sharing the coat. My son was smiling and said thank you when we arrived at school. I at first thought this was a nurturing moment for my own son. And then realized it was also a nurturing moment for me."

Frequently Asked Questions

What if I can't find a nurturing moment?

It is very common to have difficulty finding a nurturing moment, especially when first learning the practice. Sometimes being put on the spot makes it hard to think of any, but that doesn't mean we don't have them. Sometimes we try to think of only the most significant nurturing moment, making it difficult to choose one. Sometimes it's just difficult to recall the moments that bring feelings of safety or calm because our mind has a strong habit of focusing on threats in ways that crowd out the positive memories. It can be challenging to recall the positive things . . . at first. If any of these describe you, know that you are not alone. And this is why we call this "practice"!

We recognize that many of us have not had loving or ideal parents or caregivers, so we may not have access to "big" memories of nurturing individuals. Thankfully, that is not at all necessary for this practice. For those of us in this situation, we can simply recall when we have experienced any type of comfort or support in our own lives, even if not ideal or perfect and even if fleeting. We might also simply imagine how it *would* feel to experience these moments. By practicing this, each of us can learn to connect with the feeling of receiving kindness and love.

If you get stuck, try any of these helpful options:

- **Choose a really small moment.** Recalling a stranger holding the door for you, someone saying something kind, a pet greeting you with a purr or wagging tail, the feeling of sinking into a warm bath after a long day, or listening to a soothing song. What has made you smile?

- **Make one up.** If you can't think of a specific moment from your life that made you feel some sense of comfort or safety, just imagine one. What would it feel like to be protected and safe? What situation would allow you to feel these feelings? Be creative and build an image in your head, with as much detail and as many different sensations as you can imagine.

- **Create a nurturing moment for yourself—right now!**
Perhaps by placing your hand over your heart lovingly, giving yourself a hug, swaying your body, putting on a favorite sweater, taking deep breaths. Experiment with an action that provides you with that sense of safety or comfort and then sit with that, noticing how it makes you feel. Research suggests that even curling up the corners of the mouth in a smile can signal our nervous system to relax and settle down. See what works for you.

- **Think of a time when it felt good to care for another.** For many people, especially people who have spent time caring for infants, vulnerable people, or pets, a nurturing moment may come from something as simple as holding a loved one in their arms. Embracing another, or holding a baby to your chest, stimulates the release of the bonding hormone oxytocin. This hormone is a powerful neurochemical that helps us feel warmth toward others and to develop trust. Perhaps this is part of why intense memories of caring for others bring up feelings of nurturance for ourselves.

Does my nurturing moment have to be with another person?

No, the nurturing moment does not have to be with another person. There are many moments, with or without others, that can make us feel safe or nurtured. Choosing a moment involving a person (or people) can help inspire us to nurture others, but this is not necessary. Thinking of any moment when we felt a sense of safety or comfort can serve this purpose. These could be moments in nature, listening to a favorite song, sitting with a pet, or any other activity that elicits these feelings. Whether our moment is with a person or not, we spend time connecting to the value of feeling safe and comforted. This is what then motivates us to be a source of those feelings for others.

To explore this option, you can think about where you tend to feel happier or safer. Or perhaps a place that helps you regulate. This could be in your favorite chair, with a favorite blanket or pet, in your room. Or, it could be engaging in an action, like pulling on your favorite sweatpants or placing your hand on your heart.

When you've practiced this ability to connect with such a time, you may see that it is not so hard to expand to include others. Maybe ask: Is there someone who would make you smile if they walked in the room? Or whom you would call if in need?

Should I use the same nurturing moment every time?

There are benefits to both using the same nurturing moment every time, and to trying out different ones. The benefit of choosing the same one every meditation is that you become so familiar with it that it becomes easier to recall and tap into the associated feelings. The benefit of choosing different moments each time is that you are broadening your awareness of the many nurturing moments you have had in your life—many of which you might not have noticed before. Experiment for yourself and see what works best for you!

What if something distressing or difficult surfaces alongside the nurturing moment?

Sometimes memories of being nurtured are entangled with memories of loss, or of being threatened or vulnerable. No moment exists in isolation. For example, if your nurturing moment is a moment with a loved one who is no longer living, while the moment itself may be nurturing, the thought of that person could also bring feelings of sadness or grief. It's okay if difficult emotions come up alongside soothing ones.

There are a few ways to work with this. See what works for you. First, try to sustain your attention on the nurturing aspects of the moment in a way that allows them to intensify, allowing the difficult feelings to fade to the background. This is not the same as pushing them away or repressing them.

If this is not working, perhaps choose a different moment that makes it easier to connect just with the feelings of safety and comfort. If neither of those options helps, simply return to the settling practice of taking deeper breaths, noticing the contact of your body with a surface (grounding), stretching, and recentering. If the memory is particularly activating, you may even want to stop the practice for now and call a friend, drink some water, or take a walk—then try again later.

Do I have to master this module before I can go onto the next?

Not at all! In fact, over the next two modules, we will share some other strategies to support this practice, so please don't give up if this does not feel easy or relevant for you quite yet. All of us can get better at this and reap the benefits if we set our expectations realistically and approach each lesson creatively, from different angles. Don't forget the potential benefit of this module: What if you become the kind of person who has easy access to feeling secure and protected? Remind yourself that with patience, time, and effort, this is possible for anyone.

Conclusion

In this module, we began to access moments of safety during meditation and in our everyday lives. We focused on strengthening our ability to attune to our sensations and feelings, to recall and rest in nurturing moments, and to allow those nurturing feelings and sensations to support us in the present. We saw how connecting to the value of nurturing moments in our lives sparks a greater motivation to engage in compassion training so that we may be a greater source of nurturance for others.

In the next module, we will develop another foundational skill for cultivating compassion: stable and clear attention. Simply put, this is the ability to direct our attention where we want it to be, to notice when it wanders, and then to bring it back and keep it in place once again. This will help us stay connected with our nurturing moments, when that is our goal, and, more generally, supports our ability to accomplish any task that we decide is important. Stable and clear attention is a key part of any meditation practice, and it will prove essential for all the practices needed to train compassion in the modules that follow.

2

Developing Stable and Clear Attention

"With mindfulness, monitoring awareness,
and heedfulness,
Fully guard the gateways of your senses
Again and again, throughout day and night,
Examining the flow of your mind."

— ATISHA,
BODHISATTVA'S JEWEL GARLAND, 11TH CENTURY CE

Module 2

Having connected to a moment of nurturance, we can now settle and steady the wandering mind and become more skillful in responding to our emotions.

It is very natural for our attention to be pulled by distractions and strong emotions. When life events are stressful or distractions multiply, we can easily lose awareness or choice over where we set our focus. In this module, we train the mind to note where our attention is, and then enhance our ability to regulate our attention when it is pulled away by a distraction or laxity.

ENDURING CAPABILITIES

2.1 Enhancing the ability to sustain attention on our chosen task, object, or experience

2.2 Increasing the ability to notice unhelpful impulses, emotions, and distractions

2.3 Strengthening our ability to disengage and redirect the attention where we want it to be

What's At Stake

1. Think of a habit that you are working on strengthening to contribute to your wellbeing.

    ❋   Examples: eating healthier, exercising more, being kinder to yourself, staying focused, being more empathic or inclusive, or being less impulsive.

2. Think of times when you needed to focus your attention to support or strengthen this habit. Take your time and recall a real experience you have had, or one that you could imagine being real for you.

    ❋   For example, if you are strengthening the habit of exercising more, you may recall needing to shift attention away from an entertaining video and focus instead on getting ready for a walk or making it to a workout class. If you are strengthening the habit of being a more empathic listener, you may recall needing to shift attention away from your desire to interrupt someone and focus instead on what they are saying.

3. Pick one of these times and describe how easy or challenging it was to notice when something pulled your attention away and to refocus your attention.

4. Now, think back to the habit you have chosen to strengthen. Explain why this habit is important to you. How will strengthening this habit positively impact your life or the lives of others? What is at stake if you do not strengthen and maintain this habit over time?

5. If you can, think of a situation when you were especially aware of the importance of this habit while trying to put it into action. How did (or would) the awareness of that importance influence your ability to focus?

▶ Takeaway

Being able to direct our attention where we want is necessary for cultivating helpful habits and for unlearning unhelpful ones. In this exercise, we explored the quality of *heedfulness*, the heightened sense of care and attentiveness that arises when we are aware of the importance of maintaining focus. When we understand what is at stake, we become more heedful and better able to stay focused on what matters most.

We can keep this in mind as we endeavor to strengthen helpful skills and healthier habits, whether in CBCT or in other aspects of our lives. Pausing to reflect on the importance of pursuing our goals helps us to remain heedful. In each of the modules of CBCT, we will spend time attuning to the value of the Enduring Capabilities that support compassion. This is a fundamental aspect of the training, as it keeps us focused and committed.

Key Elements of the Module

Attention is a fundamental skill that we all have and use in our daily lives. But do we always have awareness or control over where it goes? Many times throughout the day, we are required to bring our attention to something in particular, whether that's a task, a conversation, written instructions, or the needs of those around us. Yet, while trying to pay attention, we commonly get distracted. Our minds wander.

Let's think about an average day in our lives. How many times do we start to send an email or text, only to realize later that we got distracted and never sent it? How often do we enter a room only to forget why we walked in? Perhaps we find it hard to concentrate long enough to study for a test or finish a project by the deadline. Or perhaps we have trouble focusing on a conversation because our minds were on something else (and the person we were talking to gets annoyed that we weren't paying attention). This is what happens when our attention needs strengthening.

A stable attention is like the steady flame that illuminates what is present and important in every moment. If the flame is flickering in the wind, it will not illuminate its surroundings well, but if we can shield it from the wind, its light will be steady and bring clarity. In the same way, a well-trained attention—protected from distractions—allows us to see clearly and correctly. Whether our intended focus is on a task, our environment, or the needs of others, we can learn to sustain our attention there and better understand what is going on. On the other hand, an unfocused mind is prone to jumping from topic to topic, losing track, or becoming emotionally dysregulated. An unfocused mind can affect our mood, contribute to our anxiety and depression, and reduce our overall happiness.

Attention is understood by neuroscientists as an essential skill for emotion regulation. They refer to this skill as *attention deployment*,[32] which is the cognitive strategy of disengaging from distressing sensations or thoughts, shifting the attention to something less disturbing, and holding it there. This allows the body and mind to calm as the attention becomes focused on something pleasant or neutral, instead of entangled in unpleasant memories or worries. In CBCT, we already began using this skill of attention deployment in the first module when we learned to direct and hold our attention on a nurturing memory or image. In this module, we continue to train this skill and apply it in other helpful ways.

Improving the quality of our attention is key to accomplishing anything important to us, including—as we shall see—the development of compassion.

In this module, we explore and train the following key factors for cultivating well-regulated attention:

1. **Mindfulness:** Remembering or "filling the mind" with an intended object of focus. Ethical mindfulness is when that object of focus is one of our important values or intentions.

2. **Monitoring awareness:** The ability to notice whether attention has wandered, which allows us to bring it back to our intended object of focus.

3. **Heedfulness:** An elevated sense of care and motivation based on an understanding and awareness of what is at stake.

Bringing Attention Where It's Needed

After completing school, Armaan began pursuing a career that his parents did not approve of. For weeks they continued to discuss it over the phone, but Armaan was determined to pursue his dream. He returned home for a brief visit, and, again, the only topic that seemed to be of interest to his parents was this new career. His feelings of anger, frustration, and sadness became overwhelming. Armaan walked out of his parents' house, got on his bicycle, and headed to the home of a close childhood friend, a place he had cycled to countless times.

As he pedaled along the side of the busy four-lane road, Armaan's mind replayed the arguments with his family over and over again, his hurt feelings over his parents' lack of support riveting his attention. He kept thinking about what he wished he had said, and what he wished *they* had said. He became more emotional, and tears began to well up in Armaan's eyes.

Suddenly, Armaan was startled by a loud horn. Distracted by his thoughts, he had drifted into the left lane. If he hadn't heard the horn, he would have crashed into a truck driving next to him. Armaan refocused his attention. He swerved back into his lane and became alert and aware of his surroundings. A quick look in his mirror showed a line of trucks speeding toward him. He felt a rush of energy as he realized he had narrowly escaped a horrible accident.

Now alert, Armaan set his attention on the task in front of him. The thoughts of the argument and difficult feelings did not go away completely, but with the understanding that his life was at stake, he no longer let them overtake his ability to focus enough to bike safely. If his attention became entangled in that argument again, it could easily lead him to veer into the road. So, as he cycled, and as the strong, ruminative thoughts around the struggle with his parents tugged at his awareness, Armaan intentionally brought his mind back to the present moment, again and again, intensifying his focus each time.

Armaan not only made it to his friend's house safely, but he also found that he was feeling a little better by the time he got there. Holding his attention in the present, even for this short period of time, had the powerful effect of calming both his body and his mind.

Attention Deployment

1. At some time or another, everyone's mind gets caught up in repeating loops of unwanted thoughts and feelings. If it is comfortable, think of a few times when this has happened to you. If you cannot think of specific examples, imagine ones that seem realistic or relevant to your own experience. Examples include:

   ❊ Rehearsing "what if" scenarios for a future event that is not in your control.

   ❊ Being unable to focus on work because of an upcoming vacation or anticipated romantic outing.

   ❊ Thinking over and over about an important conversation you need to have, or a presentation you need to give, and being unable to fall asleep because of it.

   ❊ Mentally replaying a loss or setback that you experienced.

2. Pick one from your list and reflect.

   ❊ Describe the experience of your attention getting stuck. How might you have felt or acted differently if you were able to disengage and redirect your attention?

   ❊ If you were eventually able to shift your attention to something less distracting or distressing, describe that experience and what it felt like.

▶ **Takeaway**

A steady and clear attention helps to guard against distractions, ruminations, and intrusive thoughts. It is natural that our attention will wander or get pulled by this or that, especially when there are strong emotions involved. In some cases, mind-wandering can be very helpful, as it can fuel creativity, or give our minds a rest! But in other cases, it may lead to distressing thoughts or feelings. In those moments, attention deployment can be an effective strategy to regulate our emotions and allow us to choose—if we want—to shift how we feel. The skill of attention deployment can help us to stay in our ZOW, where we feel safer and are more in control of our inner world and our choice of behaviors.

In the formal practice for this module, we take deliberate steps to exercise our skills of mindfulness and monitoring awareness. With these skills, along with heedfulness, we will be better able to deploy our attention when needed and, as we will explore in the coming modules, to attune to helpful insights and goals.

Choosing an Object of Focus for the Formal Practice

In the *lojong* tradition, training the mind in attention is compared to training a wild elephant. In ancient times, elephants were trained by being tied to a post with a rope. Whenever they tried to wander off, there was a gentle and attentive trainer who would kindly bring the elephant back to the post. This would be done over and over again. To train the skill of attention in the formal meditation, we choose an object of focus that acts as our own post. Once we choose that object, we hold our attention there, much like the rope holding the elephant. This is our skill of mindfulness. Throughout the formal practice, we will continue to check in to make sure we are still with our object of focus. This skill of monitoring awareness can be compared to the gentle and attentive trainer. And if we notice we have wandered, we can kindly bring our attention back to our object.

Traditional practices to cultivate a stable and clear attention have used some basic, readily available objects of focus. All have the quality of (1) existing in the present moment, (2) occurring naturally or spontaneously, and (3) being "neutral" or free from strong emotional content. You should feel free to experiment and change your chosen object over time. Some options include:

- **Breathing:** Find the place in your body where you feel the breath most vividly. This could be sensations of air at the nostrils, the rising and falling of the belly, the filling and emptying of the lungs in the chest, or anywhere else you experience the breath. Without controlling the breath, place your attention on that location in your body, and follow

"The faculty of voluntarily bringing back a wandering attention, over and over again, is the very root of judgment, character, and will. An education which should improve this faculty would be the education par excellence."

— WILLIAM JAMES,
THE PRINCIPLES OF PSYCHOLOGY, 1890

the sensations as they change from moment to moment, breathing in and breathing out.

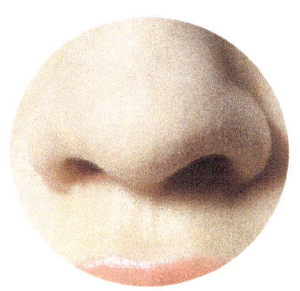

- **Sound:** When using sound as the object, bring your awareness to your ears and attune to the sounds around you. Become aware of the entire soundscape that surrounds you, allowing all the different sounds to be present without zeroing in on one or another. Without judging or categorizing the unfolding sounds or soundscape as good or bad, allow yourself to follow the changes as they unfold in the present moment. If you feel distracted by a given sound, let that feeling go and return to noticing the entire soundscape.

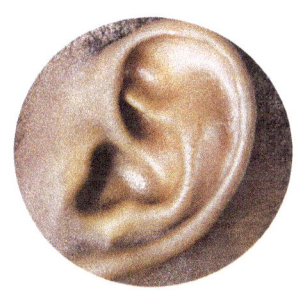

- **Other body sensations:** Choose another place in the body where you notice a specific sensation. This could be the feeling of your heart beating, or sensations in an area where your body contacts a surface—your buttocks on the floor or chair, your feet on the ground, your hands or elbows resting in your lap or on an armrest, the clothing against your skin. Gently place your attention on the part of your body you've chosen and notice any sensations unfolding in this area. Without judging or trying to change them, simply become aware of the sensations, moment to moment. If you notice unpleasant sensations, feel free to shift your attention to a part of the body that feels better.

Note:
Before beginning the formal practice, take a moment to choose an object of focus to use as an anchor for your attention.

Approaching Mindfulness Practice

As you start to practice, remember that it is natural for the mind to wander. Mind-wandering is actually an important part of this training! We can think of it like training a bicep: To strengthen this muscle, we need to release our arm. It is the act of bringing the arm back over and over again that strengthens the muscle. Similarly, when we strengthen our attention, our minds will naturally wander. This is part of the practice! It is the act of bringing our attention back over and over again that strengthens our skills of attention. When mind-wandering happens, you can have a little inner celebration or expression of gratitude, and then return to your object.

Take a moment to **find a comfortable posture and connect with your body** and current feelings. If you notice tension in any part of the body, feel free to stretch or move.

Allow yourself to **settle into the present experience**. Take a few deep breaths if that is comfortable for you. Gently inhale, and, if you like, have the sense that nourishing air is infusing your entire being. As you breathe out, see if you can release tensions and worries to some degree to allow the body and mind to settle into an unfolding sense of calm or ease.

If settling is hard today, you might want to pause and spend a few moments with the Module 1 practice.

When ready, **bring your attention to your chosen object of focus**. This might be the unfolding sensations of the breath where you notice it most easily, unfolding sounds around you, or other sensations in the body. Direct your attention to this object and see if you can sustain it there from one moment to the next.

From time to time, **briefly check in** to see if your attention is still on the object or has wandered off. If you notice that the mind has wandered to other sensations, emotions, memories, or thoughts, take this as an opportunity to practice redirecting your attention back to the chosen object of focus. Each time you reconnect, see if you can sustain the attention there for a few more moments.

If you feel sleepy or notice your energy sinking, you may adjust your posture to sit a little straighter, open your eyes wider, look up, or take a deep breath and exhale fully to clear out the drowsiness. Then, reset the focus on your chosen object, sustaining it in the present moment once again.

If you're having trouble keeping your attention where you want it to be, see if you can intensify your focus. If your mind keeps getting pulled away, remember that each time you bring it back, even if it is just for an instant, you are strengthening your attention and your flexibility. This is something to be acknowledged and even celebrated!

If you're struggling to disentangle from a thought or emotion, think about your goal for engaging in this practice and the value of strengthening attention. See if that greater heedfulness helps you to return to your object of focus.

Continue to hold your attention on your object of focus for a few more moments. Bring your attention back whenever it wanders off.

When ready, release your attention from your object of focus and **attune to your current feelings and sensations.** What shifts do you notice that arise from this practice?

Finally, reflect: How important is it to cultivate greater attention? How helpful is it to have the choice to redirect your attention when needed and to sustain it where you want it to be?

Take a moment to dedicate your practice today to those who are in need of health and wellbeing and, as you are able, expand this dedication to include a widening circle of beings on this earth.

And **conclude by setting an intention** to extend the skills and insights from this practice into everyday life.

Bringing the Skills to Life

- **Catch and shift.** Catch yourself when your mind has become distracted. Without overthinking it, shift the mind back to where you want it to be.

- **Everyday mindfulness.** Apply mindfulness in your daily activities, such as:

  - *Walking.* Focus on the feelings of your feet touching the ground as you walk, one after the other. Try this while walking a bit slower than usual, perhaps when you go down a long hallway at the office or at home.

  - *Eating.* Focus on the sensations of smell, taste, and touch while eating slowly, taking one bite at a time, and swallowing completely.

  - *Showering.* Focus on the feelings of the water—its texture, pressure, and temperature—as it flows across the body.

  - *Brushing teeth.* Focus on the feelings of the brush's bristles in the mouth as you gently move from tooth to tooth. Focus also on the brush's contact with the tongue, as well as the sensations in the mouth after rinsing.

  Please be careful! Do not choose an object of focus that will distract you from being safe. For example, if you are doing something hazardous like driving a car or truck, don't focus on the sensations of eating. While driving, please focus 100 percent on driving! Watching the breath at a red light or while stuck in stand-still traffic could safely build mindfulness—and perhaps even reduce stress—but meditating is not advisable while your attention should be on the safety of yourself and those around you.

- **Attention deployment.** Try using attention deployment when you are feeling dysregulated or stressed. This can be done in just a few moments, while alone or even during stressful social situations. When you notice you are feeling tightness or tension in the body, or that you are having stressful emotions, take a few moments to shift your attention to something pleasant or neutral. Pleasant things could include the soft sensation of your clothing, a cooling breeze, or the recalled moment of nurturance you have been working with since Module 1. Neutral things could include the unfolding sensations of the breath, your hand resting on your leg, or any unfolding bodily sensation. See if you can hold your attention on the pleasant or neutral focus for a few moments, allowing time for your nervous system to regulate. Every now and then, check in with your body and mind to notice any shifts in your sensations and feelings.

- **Attending to attention.** Establish designated times to deliberately check in with your attention. Perhaps set a reminder on your phone to prompt yourself three to six times per day. When the alert goes off, try first to note what task you are doing. Then, ask: Where is my mind during this task? If your attention has wandered away from what you are doing, try gently redirecting it back to your task. See what shifts, if any, you may notice in your feelings—as well as the quality of your experience—when you are able to sustain attention in the present moment.

  - If you have some time at the end of the day, look back and reflect on how your practice went. If helpful, write out thoughts and feelings. And remember, if you notice that your attention has wandered, don't criticize yourself—celebrate the fact that you noticed it! You are developing the "muscle" of monitoring awareness.

Personal Reflections

" As a mother of young children, getting my kids to school is so chaotic with everybody's needs—'Mom can you . . . ,' 'Mom help me with . . . ,' and the dog needing to be fed or taken outside—that every morning I felt worn out by nine in the morning. I felt pulled in 10 directions at once and it was exhausting. But by developing a stable and clear attention, I was able to address this source of stress. In the moment, I would notice the reactive sparks of frustration or worry with each new demand, and I was able to disengage and refocus on the task at hand. I started to see that the lure of multitasking was the problem, and my new clarity meant I could not only break down the morning into manageable steps, I could set a boundary, like, 'I'll be there as soon as I'm done helping your brother.' With practice, I felt more centered, present, and attentive with my kids and mornings weren't so exhausting. "

" As someone who has dealt with anxiety for over a decade, I am so used to turning to my usual coping skills that I sometimes forget the value that a moment of deep, stable attention can have. It is truly amazing how an act as simple as focusing on a couple of deep breaths can transform one's mood and remind us all that our present-day problems are more manageable than we perceive them to be. As the past week has been particularly stressful (everything was moving in the wrong direction with my work), focusing my attention on my breath, and only my breath, for even a minute has helped me ground myself and develop an action-oriented plan to keep moving forward. "

" I was completely distressed after my toilet overflowed and my bathroom smelled like a sewer. I tried so many plumbers, and it seemed nobody could get to me. I was overwhelmed by the stench and totally distressed. I was freaking out a bit. Then, I looked outside and saw it was a beautiful day, so I went to the balcony and relaxed in the sun. I focused on sensation, the warmth of it on my skin, the slight chill in the air, the ebb and flow of the gentle breeze. In time, I relaxed and refocused. I was able to shift from distress to remembering how beautiful the environment around me is. I was able to gain some perspective and realize it wasn't worth me losing my mind over this. I needed to keep going, taking one step at a time to find a plumber, and start calling friends and relatives with whom I could stay until it was fixed. "

Frequently Asked Questions

What if I find it difficult to focus my attention on my object of focus?

- **Shifting the location of focus:** If you find it too difficult or distressing to focus your attention on your chosen object, try choosing a different object. For example, if you have chosen the sensations of the breath at your nostrils, perhaps try following the sensations at your stomach, chest, or throat instead. If you are doing a grounding practice and following the sensations in your legs against a chair, perhaps shift the focus to your hand on your lap or your back against the chair. If shifting focus during your meditation isn't working, try choosing a different object altogether. For example, instead of meditating on the breath, you can try changing your object of focus to the sounds in the room.

- **Counting:** If you are focusing on the sensations of the breath in your practice and are having trouble keeping the attention there, you can try counting the breaths. Silently say to yourself "one" after a full inhalation in and a full exhalation out. Then, count "two" following another round of inbreath and outbreath. Continue doing this until you get to five or seven, and then begin over by starting again at "one." Start over anytime you get lost, but try not to be frustrated with yourself or judge yourself in any way—getting lost is just part of the experience. Finally, be careful not to overemphasize the counting process and forget all about following the sensations of the breath.

Are there other alternative objects of focus I can use in this practice?

- **A small object in front of you:** A spot on the floor, a pebble, or a candle flame can also provide an object of focus. These options are not as portable as the others and do not have the quality of changing over time, but for many people they provide a very strong and solid way to engage in this practice.

- **Hands rising and falling:** Many people enjoy moving practices, particularly when they first begin meditating. Here is one that aligns with the breath yet keeps the focus on the hands. Place one hand, face-up, below the navel, and the other, face-down, on top of it. As you breathe in, slowly raise the upper hand to chest level until the breath is complete, then reverse direction as the breath goes out. Try to synchronize the timing of the hand motions to correspond with the breath (bringing the hand up on the inhalations and bringing it down on the exhalations) while maintaining attention on the movement and feelings in the hands.

- **Flickering flame of a candle:** Some people enjoy the visual experience of looking at a candle flame, which, like the breath, is constantly changing yet always there.

- **Return to the earlier practices:** Settle the body and mind with a few deep breaths or return to your moment of nurturance. Returning to earlier practices is always an option, especially as you learn the later practices. Learn to notice when this may be helpful for you and always give yourself this option.

If you are very uncomfortable, or if you find that meditating on any of these objects causes you any distress, please stop. Get up and do something pleasant, familiar, or distracting.

What should I do when strong or surprising thoughts and emotions come up in the practice?

If surprisingly powerful emotions, sensations, or thoughts arise during meditation, or if past traumas come to the front of the mind, take notice. Don't think that you should "push through" or suppress or "just allow" these experiences to happen. Meditation is not about unleashing unwanted experiences, but rather is about learning to voluntarily make choices within our mental experiences. Always take care of yourself and respect your limits. Sometimes meditation shines a light into long-hidden areas of our inner world, and this may feel quite intense. In choosing to open yourself to such experiences (or not), it is important to learn to do this gradually by disengaging and protecting yourself from becoming flooded by old memories or feelings. Working through very strong emotions or remembered traumas is better done with a trusted person or trained psychotherapist and is not the goal of compassion training.

Conclusion

In this module, we began to understand the value of developing stable and clear attention. We reflected on the role attention plays in cultivating important habits and greater resilience, which enhanced our heedfulness. We then learned to deliberately train our attention through a formal practice aimed at strengthening mindfulness and monitoring awareness, and we explored ways to bring these skills into our daily lives.

In the next module, we will point our polished lens of attention toward our inner world of thoughts and emotions to gain greater insight into how our minds operate. We will explore the real possibility of freedom from habitual unwanted mental patterns and reactivity.

Enhancing
Self-Awareness

*"Between stimulus and response, there
is space. In that space is our power to
choose our response. In our response lies
our growth and our freedom."*

— UNKNOWN
(ATTRIBUTED TO VIKTOR FRANKL)

Module 3

Having developed a stable and clear attention, we can now direct that attention to our inner world of feelings, thoughts, and sensations in order to have more choice over otherwise habitual reactions.

Often, our focus is on the things going on around us, and what is happening within us can go unnoticed. We may even be unaware of how we habitually respond to situations. In this module, we gain a greater awareness of these unfolding mental experiences and learn to disengage from harmful pre-programmed impulses, such as projections, judgments, or over-identification with our thoughts or feelings. Becoming aware of our thoughts and feelings can help us choose how to respond to them, reducing the potential for conflict and increasing the opportunity for making meaningful connections and positive change.

ENDURING CAPABILITIES

3.1 Enhancing awareness of the patterns of thoughts and emotions in our inner life

3.2 Strengthening the ability to distinguish reality from our projections

3.3 Deepening the understanding that thoughts and emotions are fluid and changing, not fixed or solid

3.4 Increasing the gap between impulse and behavior, allowing greater choice and flexibility in our responses

Catching the Spark

Before beginning this activity, take a moment to review these two stories from CBCT participants:

> *"I was getting ready for an event when I suddenly got a migraine. My focus narrowed in on the pain, and I could feel the urge to get upset. It was almost as if I could see the thoughts of frustration that wanted to take over heading my way. Thoughts like: 'Why is this happening? This is going to ruin my whole night,' and 'I hate getting headaches, this is horrible!' I knew from the many headaches I've had in the past that getting caught up in those types of thoughts usually made the pain worse (and my mood too!). So, I just noticed them trying to bounce into my mind, and I let them bounce right back out. This was liberating for me—to know that I could notice an urge, one that is actually a habit of mine, and choose to not give any fuel to it. A choice that in the end left me feeling a lot better."*

> *"I am someone who experiences road rage quite often. One day when I was driving, someone cut me off, and I instantly noticed my usual impulse to assume they were rude and to get angry. I started to feel my face getting a little warm as these emotions bubbled, but as soon as I noticed that, I paused and took a breath. I acknowledged my impulse to judge the other person and to feel annoyed, but then let it go. Instead of my usual response of making rude gestures or yelling, I remained calm and kept driving."*

These stories demonstrate situations in which people were able to catch sparks before they turned into fires. By catching the impulses to project—to judge, over-identify, assume, or interpret situations—and letting these impulses go, these CBCT participants stopped fanning the sparks and prevented unneeded distress and harmful responses.

1. Describe a situation in which you succeeded in catching a spark before it turned into a forest fire.

    ❀ What event instigated the spark?

    ❀ How did you manage to catch it and stop it from growing?

2. Describe any impulses you had to project onto the situation. In what ways would they have fanned the spark into a fire?

❋ For example, in the first story above, it was the urge to judge the headache as "the worst thing possible" that would have led to more pain and distress. In the second story, it was the impulse to assume the person cutting them off "must be a jerk" that would have led to anger and yelling.

3. How did it feel to catch the spark and prevent the fire? Describe any emotions or sensations associated with that choice.

4. What value would come from strengthening this ability to catch the spark? In what ways would improving this skill impact different areas of your life?

▶ **Takeaway**

"If you are distressed by anything external, the pain is not due to the thing itself, but to your estimate of it; and this you have the power to revoke at any moment."

— MARCUS AURELIUS

All of us, at times, tell ourselves stories that are not true or are at least exaggerated. This can cause suffering. Just like a little spark can be fanned and grow into a raging forest fire, our difficult thoughts and emotions can be fanned by our own projections, causing unnecessary emotional suffering and sometimes driving hurtful responses. However, we all have the ability to catch those sparks before they turn into fires. And if we catch them when they are small, they are easier to put out. Awareness gives us choice; it allows us to see a potential reaction that is harmful and choose to not engage in it. In this module, we strengthen this capacity, fostering greater resilience and self-agency as we move through our lives.

Key Elements of the Module

If you have ever spent the night wide awake thinking about something disturbing that happened earlier in the day, then you've experienced the drawbacks of your mind being taken hostage by rumination. At times, our minds are hijacked by the impulse to judge what comes up in our minds, to over-identify with our thoughts or feelings, or to cling to the good and push away the bad. The problem with this is that our actions wind up being controlled by pre-programmed reactions that may no longer be helpful in the current situation. These reactions may even be harmful, though we may not be consciously choosing or even noticing them.

A *projection* is when the mind generates an appraisal that is distorted or does not align with the actual facts of an event. For example, if someone does not answer our phone call, we might think they don't like us anymore when, in fact, their battery just died. Projections happen all the time, but fortunately, we can catch them and refrain from fanning the sparks of emotional reaction into a larger fire.

> In CBCT, we use the term "projection" to refer to any distorted or narrow cognitive appraisal that our mind projects onto the world. This definition includes, but is not limited to, the specific use of "projection" that is common in psychotherapy: a defense mechanism in which someone attributes unwanted characteristics, thoughts, feelings, or motives onto another person.

In the previous chapter, we saw that one great option to help us tame impulses is attention deployment, shifting our attention away from a distressing thought and anchoring it somewhere pleasant or neutral. In this module, we explore another emotion-regulation skill, sometimes referred to as *self-distancing* or *non-appraisal* by scientists.[33] This is the ability to observe our mental experiences without judgment and without becoming entangled in them. In the formal practice, we will learn to notice when we have become ensnared by a string of distortions, release that string, and simply witness what arises without judgment. This allows us to more clearly see what's happening.

With greater awareness of our inner experiences, we create a space that allows for more choice. If we see that our mental patterns are helpful, we can make the choice to continue to engage with them. If we decide they are not helpful, we are better able to let them go. For example, when we notice judgments that may harm others, we can acknowledge their presence without feeding their intensity. We can more easily let them pass by. Or when we notice an impulse to act in a way that may damage our health, we can try to do the same. As we strengthen our mental awareness and develop this ability to choose, we enhance our own agency. This makes us better able to lay the foundation for our own wellbeing and to contribute to the wellbeing of others.

Becoming Aware of Mental Patterns

Sasha has had a difficult relationship with one of her parents. Since childhood, she has been treated harshly and critically, being blamed for things that were not her fault. She grew up hearing only about what was wrong with her, frequently criticized and even humiliated in front of her peers.

Now an adult with a thriving career, Sasha was working on a project and was tasked with giving a presentation to her colleagues. In the middle of her talk, her supervisor interrupted with a question and offered an alternative point that was a bit contrary to what Sasha was presenting. Sasha felt her face turn red and responded with a sarcastic comment before abandoning the presentation and stomping out of the room.

Because of her experience growing up, Sasha was quick to assume that her supervisor's interruption was an attack. This projection sparked the same defensiveness and anger that had been habitual since childhood. When she was interrupted in the meeting, she was overwhelmed by thoughts like, "This is rude," "My boss is disrespecting me," "I can never do anything right," and "I am never valued."

Sasha's supervisor had experience in conflict resolution, so she followed her out of the room to talk about what had just happened. She understood that Sasha was struggling with a projection, and her first action was to apologize and offer her a sense of safety. She let Sasha know how much she valued her work and her perspective, and that she was very happy with everything Sasha was doing. She explained that she simply meant to offer feedback to aid in Sasha's success, not to tear her down. That conversation cleared up the misapprehensions, and Sasha apologized for jumping to the wrong conclusions. It was at that point, when Sasha began to see the reality of the exchange, that she understood that her supervisor's feedback could enhance her own ideas. She thanked her for the help, and they returned to the conference room together.

After many years, her supervisor announced her retirement. Sasha wrote her a long letter, thanking her for that exchange. She explained how important it had been in starting down the path of understanding the patterns of her mind. Sasha concluded the letter with the following: "You helped me realize that I was stuck in patterns from my childhood that were holding me back. Your kind response sparked this awareness in me, and I saw that I could begin to make different choices. Honestly, it changed the course of my life, and I will be forever grateful."

Examining Our Emotional Scripts

In his book *Emotional Awareness*[34] (written with the Dalai Lama), Paul Ekman describes *emotional scripts*—the concept that emotional responses can become like scripted patterns operating in our lives. From as early as childhood, we can start assigning roles and interpretations to people and situations in our lives, which leads us to replay these scripts repeatedly, trying to make the story of our current reality fit into them. It's as though we are always unconsciously on the lookout for circumstances that seem familiar, and when we connect with the familiarity, out pops an old script, like how Sasha's misinterpretation of her supervisor's intentions replayed an emotional script she had with her parent.

1. Take some time to recall an unhelpful pattern or emotional script you've seen in your own life. Think of situations that tend to elicit a similar emotional and behavior response automatically, perhaps one disproportionate to what is needed. See how clearly you can describe the pattern, by filling in these blanks:

   Typically, when this happens [event]: _____,
   I tend to react by feeling [emotion]: _____,
   which often leads me to say or do [action]: _____.

   Here are some examples from other CBCT participants:

   ❀ "When I spend too much time alone, I start to feel down, and I find myself drawn to eating candy or desserts."

   ❀ "When I am around [this person], I tend to get more irritable and am more likely to use an angry tone of voice and start an argument."

   ❀ "When I am around people who talk about current trends, I feel like I don't belong. I make jokes and act like I think it is silly to think about those things."

Note:

Don't forget to be kind to yourself! It is normal to have patterns like these. We all have habits that are helpful, and some that are unhelpful. This isn't about being harsh toward ourselves for having these patterns, but about making them visible so that we may find a way to interrupt any harmful consequences that arise from them.

> ❋ "When my spouse has a new idea about how to spend our money, I feel disrespected and seek flaws in my spouse's logic and want to insist on my way."

2. Reflect on the good that might come from catching this pattern while it is playing out. What benefits might come from becoming better at catching ourselves in these instances and interrupting emotional scripts?

3. Brainstorm and jot down at least one step you can take to interrupt the scripted pattern when it happens next. Consider how you might apply the skills of attention deployment or self-distancing.

"Emotions often, but not always, occur in scripts that distort reality. Uncovering a person's script can be helpful, alerting him or her not to continually play the same dull script again and again."

— PAUL EKMAN,
EMOTIONAL AWARENESS,
2008

▶ Takeaway

When patterns are so deeply conditioned, we may not even be aware of them. This activity helps to make those patterns visible so that we stop unconsciously replaying them throughout our lives. With greater awareness, we can let go of automatic projections and the responses that result. This takes time, but with training, we can unlearn these habits as we strengthen our ability to pause and see things as they are.

Non-Judgmental Awareness

1. Think of moments in your life when your view of a situation changed significantly, perhaps even multiple times. Pick one and describe how your feelings shifted over time as your judgment of the situation changed.

   ❀ Example: Imagine you did not get an opportunity you wanted. You might have thought it was the end of the world at the time but then discovered that not getting the opportunity led to something even better. You might have then felt relief and joy. Later, that new opportunity might have proved to be more challenging than expected, and your thinking might have shifted to feeling defeated and considering it a bad move.

2. What did it feel like to have your emotions constantly shifting as judgments shifted? How did this affect your overall sense of groundedness or wellbeing?

3. What benefit could it bring to respond to the events in your life with non-judgmental awareness instead of clinging to the notion that something is *all* good or *all* bad?

   ❀ If helpful, imagine and describe how the situation you reflected on would have differed if you had maintained this equanimity. How would this have altered your emotions and even behaviors?

▶ Takeaway

Over-identifying with the various thoughts that flow through our minds has many downsides. When our inner narratives get stuck on one story, or constantly toggle between extremes like, "This is the best," and "This is the worst," our emotional state will be at the whim of life's ups and downs—our moods and actions will follow these emotional swings. We will spend our energy putting out fires, with less time to discover and focus on what is more lasting and truly important to us.

Starting with Sensations

To get a taste of the Module 3 formal practice, let's start with a body scan, widening the lens of our focus to include all our unfolding body sensations.

1. Begin by bringing your awareness to your toes and noticing the sensations that naturally arise there. For some people, directing attention to sensations can be activating in unhelpful ways. Feel free to shift to another practice if this one does not suit you, such as recalling a nurturing moment or grounding (noticing the contact of your body with a surface).

   ❋ As you become aware of these sensations, note any automatic judgment of those sensations as pleasant, unpleasant, or neutral.

   ❋ If you find you are judging them as good or bad, see if you can gently soften that judgment and try to accept the sensations without labeling them as wanted or unwanted. Allow them to arise in your awareness and then to pass and fade naturally.

2. When ready, you can then move the awareness up through the body, stopping at each point and repeating the process. Go from toes to feet, to legs, to belly, to chest, to back, to arms, to shoulders, to neck, to face, to eyes and ears, to scalp.

   ❋ In each place, pause for 10–15 seconds and notice the sensations, also noticing when the mind sees them as pleasant or unpleasant or labels them as good or bad.

   ❋ Maybe you will even notice your mind racing and telling stories, like, "That is where I hurt my knee when I was younger," or "That rumble in my stomach means I am hungry." When you notice such mental interpretations or reactions, be glad you noticed it, accept that it is happening, and return to observing the sensations without preference for one or another.

3. Once you've finished attuning to your sensations, describe what this experience was like. Consider the following questions to help guide your reflection:

❀ What sensations did you notice? Were they pleasant, unpleasant, or neutral?

❀ As you noticed the sensations, what thoughts came up (i.e., memories or thoughts of the future)?

❀ What feelings did the sensations and/or thoughts elicit (i.e., anticipation, fear, or curiosity)?

❀ If you were able to disengage from distraction, describe that experience. How easy or challenging was it to notice and disengage?

❀ What did it feel like to try to notice sensations without becoming entangled in them?

▶ **Takeaway**

In this activity, we learned to accept body sensations for what they are. In doing so, we were able to withhold the labeling of experiences as completely pleasant or complete unpleasant. This is a great starting place for applying this same process to thoughts, emotions, and other mental experiences. This is not to say that we should apply this non-judgmental awareness all the time. We strengthen this capacity so that we can use it if and when see it as beneficial.

Metaphors for Understanding the Mind

The Sky

When we engage in the Module 3 practice, it can be helpful to liken the mind to the sky—vast, open, and ever-present. Our mental experiences—sensations, thoughts, memories, feelings—can be thought of as the clouds that pass through the sky. Sometimes, these clouds are light and fluffy, while at other times, they are quite

"Whatever thoughts may arise, do not stop them, but recognize their movement and place your mind unwaveringly upon them."

— Panchen Lobsang Chogyen, Root Stanzas on Mahamudra, c. 150 CE stormy or threatening. At times, clouds may even seem to fill the entire sky. Yet, clouds do not mean that the sky has gone away. The sky is always there, vast, spacious, and accepting. If we are patient, we know that the clouds will pass and we'll again see the blue sky. The mind is just like this.

We are going to practice simply witnessing our mental experiences arise and pass in our minds, without clinging to them, pushing them away, or preferring one over another. We stay mindful that the mind, like the vast sky, is always there, even on the stormiest days. We can remind ourselves that, like clouds, none of our mental experiences are as solid or permanent as they may seem. We can also remind ourselves that we are not defined by any one thought or feeling that comes into the mind, just as the sky is not defined by any one cloud that passes through.

The Ocean

Another helpful analogy for this practice is that the mind is like an ocean—incredibly vast and deep—and mental experiences are like the waves that move on the surface. Depending on the weather conditions and wind speed, the waves may be gentle and serene, or they may be unwieldy and wild. So often in our lives, we feel as though we are caught up in these waves and getting thrashed around. We may even feel that we *are* the waves and have no control over what is happening (like when we are out of the ZOW).

Just as the depths of the ocean are clear and still, unaffected by the waves crashing on the surface, an underlying stillness can be found in non-judgmental awareness. This practice can help in moments when we become entangled with a wave or feel overwhelmed by it. It can help us to go deeper into the mind, creating stability and space to see what is happening more clearly than we would have if we were at the surface, being thrashed around. In this practice, we may also begin to sense that, like waves, none of our mental experiences are solid or permanent. With time, they can eventually settle back into the calm depths of the mind.

Beginner's Mind

Holding back our habitual mental projections is easier said than done. So too is describing what this practice feels like. Luckily, ancient contemplative approaches provide time-tested techniques, as well as a number of evocative metaphors to help. Sometimes the non-judging state is called *beginner's mind*: We try to perceive all these things like a child seeing a vibrant mural or vast landscape for the first time, without preconceived notions. The child notices each experience through fresh eyes, and they have no judgments about it. They just take it in.

To cultivate beginner's mind, we observe the inner canvas of the mind without getting entangled in or overly engaged with any particular thought, sensation, emotion, image, or memory. This is another way of understanding the key skill of self-distancing (non-appraisal). Think of this practice as shifting from *mindfulness of an object* to *mindfulness of the mind itself*. As we turn our attention to the mind, we ask: Instead of engaging, can I just witness each moment without projecting?

At first, this awareness may feel unfamiliar and awkward. That is normal. This is not something we expect to get perfect. In fact— and especially in this practice—having a goal of getting it right will interfere with being able to do it at all. We will either grab too tightly onto a passing thought, or be too relaxed and space out, or be swept up in daydreams. The not-too-tight, not-too-loose quality we are looking for is the same kind of vibrant, relaxed alertness we need to balance on a tightrope or on a log floating in a river.

Take a moment to **find a comfortable posture and connect with your body** and current feelings. If you notice tension in any part of the body, feel free to stretch or move.

Allow yourself to **settle into the present experience**. Take a few deep breaths if that is comfortable. Gently inhale, and, if you like, have the sense that nourishing air is infusing your entire being. As you breathe out, see if you can release tensions and worries to some degree to allow the body and mind to settle into an unfolding sense of calm or ease.

If settling is hard today, you may want to pause and spend a few moments with an earlier practice.

When ready, **open your attention** to the unfolding inner world of thoughts, memories, and emotions, without holding onto or pushing them away, simply witnessing as they come and go.

While observing your present-moment experiences, you may **let the field of your mind be like a vast sea**, with stillness deep down, relating to the unfolding mental activities as if they are the ripples or waves of your mind. Waves unfold on the surface of the sea when the conditions for them are there and subside into calmness when those conditions subside.

You may notice patterns of thoughts, concerns, or emotions that replay frequently. See if you can simply make note of them. As you **observe these wave-like mental experiences without identifying with them or judging them as good or bad,** they may gradually subside into stillness.

If this happens, you may simply rest your awareness in the unfolding calmness of the mind. If they do not subside, you continue to observe the mental experiences as they arise and pass.

***

While observing the flow of your inner world, **if you notice that you are caught up in an emotion or a string of thinking or stories,** see if you can release that entanglement and return to being a neutral observer of your inner world. Little by little, as the gap between one thought and another expands, you can rest your awareness in that expanding space of the mind.

***

Finally, reflect on how helpful it can be to have more space between your impulses and your responses to them. As a spark will not grow into a forest fire unless it is fanned by the wind, your impulses will not grow into emotional forest fires if you do not fan them with excessive judging and projections.

***

Take a moment to dedicate your practice today to those you know to be in need of health and wellbeing and, as you are able, expand this dedication to include a widening circle of beings on this earth.

And **conclude by setting an intention** to extend the skills and insights from this practice into everyday life.

***

Bringing the Skills to Life

- **Catch the spark.** Catch yourself when your mind has become entangled (in thought, worry, emotion, memory, or anticipation) and shift to recall that these are not solid realities but changing, temporary mental experience. See if you can allow them to come and go, without fanning the sparks into fires.

- **Find calm within the storm.** Try self-distancing when you are feeling dysregulated or stressed. Self-regulation using self-distancing can be quick and can be done while alone or even during stressful situations or conversations with other people. When you notice that you are feeling tightness or tension in the body, or that you are getting caught up in rumination or stressful emotions, take a few moments to step back and allow your thoughts, emotions, and sensations to come and go without automatically engaging with or judging them. As you create space between yourself and your unfolding mental experiences, you may notice a greater sense of relaxation and calm. This will not work in every situation, so approach it as an experiment. If it is not working for you, you might try going back to the previous modules' emotion regulation strategy of attention deployment—bringing the attention to something pleasant or neutral and holding it there.

- **Map your inner landscape.** As you become more aware of your thoughts this week, keep a list of those that seem to come up over and over again, paying special attention to thoughts that seem to come with emotional scripts. Remember, for now, you aren't trying to fix or stop these thoughts; we'll explore ways to shift our mental patterns (if we want to) in later modules. But noticing them, and getting better at disentangling from automatic impulses, is the first and most important step!

Personal Reflections

" One big insight I had while learning Module 3 is that I had always thought that, to meditate, I had to push away upsetting thoughts or annoying sensations and just grab after the positive. I realized that it was setting up an enormous amount of tension and judgment. So, when the instruction came to accept the thoughts, emotions, and sensations as they are instead of clinging to things I thought were positive or pushing away things I didn't think were appropriate, I really relaxed. I was able to let things float away, and naturally, they did. "

" I have a very demanding job. I am a high-level manager in a big company with many individuals reporting to me. All day long, my staff comes into my office with problems, and usually they are upset. This is incredibly stressful. I found the idea that there was (or the possibility of) a space or gap between stimulus and response revolutionary. Rather than responding immediately to others at work, I would pause, notice if I was getting activated from their distress, and take a breath or two. That space became my saving grace. I am now able to respond to each person or situation from a place of calm and clarity. Previously, I would be exhausted at the end of the day; now, I have the energy to take a walk when I get home and feel better overall. "

" I was going to the dentist for a routine checkup. Sitting in the waiting room, I realized my legs were shaking and my mouth was getting dry from anxiety. At first, I didn't know why. But by noticing the feelings, I realized I had been worrying for 30 minutes, all the way on the trip to the dentist, about what she might discover and how much money and pain may result. I was as stressed as if these things had already happened, even though I really didn't know if they would happen or not. Once I saw the worrying for what it was, suddenly I chuckled, and I was able to shake it off. After I stopped dwelling on stories about the future that were probably not even going to happen, my body calmed down, and my brain calmed down, and I was able to relax and read a magazine while I waited. "

Frequently Asked Questions

What if my thoughts won't stop?

First of all, congratulations on noticing that your thoughts won't stop! This is evidence that you are already benefiting from the Module 3 practice. It's true for all of us that, at times, thoughts won't stop. Just noticing this is a success!

Remember that the goal of CBCT is not to stop our thoughts, but to practice relating to activities in the mind in different and more helpful ways. Instead of wishing all these thoughts would stop, try to allow them just to come and go and, instead of getting caught up in them, remain as a witness to them. It can help to silently repeat to yourself: "This is just thinking," or "This is just mental experience." You might also try labeling thoughts as you notice them: "Thought." "Thought." "Thought." You can also try categorizing each different experience: "Sensation." "Image." "Feeling." "Thought." Labeling each experience gives the mind something to do, helping it avoid getting entangled or automatically pushing away the waves of inner experience. Scientists suggest that a thought lasts about 2 or 3 seconds, so this means that during 1 minute of time, we have an opportunity to notice 30 unique mental experiences—maybe even more!

This practice seems too difficult, like being thrown into the deep end of a pool. Are there any options that would allow moving into the practice more slowly?

There are many options! Along with the labeling exercises described in the answer to the prior question, try one of these:

5-4-3-2-1

To help the mind settle into accepting whatever arises and passes, especially on those days when things seem very unsettled, try this approach. To yourself, slowly name five colors you see in the room, then four sounds that you can hear, then three sensations of touch the body can feel, then two smells, then one taste. Cycle patiently through this once or twice. Next, see what it is like to add thoughts. After one taste, ask the question, "What thought am I having?" and see what you notice. Maybe there is a sequence of thoughts, as opposed to just one. Whenever you like, you can move back to the 5-4-3-2-1 naming practice without adding the observation of thought.

SIFT (Sensations, Images, Feelings, and Thoughts)

This exercise is adapted from the work of psychiatrist Dr. Dan Siegel, author of *Mindsight*[35] and many other books on mindfulness practices. Like the 5-4-3-2-1 exercise, this strategy helps you become aware of mental experiences one step at a time, giving the practice more guidance and making it less overwhelming. Instead of opening our awareness to all types of mental experiences immediately, start this practice by just focusing on body sensations (S), then add mental images (I), then feelings (F), and finally thoughts (T). By the end, you are open to the rising and passing of all these mental experiences.

Begin by focusing on the body, noticing whatever sensations arise. You might notice a breeze against your skin, a tightness in the shoulders, or an itch. Simply witness those sensations as they come into your awareness without clinging to them. After a few breaths, widen this lens to include any images that arise in the mind. You may first notice visual images (faces, scenes, colors, shapes), but you may also have sound images, such as a song that plays over and over in the mind. See if you can relate to these images with acceptance, without judging them as good or bad, and without trying to figure out why they are there. Then, after a minute or so, expand the lens to include feelings. These may be feelings like fatigue, hunger, or boredom, but could also include more complex emotions like sadness, joy, anticipation, or anxiousness. Either way, the experiment is to simply notice and relate to each of them with acceptance, without needing to change them or chase them. Finally, observe your thoughts. These are usually the mind's ongoing narrative, explaining, planning, celebrating, or criticizing. Our narrative is like a running commentary in the mind and is usually there if we look for it. However, the narrative doesn't appear as though we are reading a story in a book. Rather, it often unfolds as a few words, partial sentences, a combination of words and images. Simply allow them to flow; relate to them with acceptance and maybe even a sense of humor.

Wouldn't it be dangerous to stop appraising things as good and bad?

It would indeed be dangerous if we stopped appraising altogether, but that is not our goal. Our brain's appraisal system is powerful and exists for good reasons, and we are not going to stop it from looking out for us. When there is a real threat, we will still appraise it as a threat. By enhancing awareness of our inner life through this practice, we get better at noticing when the mind is appraising things narrowly or even incorrectly.

As we explored in Module 1, we have evolved to have a negativity bias—to pay more attention to the negative rather than the positive or even the neutral.[36] This has been important in helping us to survive, helping us scan for and identify dangers so we could quickly respond. If we were to come across a tiger or a snake, for example, it would be important for us to judge that as dangerous so we could fight or run away. However, in our modern world, most of us luckily do not face the same threats daily. Yet, we may still operate from this negativity bias, responding to situations and people in our lives as if they are life-threatening when, in many cases, they are not. This tendency to narrow our focus and to over-rate dangers has become a harmful habit that can ramp up our stress in the short term and chronically.

Paul Ekman explains that "our appraisal system can both save our lives and make us miserable. The issue, if we want to improve our emotional life, is to introduce awareness into it, to become aware that the impulse has arisen, and then choose whether to engage with that impulse or to let it pass."[37] When we judge things as completely good or bad, we automatically cling to them or try to get rid of them. If we judge a headache as "all bad," for example, we may then spiral into a fixed narrative around that—making the pain worse, along with our mood. Our automatic judgments, projections, and impulses often lead to unwanted outcomes, feelings, or behaviors. Becoming more self-aware allows us to act more thoughtfully. We gain clarity and control over our experiences and actions. For instance, if the headache is leading to a spiral of anxiety, we can catch that, disengage from the spiral, and allow ourselves to examine the situation more clearly. If it is alerting us to something that needs medical attention, we can then take the necessary steps to address the issue without fanning the flames of our concerns into a fire of unhelpful reactivity. Holding back from judgment, therefore, gives us the space and calm to discern what next steps should be taken.

Conclusion

In this module, we turned our attention to witnessing thoughts, feelings, and other elements of our inner lives without judgment. We saw how this can help us gain a clearer view of our inner world and provide insight into our mental experience. As we made these patterns and habits more visible, we also learned that we can become less controlled by them.

In the next module, we will begin to use these insights to inform our growth over time. With greater self-awareness we will make visible both our helpful and unhelpful habits, transforming unwanted ones through the process of analytical meditation—a mode of practice that we will engage in throughout the remaining modules. This powerful approach will help us identify and foster healthier mental habits to generate positive change in our lives and in the lives of others.

4

Cultivating Self-Compassion

Part 1: Accepting Our Vulnerabilities with Kindness

"No one ought to feel annoyed with themselves. It just adds to the frustration. I mean, we are human beings, fallible human beings."

— THE MOST REVEREND DESMOND TUTU,
THE BOOK OF JOY, 2016

Module 4

Building on the practice of relating to our thoughts, emotions, and other experiences without judging, repressing, or over-identifying with them, we can now learn to see our ups and downs from a broader perspective and develop the ability to respond to ourselves with greater understanding and kindness in the face of our setbacks.

It's natural that things go wrong in life; we will inevitably face adversity and a degree of emotional distress. When our views of our personal setbacks and failures become exaggerated or distorted, this can fuel reactions of excessive self-criticism and self-blame, which amplify our distress. How we marshal our internal resources to face difficulties directly impacts our well-being. In this module, we cultivate the fortitude to accept the inevitable vulnerabilities of our human condition, opening the possibility of responding with greater kindness and resilience when things go wrong.

ENDURING CAPABILITIES

4.1 Sustaining awareness that we are not alone in having setbacks and limitations

4.2 Maintaining the broader perspective that, while we may have limitations and challenges, we also have strengths and opportunities

4.3 Applying a systems-thinking perspective to setbacks, understanding that there are many contributing factors to any outcome that are not all within our control

Talking to a Friend

The following is an adaptation of an exercise from the leading program in the field of self-compassion, Mindful Self-Compassion.

Note:

For more information on Mindful Self-Compassion, see page 112.

1. Think of a good friend, a loved one, or someone for whom you have a lot of warm feelings, and remember (or imagine) a time in which they faced a setback.

    ✱ Examples: a mistake they made, a situation in which they failed, or a recognition of their faults or perceived inadequacies.

2. Take some time to reflect on what your chosen person experienced in that moment.

    ✱ How are they feeling? How do they feel about themselves? What's their overall mood, and how do they feel about the future in this moment? Are they being overly hard on themselves, and how does this affect their ability to move forward?

3. Take a few minutes and think of three to five things you said (or would say) to your friend in response to this difficult situation. Write them down.

    ✱ What feelings underlie your response toward your friend? Recall or imagine the tone you would take when responding to them.

4. Now, think of yourself experiencing a similar setback and write down three to five phrases that you tend to (or would) say to yourself when you're in that situation.

    ✱ What feelings underlie your response toward yourself? What kind of tone are you taking with yourself?

5. Finally, compare the two sets of responses. What do you notice?

    ✱ What differences, if any, do you notice between the phrases used?

❀ What differences, if any, do you notice in the attitude that underlies the kind of advice or response given?

❀ If you noticed that you are harsher toward yourself than toward others, what feelings does this bring up? How might this awareness change the way you relate to yourself in the future?

▶ Takeaway

How we respond to ourselves in the face of our setbacks and struggles varies. As we bring our awareness to our own tendencies, some of us may find that we are naturally understanding and kind with ourselves in difficult moments; we may consider self-compassion to be a strength of ours. But many of us find that we are more likely to be harsh on ourselves when things go wrong. Even if we naturally offer understanding and kindness to others in similar situations, we may struggle to offer that to ourselves.

In this activity, we may have discovered that we were harsher on our friend than on ourselves. We will spend more time examining those responses in the later modules of CBCT as we turn our attention to how we relate to others. This activity is focused on making visible how we relate and respond to ourselves and specifically noticing if we tend to be overly condemning or self-shaming.

It's surprising how overly critical we can be about our own flaws or errors. Sometimes we default to judging ourselves as incompetent when we do something as mundane as forgetting our keys. In some cases, we may even choose to respond this way because we believe that harping on our weaknesses will help us to improve. However, research suggests that the opposite is true—those who are more self-compassionate in the face of setbacks are more likely to succeed long-term than those who are more self-critical.[38]

Making visible how we respond to ourselves in the face of our setbacks and vulnerabilities gives us the opportunity to make a choice: If we find our responses to be helpful, we can continue to engage in them; if not, we can begin working to transform them and cultivate greater self-compassion.

Key Elements of the Module

Attention, self-awareness, and resilience all support self-compassion. Consider how, as stormy winds quiet, a lake becomes more tranquil and clear. When the lake's surface is calm, it makes it easier to see what is deep below and offers a clearer reflection of the surrounding environment. Similarly, with the calm and clarity we developed in previous modules, it becomes easier to see the deep patterns of our minds. In this module, we begin to make these patterns visible so as to reinforce our healthy habits and unlearn harmful ones. The calm that we learned to access more easily in the earlier modules helps us to see the reality of our human condition more clearly. And as we will see, this is the key to cultivating self-compassion.

Self-compassion springs from the genuine desire to free ourselves from distress and dissatisfaction. As we engage in the activities of this module, it is important to remember and connect with this *fundamental desire for wellbeing*—our deep aspirations as human beings to flourish, to be safe, and to be free from suffering and harm. As we remain mindful of this fundamental longing, we feed our motivation to cultivate greater self-compassion,

Self-compassion is an inner fortitude that fosters an abiding attitude of kindness toward the self in the face of life's adversities, and a commitment to identify and alleviate the underlying causes of our suffering.

strengthening habits that will alleviate suffering and contribute to our wellbeing.

CBCT divides self-compassion into two parts. Module 4 (Part 1) focuses on accepting our setbacks and vulnerabilities with greater understanding and kindness. Given how many of us naturally respond to our setbacks with excessive self-criticism and self-blame, Module 4 aims to soften those harsh responses by deepening the understanding that we are not alone in having setbacks, broadening our awareness to also recognize our strengths, and reminding ourselves that we are not in full control of every situation. Module 5 (Part 2) then turns to how we can find meaning in life's struggles. These perspectives, over time, foster greater responses of self-compassion. Both modules give us an opportunity to familiarize with and cultivate perspectives that can prevent additional distress when we face unwanted challenges.

As we familiarize ourselves with these perspectives, over time they can become the natural way that we understand and view the ups and downs of our lives. As we shift our disposition, we reinforce a new habit: an effortless, self-compassionate response in the face of challenges.

This process of shifting and broadening perspectives is referred to as *cognitive reappraisal*.[39] Like attention deployment and self-distancing, cognitive reappraisal is also considered an emotion regulation strategy by neuroscientists. It is another skill for managing our emotional and behavioral responses, and it is key to growing compassion.

This is the first module in CBCT where we turn to *analytical meditation*, a method that employs cognitive reappraisal of life events. This mode of practice gives us options to shift our perspective in order to alter emotional and behavioral responses. We will use this mode of meditation in each of the remaining modules.

As we strengthen our resilience through the cultivation of self-compassion, this also puts us in the position to be there for others. We can think of this as putting our own oxygen masks on before assisting others, as passengers are instructed to do on flights. By taking care of ourselves, we are better able to take care of others. This recognition makes a turning point on the journey toward developing compassion.

The Tale of Kisa Gotami[40]

Kisa Gotami lived in a village in ancient India and was mother to one young child. As in many ancient societies, there was high pressure for women to have and raise children. Kisa grew up feeling the weight of this expectation and was thrilled when she gave birth to her first child.

At the age of three, her child unexpectedly got sick. The sickness progressed quickly, and despite all her efforts, her child soon passed away. Kisa was overcome with grief and suffering. She blamed herself for not being able to prevent this tragedy and felt that she failed in her role as a mother.

From that place of grief and despair, Kisa set out to find a way to revive her child. She carried the body through the village, begging everyone to help her bring the child back to life. She went to every doctor she could find, but nobody could help. After a few days, someone suggested she take the body to the Buddha.

When Kisa found the Buddha and explained the situation, he told her he could help. "Leave your child here, then go find a handful of mustard seeds and bring them back to me," the Buddha instructed.

"Yes, of course," said Kisa, feeling immense relief. She placed the body down and eagerly turned to go collect the seeds.

"But wait," said the Buddha. As Kisa paused and turned, the Buddha added, "It is most important that these seeds come from a household that has experienced no loss."

Full of hope, Kisa ran back to the village. She knocked on the door of the first home she came to and asked for mustard seeds. The owner agreed, but when Kisa asked if the household had experienced any loss, the man said he had recently lost his aunt to pneumonia. Disappointed, Kisa moved on.

At the next house, an elderly woman also agreed to give her some seeds but said she had lost her husband several years ago. After that, at yet another home, a young man said he had lost his mother. At another, someone lost a sister, then a brother. Further down the street, one person had also lost their young child. Kisa travelled throughout the whole village, listening to one person after another tell stories of losses and personal grief.

Kisa eventually realized that she was not alone in her loss. Far from it, in fact. Again and again, she found she shared grief with so many others, perhaps *all* others in the village, perhaps everyone in the world. She began to feel a deep connection with each of the people who kindly shared their stories of death and loss. Kisa then came to understand that her loss was not her fault; it was not evidence of being a bad parent or flawed person. She began to see that uncertainty and loss are a part of every life. Her burden of shame and self-blame was lifted and her experience of loss no longer isolated her but, to the contrary, became a path to connection.

Kisa returned to the Buddha without the mustard seeds but thanked him for opening her eyes to this broader perspective that relieved her of the crippling despair. She gathered her child's body and held a funeral, where the whole village came to share in her loss. Although still suffering from the grief, she was able to let go of crippling perspectives of failure and fault.

Even as she began the difficult task of planning her next steps, she was strengthened and encouraged by the wisdom gained from her search for the mustard seeds: loss, imperfection, and vulnerability are part of every life.

Kisa's story illustrates the power of recalling our shared human condition. We will all experience some pain, loss, and suffering at some point in our lives. We are all vulnerable. To ignore or reject this reality is to set ourselves up for experiencing even more pain as we confront these experiences regardless. By contrast, when we are mindful that difficulties are a part of every life, we will not take those problems quite so personally, adding to our distress, when they inevitably happen. We can ultimately see that "personal" setbacks are not only happening to us but are similar to those of many others. This greater understanding and acceptance of our human condition can then bring relief from harsh self-judgment, excessive self-criticism, and extreme feelings of isolation—responses that only serve to magnify the inevitable pain that is part of any life.

I'm Not the Only One

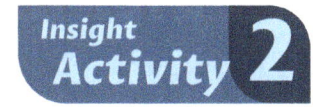

1. Think about and describe a time when you were hard on yourself for making a mistake, or when you were distraught after a setback, but then realized you were not alone. Consider the following examples:

   ❀ Experiencing a breakup and being harsh on yourself for struggling to get through it, but then hearing a heartbreak song and realizing you weren't alone.

   ❀ Making a mistake at work or with your family and beating yourself up over it, but then having a conversation where you realized you were not alone and that such mistakes are made by all of us.

2. What did this realization feel like? How did it change your attitude or shift how you relate to yourself?

3. How can you apply this insight moving forward in your life? In what types of situations would this perspective be most helpful? What benefits might come from holding this perspective when you face challenges?

▶ Takeaway

It's inevitable that we will lose things, miss opportunities, make mistakes, and end up in situations and with feelings we don't want. Though we may have deep aspirations to be free of these problems, both success and struggle are part of the full spectrum of being human. In such human moments of struggle, we often feel that problems are the only things that are happening and think, "This is only happening to me." But if we step back and look at the situation from a broader perspective, we might ask, "Is it just me, or do others also go through setbacks and struggles?"

Discovering that we are not alone in making mistakes, experiencing setbacks, or struggling with our emotions helps us to see through distorted perspectives, such as, "I'm a total failure because of this mishap." This prevents us from reducing ourselves to one situation and helps us to see ourselves more fully and realistically. This awareness can then bring a sense of belonging and relief, leading to responses of understanding and resilience instead of excessive self-criticism, self-blame, helplessness, or defeat.

Making Strengths Visible

This exercise was adapted from psychologist Dr. Ryan Niemiec's book, *Character Strengths Interventions: A Field Guide for Practitioners*.[41]

1. Reflect on a specific situation or time when you were at your best and functioning well. This could be something recent or from your past, related to your work life, school, relationships, or anything else.

2. Describe this situation or time, deeply emphasizing how you engaged and acted at that time, as well as any outcomes that resulted.

3. Read through the story you've written and identify which of your strengths were used in that situation. (Feel free to refer to the list of character strengths in the box below or come up with your own.)[42]

▪ Appreciation of beauty	▪ Hope	▪ Perseverance
▪ Bravery	▪ Humility	▪ Perspective
▪ Creativity	▪ Humor	▪ Prudence
▪ Curiosity	▪ Judgment (wisdom)	▪ Self-regulation
▪ Fairness	▪ Kindness	▪ Social intelligence
▪ Forgiveness	▪ Leadership	▪ Spirituality
▪ Gratitude	▪ Love	▪ Teamwork
▪ Honesty	▪ Love of learning	▪ Zest

4. What does it feel like to notice these strengths?

5. How might greater awareness of your strengths be helpful in your everyday life? How might this awareness be helpful in challenging moments—during setbacks, mistakes, or failures?

▶ **Takeaway**

Some of us may have noticed more positive feelings from simply reflecting on our strengths. Not everyone will notice such feelings the first time doing this exercise, but psychologists have found that strengths-based interventions—ones that focus on bringing awareness to and enhancing positive qualities—do tend to increase our positive feelings and wellbeing overall,[43] and have been found to reduce stress, depression, and physical symptoms.[44]

This shift from a narrow focus on our weaknesses to a genuine acknowledgment and appreciation of our strengths is a powerful reappraisal to support self-compassion. Broadening our awareness to see that we are more than our limitations, that we also have strengths and opportunities, serves as an antidote to negativity bias. We can gain relief from some distress by allowing ourselves to enjoy the positives within and around us. Focusing on what we have done well, and can do well, will also be a launching point for cultivating our self-agency, which we will explore in depth in Module 5.

 **What We Can (and Cannot) Control**

1. Call to mind a few different moments when things did not go the way you wanted them to go, despite your efforts, and that led to self-blame. Please pick moments that are not too overwhelming or distressing to recall.

    ❋ Perhaps you made a New Year's resolution but struggled to keep it, or perhaps you hoped a relationship would work out and it did not. Maybe you applied for a job and were passed over or planned a relaxing vacation that did not turn out as expected.

2. Choose one of these moments and apply a systems-thinking lens by writing down as many of the following factors as you can.

    ❋ What factors directly contributed to this incident?

    ❋ What factors indirectly contributed?

    ❋ Which of these factors were within your control?

    ❋ Which were outside of your control?

3. Describe any emotional shifts or insights that emerged from the recognition that the outcome was not fully in your control.

    ❋ Examples of emotional shifts: reduced self-blame or obsessiveness, or increased lightness or relief.

    ❋ Examples of insights: If I am not 100 percent in control, how can I be 100 percent to blame? It's not helpful to try to get everything perfect, since there is no human that can control everything; I can let go of trying to control things (or people) that I don't have influence over.

▶ Takeaway

Many of us go through life thinking we have full control over what we pursue and engage in. Even if this is not the case, that assumption may still creep in when things don't go how we want them to. If we think that it is our efforts alone that contribute to an outcome, and things do not go well, we may feel confusion, frustration, or even despair and react with excessive self-blame and self-criticism. If we believe that we are in full control, then we will naturally give ourselves all of the blame when things don't go as planned.

In this exercise, we applied *systems-thinking*, the process of holistically examining the many factors that contribute to any outcome. This helps us get beyond a narrow, sometimes self-focused view to see the full situation more fully. This view can bring a more reasoned understanding of our ability to affect any given circumstance. Clearly, just as some factors provide us the opportunity to influence the situation, other factors lie beyond our control. Though this may seem counterintuitive at first, the acceptance that we are not in full control can relieve—and even prevent—distressing emotions that would otherwise arise in the face of setbacks, especially the bigger ones.

As we make visible the many factors that lead to unwanted outcomes, we must be careful not to swing to the other extreme and shift the blame entirely away from ourselves and onto other people or circumstances. Neither view considers the full picture. By recognizing that no single person is in full control of their circumstances, we can soften the harsh blame that can arise toward both ourselves and others. This key insight will be explored further in Module 6: Expanding Our Circle of Concern.

"You may not control all the events that happen to you, but you can decide not to be reduced by them."

— MAYA ANGELOU,
LETTER TO MY DAUGHTER,
2008

Benefits of Self-Compassion

"While the motivational power of self-criticism comes from fear, the motivational power of self-compassion comes from the desire to be healthy. Self-compassion recognizes that failure is not only inevitable, but it's also our best teacher, something to be explored rather than avoided at all costs. Self-compassion also allows us to acknowledge areas of personal weakness by recognizing that imperfection is part of the shared human experience. We can then work on improving ourselves, not because we're unacceptable as we are, but because we want to thrive and be happy."

— KRISTIN NEFF, PHD, CO-DEVELOPER OF MINDFUL SELF-COMPASSION

Self-compassion is relatively new as an area of contemplative practice, but hundreds of studies showing its benefits are proving that it is a well-grounded approach. Since 2003, the field has been led by Dr. Kristin Neff at the University of Texas and psychologist Dr. Christopher Germer at Harvard. The two have created research measures for self-compassion and have helped to establish the term, as well as highlight its importance for human wellbeing. Their program, Mindful Self-Compassion (MSC), shares several of the core practices of CBCT, especially those in Module 4. They focus on the importance of recognizing our shared human condition, as we have been exploring here. Here, we detail just some of the findings on the benefits of self-compassion as discovered through Neff's and Germer's work, and that of many others who have stepped into the field of self-compassion research.

In one study, Neff and her colleagues worked with veterans returning from the wars in Iraq and Afghanistan. Clinical psychologists determined that nearly half of the veterans (42 percent) experienced symptoms of PTSD. Using a 26-item self-report questionnaire that included statements like, "I'm tolerant of my own flaws and inadequacies," Dr. Neff and her colleagues then rated participants' levels of self-compassion. The study concluded that the more self-compassionate veterans were, the less severe their PTSD symptoms were.[45]

"In general, studies like this suggest that self-compassion attenuates people's reactions to negative events in ways that are distinct from and, in some cases, more beneficial than self-esteem," the researchers found. In other words, without the pressure to be superhuman, it is easier to accept feedback and criticism; it is much harder to learn and improve when you believe you already know everything. Self-compassionate people, furthermore, tend to ruminate less because they can "break the cycle of negativity" by accepting their own imperfections.

Note:

For more information on Dr. Kristin Neff's research and on Mindful Self-Compassion, the contemplative training program she co-developed with Dr. Chris Germer, visit self-compassion.org.

RESEARCHED BENEFITS OF SELF-COMPASSION:[46]

- Greater resilience

- Less anxiety and depression

- Reduced rumination

- Less suppression of difficult emotions

- Greater ability to cope with early childhood trauma and chronic physical pain

- Greater happiness, optimism, curiosity, creativity, enthusiasm, inspiration, and excitement

- Positive association with emotional intelligence, wisdom, life satisfaction, and feelings of social connectedness

- Promotion of personal improvement[47]

Cognitive Reappraisal Strategy

Holding Back from Shooting the Second Arrow

> A teacher asks her student, "If a person is struck by an arrow, is it painful?"
>
> The student says, "Yes, that would be very painful."
>
> The teacher then asks, "If a person is struck by a second arrow in the same place, is that even more painful?"
>
> The student responds, "Yes, of course. If someone is struck again in the same spot, that would be much more painful than being struck only once."
>
> The teacher replies, "In life, we cannot always control the first arrow. However, the second arrow is our reaction to being hit by the first arrow. If we can avoid shooting that second arrow, we take an important step toward the relief of much additional suffering."

There are challenges in life that are inevitable: All of us experience setbacks, failures, illness, and loss—these are natural and universal aspects of life. Think of these experiences as the "first arrow" in the story above. We will experience some pain that we cannot control, but at times, we may engage in further harmful emotional or behavioral reactions to the setback. This is the second arrow, amplifying the initial pain of the situation. When we fall down, we may react by feeling frustrated with ourselves and engaging in harsh self-criticism that erodes our self-confidence.

Module 4 and the Emotion Timeline

The diagram below uses a simplified version of Paul Ekman's emotion timeline to explore how our appraisals of certain situations fuel emotional and behavioral responses. Shown are some common appraisals that occur when confronted with events such as setbacks, limitations, and mistakes. Can you relate to these appraisals, as well as the emotions and behaviors that come after them?

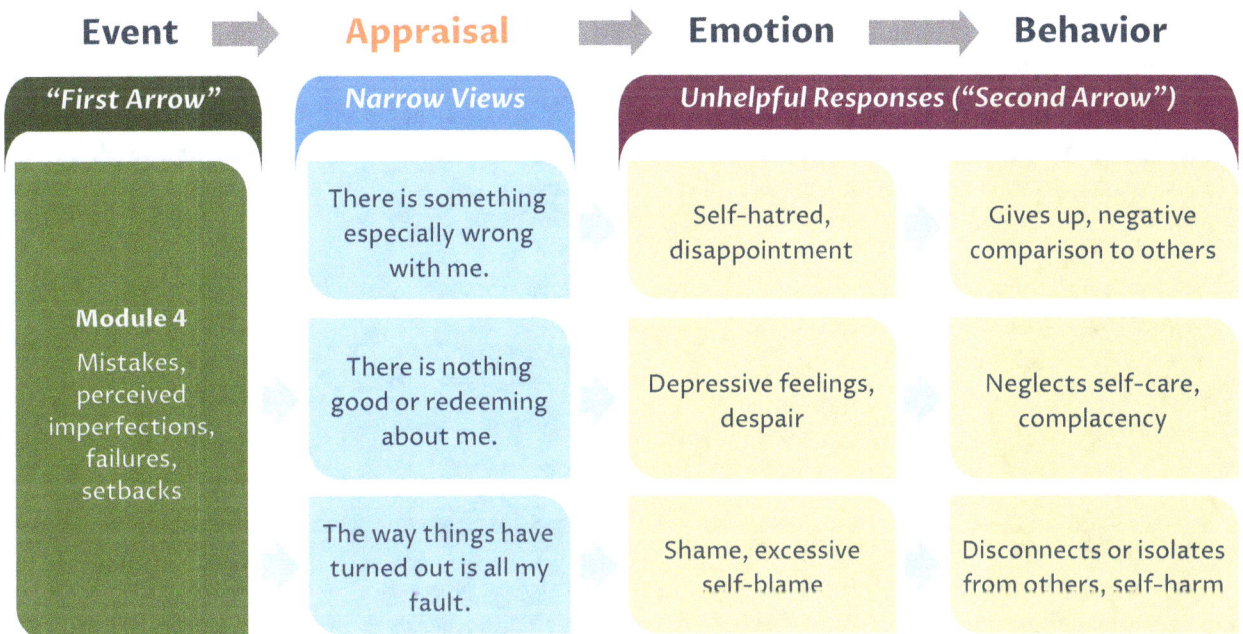

Understanding that our appraisals influence our responses gives us a point of entry for making lasting change; we are given the opportunity to alleviate the "second arrow" of added distress. Through the process of analytical meditation, we examine to see if we have any narrow views shooting that second arrow. We then familiarize ourselves with broader perspectives so they can eventually become our natural outlook, resulting in healthier emotions and behaviors that are effortless and spontaneous.

It would be incorrect to blame all our struggles on our own appraisals because those appraisals rely so much on our context, culture, and societal expectations. As social beings, none of us could expect to be free from these influences, even as we can gain greater awareness of them. However, understanding the emotion timeline can help us take steps to disarm some of those painful second arrows. Consider what happens in the "reappraisal" timeline below, compared to the one above:

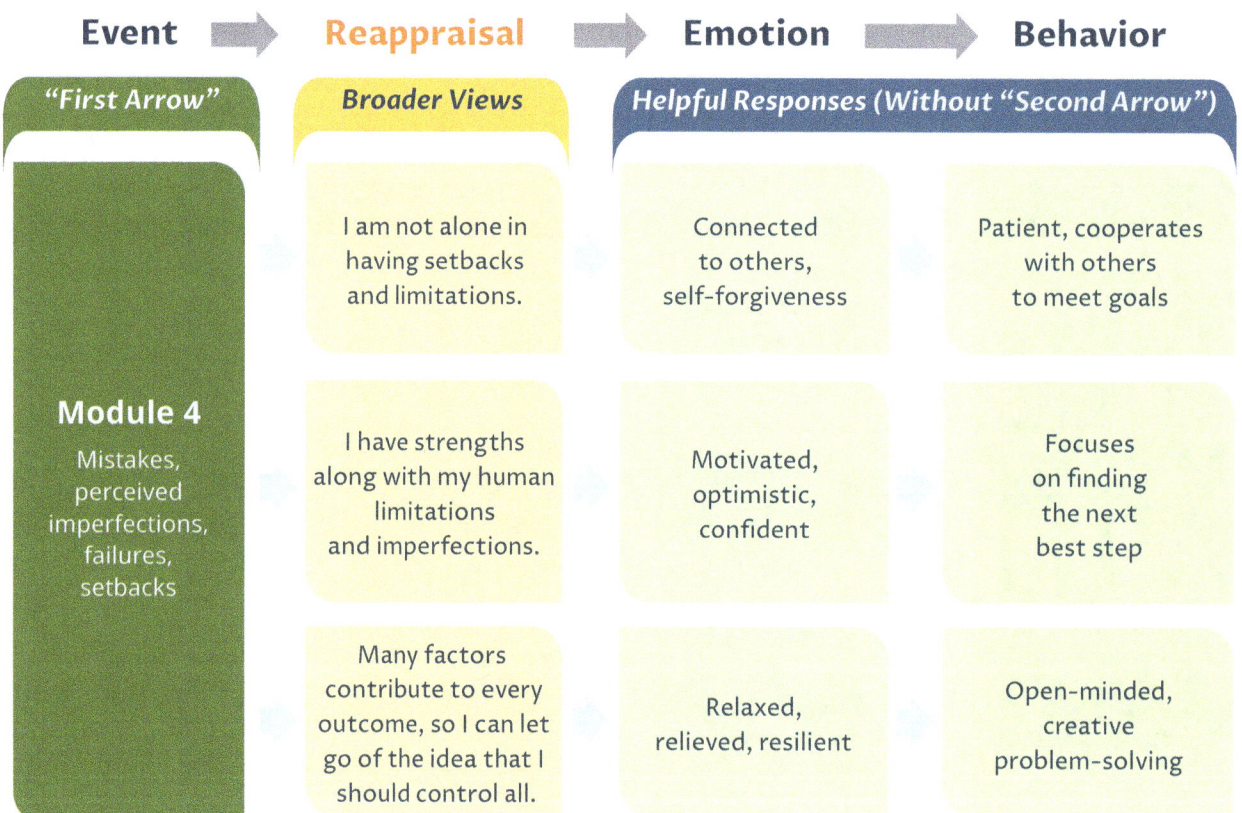

Event	Reappraisal	Emotion	Behavior
"First Arrow"	*Broader Views*	*Helpful Responses (Without "Second Arrow")*	
Module 4 Mistakes, perceived imperfections, failures, setbacks	I am not alone in having setbacks and limitations.	Connected to others, self-forgiveness	Patient, cooperates with others to meet goals
	I have strengths along with my human limitations and imperfections.	Motivated, optimistic, confident	Focuses on finding the next best step
	Many factors contribute to every outcome, so I can let go of the idea that I should control all.	Relaxed, relieved, resilient	Open-minded, creative problem-solving

The simple shift from narrow appraisals to more holistic reappraisals can dramatically change the emotions and behaviors that follow, often alleviating added distress that we want so badly to avoid. Our power to make helpful reappraisals supports our self-agency, as we will explore further in the next module.

Take a moment to **find a comfortable posture and connect with your body** and current feelings. If you notice tension in any part of the body, feel free to stretch or move.

Allow yourself to **settle into the present experience**. Take a few deep breaths if that is comfortable. Gently inhale, and, if you like, have the sense that nourishing air is infusing your entire being. As you breathe out, see if you can release tensions and worries to some degree to allow the body and mind to settle into an unfolding sense of calm or ease.

If settling is hard today, you may want to pause and spend a few moments with an earlier practice.

When ready, **spend a few moments** connecting to your **deep desire for wellbeing and freedom from harm**.

Take some time to **reflect on how you tend to respond to yourself when things do not go well.** What thoughts or stories arise in response to mistakes or perceived inadequacies? What emotions tend to arise in those moments?

Though setbacks and mistakes are natural, and the emotions that come from them are also natural, at times the flames of these emotions can be fanned to a self-defeating level. Frustration may turn into excessive self-criticism. Disappointment may turn into harsh self-blame. You may even notice your inner critic saying things like, "I am a failure," "I am useless," or "I am no good."

Consider: **If you are currently experiencing a setback, mistake, or perceived shortcoming**, what thoughts or emotions arise when you focus on this unwanted situation? How do you speak to yourself about it?

If you notice distressing emotions or harsh inner responses, see if you can **look at your situation from a broader perspective**.

Are you the only one facing difficulties, or is this a shared human situation? Is there anyone who does not make mistakes from time to time?

How does it feel when you take time to **make visible your shared human condition**? Is there a shift away from "I'm the only one" and toward "I'm not alone"? If so, what does this shift feel like?

⌒

Sometimes, in the grip of excessive harshness and self-blame, we may feel, "There is nothing good about me." But **making mistakes does not reduce us to being a mistake**. We may not be good at everything. Nobody is. But each of us is good at something.

⌒

Take a few moments to **reflect on your strengths** and what you can appreciate about yourself, making visible the things that are going well or going better in your life.

⌒

Consider: How do these broader perspectives shift your feelings about current challenges? See if you can notice an **emerging sense of self-acceptance or even kindness** in the face of your shortcomings. And, if possible, sit with these feelings toward yourself, perhaps **seeing them unfold as a soft, soothing light at the center of the chest**. If you like, with each in-breath, you can let this light and all that it represents expand, nourishing your whole being.

⌒

Finally, reflect on how helpful it can be to be able to see the ups and downs of life from a broader perspective. How might this contribute to our wellbeing and support our relationships with others?

⌒

Take a moment to dedicate your practice today to those you know to be in need of health and wellbeing and, as you are able, expand this dedication to include a widening circle of beings on this earth.

And **conclude by setting an intention** to extend the skills and insights from this practice into everyday life.

⌒

Bringing the Skills to Life

- **Embrace the human condition.** Catch yourself when your inner critic engages in harsh self-judgment or discouraging thoughts about your mistakes or setbacks. Make a shift by reflecting on our shared human condition; recall that everyone makes mistakes, and every life has limitations as well as opportunities.

- **Soften the inner critic daily.** In your everyday life, notice things that you might criticize yourself for doing when, in fact, they present very human limitations and imperfections. See these as opportunities to show yourself kindness; try to find one every day! Here are some examples of things that regularly happen, which present an opportunity to soften that harsh inner critic:

  ❀ Dropping or breaking something

  ❀ Burning something while cooking

  ❀ Misplacing your keys or your phone

  ❀ Oversleeping

  ❀ Spilling something on the floor

  ❀ Forgetting to call a family member or friend on a special occasion

  ❀ Saying the wrong thing and wishing you could take it back

  ❀ Noticing a new wrinkle on your face when you look in the mirror

  ❀ Worrying that you are unable to get your spouse, child, or roommate to clean the dishes

Personal Reflections

66 While living with and caring for my 80+-year-old mother and my 100+-year-old grandmother, patience has been in short supply. I felt terribly guilty when I would become frustrated with them. The practice of self-compassion has been essential to reframe my sense of guilt, anger, self-judgment by recognizing that they were normal in the situation. Instead of condemning myself for being human, I was able to accept my shortcomings. It made me feel freer, lighter, and more capable of continuing to care for them both. 99

66 I wish I had understood self-compassion when I was younger! I was often biting off more than I could chew, taking too many difficult classes at once, and failing in areas that had been otherwise easy for me. I was stubborn and determined to load up on Advanced Placement courses . . . Instead of dropping one or two and balancing my schedule when things got too intense, I pushed on. It was a disaster for my health and for my grades. I had thought I was being brave by doing so much, but it was braver in the end for me to admit that I had taken on too much and find a way to make better choices. When I admitted that I had weaknesses, and when I stopped worrying about what others thought of my dropping courses, I felt so much better. 99

66 You can't control every factor no matter how hard you try—that was my aha moment. When things went wrong at work, I turned the blame on myself, and looked for the holes I should have plugged, the solutions I should have found to prevent anything from going wrong. But there's so much freedom in realizing that most of the time, no matter how hard I try to control things, so much is out of my control. 99

Frequently Asked Questions

What is self-compassion not?

- **Self-indulgence:** Self-indulgence is an excessive gratification of our immediate desires, and it can undermine our motivation to take on difficult or long-term tasks. Often, self-indulgence contributes to the suffering we want to avoid, and in this way is the opposite of self-compassion! For example, let's say we like chocolate. We might eat a piece or two on a tough day to feel better, which is not a problem. But if we eat the entire bag of chocolate, we're likely to feel unwell in the short-term, and if we keep over-indulging in sweets, we might even suffer long-term health problems. This is not to say that we should never enjoy ourselves or engage in self-care, taking vacations when we can, enjoying entertainment, taking warm baths to relax, eating good food, etc. Those are really important for our wellbeing, but indulging in too much of any of these things can end up causing us harm, which is opposite to the goal of self-compassion.

- **Complacency:** Complacency is a form of self-satisfaction that can prevent us from seeing the many opportunities for growth that life can offer. Self-compassion involves responding to our imperfections and vulnerabilities with kindness, but it also includes strengthening our motivation to learn from our struggles and to grow, which will be the focus of Module 5: Cultivating Self-Compassion: Part 2. Complacency leads to staying stagnant, whereas cultivating self-compassion is the process of transforming our habits to contribute to our own long-term wellbeing and the wellbeing of others.

- **Self-pity:** Self-pity often comes from comparing ourselves to others, thinking, "They're in a great place, or doing so well, and I'm not, poor me!" Cultivating self-compassion, on the other hand, involves seeing what we share with others, not only how we are different. We're all vulnerable to challenges in life; we're not alone in that. This perspective can be relieving and encouraging, inspiring us to keep trying, whereas self-pity, if sustained, often leads us to feel worse about ourselves and to give up.

- **Self-esteem:** Self-esteem, though generally a good thing, is different from self-compassion. Self-esteem refers to a sense of self-worth or seeing oneself as valuable. There is a lot of research on this, highlighting its value and benefits. But in some cases, our self-esteem can depend on competing with others, or judging others as less worthy. Self-compassion is distinct from this type of self-esteem because it does not rely on changing circumstances or putting ourselves above others. Rather, it depends on the recognition of the human reality and vulnerabilities that we all share.

When will I feel changes from the practice?

The familiarization process takes time, so be patient. It is worth the time and effort. Recall the three levels of understanding that we move through in CBCT: The first level is Content Knowledge, the second is Personalized Insight, and the third is Embodied Understanding. If the content knowledge doesn't have a chance to become absorbed on a personal level, then the insights cannot become embodied. (This process can be reviewed in detail on pages 10–13.)

The insight activities and the formal practice give us the chance to engage, intentionally and regularly, with this process of familiarization. It is not that insights can't also become familiar to us through informal practices, but deliberate formal practice provides a stronger focus and opportunity for the aha moments to arise. These moments shift the content toward personalized insight, the second level of understanding. As the term indicates, this happens when the content knowledge hits you at a deeper level and you have a *felt sense* that what you are learning is true—really true—for you.

What should I do if I get pushed out of my ZOW?

Remember and rely on the previous three practices.

This practice, like any practice, may bring up thoughts or feelings that push you out of your ZOW. You can return to any of the earlier practices of CBCT at any time, no matter which module you are practicing (for example, return to Module 1 by imagining a nurturing moment, or Module 2 by focusing on a bodily sensation). That is how CBCT is designed, and why the modules are organized in this sequence: The earlier practices provide support for the later ones. If at any time you feel especially activated or getting stuck outside the ZOW, please respect what you are feeling, stop the practice, and shift to another activity—maybe taking a walk, getting a drink of water, or another "Help Now!" strategy (see page 32)—to help re-regulate and move back into your ZOW. Or you may move on to the next module. Either way, you may return to the practice at time when you feel more settled and ready to try again.

Conclusion

In this module, we began to strengthen self-compassion by making visible and accepting the vulnerability of our human condition. We saw how this acceptance alleviates the harsh reactions of excessive self-criticism and self-blame, reactions that can magnify our distress in challenging times, pushing us toward feeling overwhelmed or giving up. We engaged in the analytical process, using cognitive reappraisal to deepen and maintain more holistic perspectives, and to free ourselves from narrow judgments and interpretations.

In the next module, we will continue to deepen perspectives that foster more helpful responses in the face of our challenges, leading to greater resilience and self-agency. The acceptance of our human condition gives us the confidence and ability to face inevitable struggles and to find meaning in them.

Cultivating
Self-Compassion

Part 2: Finding Meaning in Our Vulnerabilities

*"If there is meaning in life at all, then
there must be meaning in suffering.
Suffering is an ineradicable part of life.
Even as fate and death. Without suffering
and death, human life cannot be complete."*

— VIKTOR FRANKL,
MAN'S SEARCH FOR MEANING, 1946

Module 5

With greater understanding and acceptance that challenges are a natural part of life, we can explore the potential to transform those challenges into growth, meaning, and purpose.

We've explored ways to soften excessive self-criticism and self-blame by making visible our human condition. This awareness helps us respond to our setbacks with greater understanding, acceptance, and resilience. In this module, we ask: How can we move forward? Can we transform our vulnerabilities into opportunities for meaning-making? To be sure, moments of struggle are hard, but they can also be opportunities for growth. They can provide a chance to connect to our deeper values and goals, as well as to inspire empathy for others going through similar challenges. Seeing this potential can provide additional relief when we experience setbacks—it might make us feel less helpless and overwhelmed. Of course, this does not deny the hardships or mean that they are good, but this broadened perspective can act as a powerful path to greater resilience and self-agency.

ENDURING CAPABILITIES

5.1 Sustaining the awareness that we can grow and learn from our mistakes, failures, and setbacks

5.2 Using adversity as a way to clarify our core values and purpose

5.3 Enhancing sensitivity and compassion for others who share our experiences of vulnerability

5.4 Strengthening self-agency and fostering confidence in our ability to alleviate our distress

Opportunities for Growth

Insight Activity 1

1. Describe a time when an unwanted challenge, roadblock, or mistake led to something positive—a strengthened skill or quality, a valuable insight, a better situation, or a helpful path. Perhaps it was even an important turning point in your life.

    ❋ Example: "When COVID hit, I didn't get the job I wanted. I felt like giving up. Opportunities for people like me—just out of college—were really drying up. But I've always been interested in agriculture, so instead of getting depressed about my situation, I became a farmer's apprentice. And I got hooked. I went on to start my own farm and business. There's no question that the setback of not getting that job turned out to be the best thing that could have happened to me."

2. See if you can recall what you felt as you were experiencing the unwanted challenge or mistake before you recognized that this may lead to something positive. What are three words that you would use to describe the difficult emotional state?

3. How do you feel about the difficult situation now that you've seen the positives it has led to?

4. Describe any insights that may have come up in this reflection. How might those insights influence how you respond to your struggles, mistakes, or perceived limitations as they come up in the future?

▶ **Takeaway**

In the last chapter, we began to accept our failures and setbacks as an inevitable part of life and, with that, softened our harsh, habitual responses. We now take it a step further by looking at these experiences with a growth mindset—to see how we can learn from our mistakes and discover new strengths and opportunities from our challenges.

"When one door of happiness closes, another opens. But often we gaze so long at the closed door we don't notice the one opening."

— HELEN KELLER, *WE BEREAVED*, 1929

From the outside, Thomas Edison's invention of the lightbulb seems like a single, grand, successful act. He built it, he switched on the power, and there was light. However, there is more to the story. In his words, he made several hundred attempts that didn't work. An interviewer asked him, "How do you feel after all of your failed attempts?" His response was, "I didn't fail. I learned hundreds of ways not to invent the lightbulb."[48] Just as babies learn when they try to walk, or how we learn to read or ride a bike, Edison expresses a common human experience: We try, fail, *learn*, and try again.

Some of us may have had experiences that seemed horrible when we were going through them, but eventually we went on to appreciate them. As we explored in Module 3, we often are quick to judge things as good or bad. This judgment is natural—even helpful in some cases. That said, acknowledging that we do not always know where these things will lead is also important. The more open we are to the possibility that even the hardest things in life can lead to something positive, the less intense our distress will be when those challenges arise.

With a growth mindset, we can find meaning in the inevitable struggles we experience. This is not to say every cloud has a silver lining or that the struggles we experience are always good for us. However, even in situations where the setback is 100 percent negative or harmful, a growth mindset orients us toward steps we can take to move forward in the most helpful way.

In some cases, struggles can and do limit growth and make moving forward especially challenging. In other cases, we may find a shift in perspective beneficial—maybe from thinking that there is *nothing* good that could come from a setback to realizing that it actually served us well in some way. Recalling and reflecting on past moments, when we found greater strength, improvement, or something beautiful following something more difficult, can help us feel encouraged and find creative ways forward when we face future setbacks. The reminder that we came through challenges in the past, and perhaps even grew from them, can provide a greater sense of resilience, calm, and courage to persevere when struggles inevitably come our way.

Key Elements of the Module

Self-compassion springs from the genuine desire to free ourselves from distress and dissatisfaction despite the reality of life's inevitable struggles. To support this process, Module 4: Cultivating Self-Compassion: Part 1 focused on accepting our setbacks and vulnerabilities with greater understanding and kindness. Module 5: Cultivating Self-Compassion: Part 2 focuses on how we can find meaning in these difficult situations. Both modules allow us to familiarize ourselves with perspectives that can mitigate additional pain when we face challenges.

Have you ever experienced a setback when all seemed lost or doomed, but later—perhaps months or even years later—you came to appreciate what you learned and how you grew from it? When experiencing loss or a failure, did you find that it helped you connect more easily with others who had faced something similar, or helped you clarify what is most important in your life? Have you ever felt helpless when facing a challenge but later realized that there was a step forward that could be taken—something worthwhile that could be done—even if it was small?

These experiences point us to the reality that we can find meaning in our setbacks and tap into our *self-agency,* our ability to act and make a difference. Finding meaning in our vulnerabilities is not about viewing our struggles as a positive or even claiming that there is *always* a silver lining. Rather, this is about shifting how we view and respond to our challenges when they occur so that we can move forward and avoid getting stuck in feelings of anxiety or helplessness. While there are many factors of life that are out of our control, there is almost always something we can do to address the underlying causes of our suffering and to contribute to our own wellbeing. In this module, we continue to shift the way we view our setbacks, alleviating unhelpful emotional reactions such as anxiety or helplessness. As we broaden our perspectives and make visible the many opportunities that can come from our setbacks, we transform our response from despair to purpose, from powerlessness to empowerment, from inaction to action.

Self-compassion is an inner fortitude that fosters an abiding attitude of kindness toward the self in the face of life's adversities, and a commitment to identifying and alleviating the underlying causes of our suffering.

"Man is ready and willing to shoulder any suffering, as soon and as long as he can see a meaning in it."

— VIKTOR FRANKL,
THE FEELING OF
MEANINGLESSNESS:
A CHALLENGE TO
PSYCHOTHERAPY AND
PHILOSOPHY, 2010

Making Meaning from Adversity

Malala Yousafzai was born in Mingora, Pakistan, in 1997. Despite the more limited opportunities available to women in her village, her father prioritized her education and worked hard to give her every opportunity that would be afforded to a son. In 2008, the Taliban, an extremist group, dominated the village, imposing many rules and restrictions and enforcing severe punishments for those who disobeyed. After years of attending her beloved school, Malala and her female classmates were forbidden to continue their education.

Four years later, when Malala was 15, she began to speak out. She saw this injustice as an opportunity to advocate for girls, and specifically for their equal right to education. She found meaning and purpose in this pursuit, but her adversity soon worsened when her outspokenness made her a target of the Taliban authorities. They sent soldiers to kill her, and she was shot in the face at close range.

Fortunately, the bullet missed her brain, and she was able to flee to England for lifesaving treatment. Her family settled there, but not into obscurity. "It was then I knew I had a choice: I could live a quiet life, or I could make the most of this new life I had been given. I determined to continue my fight until every girl could go to school."[49] The greater suffering Malala experienced did not stop her from aspiring toward a goal. In fact, it sparked even greater resolve to continue the fight and lent an importance and urgency to her work.

In 2014, at only 17 years old, Malala became the youngest recipient of the Nobel Peace Prize in history. She had launched a

"Let us bring equality, justice, and peace for all. Not just the politicians and the world leaders, we all need to contribute. Me. You. It is our duty."

— Malala Yousafzai, Nobel Peace Prize Acceptance Speech, 2014

global initiative for educating girls, completed her education at Oxford University, and started the Malala Fund. To this day, she travels around the world fighting for the rights of girls to determine their own future by way of access to education.

We do not all need to become renowned activists like Malala, but we all have the potential to harvest meaning from our hardships in ways that benefit ourselves and even help others. Certainly, challenges have a way of creeping into our lives, affecting our health, wellbeing, relationships, goals, and careers. While these moments can derail us, making us feel helpless or stuck, we have the ability to shift our focus to see how they can empower us to make a difference. In other words, we can use that hardship to fuel a greater commitment to growth and change.

Connecting to Our Values

1. Write down 5–10 of your top values—the ones that guide your life and contribute to your happiness and wellbeing.

   ❋ It could help to think of qualities you value that you would want a biographer to highlight when telling your life story, or what you would want said in a speech about you on your retirement or your 100th birthday.

   ❋ Examples: healthy relationships, professional success, generosity, patience, wellbeing, friendships, independence, honesty, financial stability, creativity.

2. From the list, identify the three values that are most important to you.

   ❋ What themes, if any, do you notice in the values you chose?

   ❋ What feelings or body sensations arise as you connect to these values?

3. What benefits might arise from connecting to your values more often? In what ways might this contribute to your wellbeing and happiness?

▶ **Takeaway**

Two things that have been found to contribute to our happiness are (1) sustaining purpose and meaning through living by our deeper values and (2) having high quality relationships and meaningful connections with others.[50] These two things go hand in hand. Many of us find, through deeper reflection, that our core values tend to be other-oriented. Living by these values thus contributes to our happiness not only by providing a greater sense of meaning in life, but also by enhancing our relationships. Connecting to and remaining mindful of our values is, in this way, a true act of self-compassion; it protects us from experiencing the heightened distress that comes from a lack of meaning or purpose and from isolation or conflict with others.

The good news is that connecting to our values is something we can do at any point—whether we are doing well or confronting challenges. In fact, often our challenges push us to question what really matters. However, we do not need to wait for hardship to give us this opportunity. We can take moments regularly to reconnect to our core values, as we did in this reflection, and cultivate a more durable sense of our life's purpose.

Clarifying Our Needs

As humans, we have many real needs, both physical and psychological. When these needs aren't met, we naturally feel distress. Such distress alerts us to something being amiss and motivates us to act. Yet, sometimes, we feel distress at failing to get something that is not really essential for our wellbeing. For this activity, we refer to these perceived needs as *wants*.

This insight activity helps distinguish our needs from our wants. Making the distinction more visible allows us to put more energy into pursuing what we need. In turn, it also frees us to pursue our wants with less worry, softening our distress when we do not get them because we know that they are not truly essential.

Please be aware that this is not always a relevant exercise for everyone. Especially if you are in the midst of a difficult life circumstance, feel free to take this lightly or simply skip the exercise.

1. If you are able, write down a list of experiences where you struggled or failed to get something you really wanted and then later realized this was not something you needed after all. Pick one from this list for further reflection.

   ❀ What words would you use to describe how it initially felt to lose those things or not achieve them?

   ❀ How did your feelings change when you realized this was a want more than a need?

2. Now, list four or more things you *currently* want, but do not have.

   ❀ Looking at this list, identify if there are any wants that you really need—things that reflect your deepest values or that you could not flourish without. Then, identify the things you want that would be nice to have, but are not essential.

      ❧ To further clarify wants versus needs, look at

the non-essential wants you identified, and then consider if any reflect an underlying, deeper need.

↪ Consider, for example, that the desire for a vacation may point to the need for more balance in your life, or greater connection with loved ones.

❀ How does it feel to distinguish wants from needs? How might this distinction influence what you prioritize, going forward? How might it influence how you feel when you don't get things you want?

3. Drawing on these insights, what advice or wisdom would you call upon the next time you do not get something you want and find yourself experiencing feelings of frustration or desperation? Write this out in a sentence or two, giving yourself advice as if you were speaking to a dear friend.

▶ Takeaway

We all want to live long and well, and avoid suffering, but often we get confused about what will help us achieve these goals. In *A Guide to the Bodhisattva's Way of Life,* Shantideva offers the following observation:

Although we wish to be rid of our suffering
We seem to be chasing after suffering itself.
Despite our wish for happiness, out of confusion
We destroy our own happiness as if it is our enemy.[51]

This is as timely today as it was a thousand years ago. We still confuse what contributes to wellbeing and what gets in the way of it. One way to avoid this is by taking time to distinguish between our wants and our needs. Again, there is nothing wrong with wanting things, such as tasty desserts, more money, or a nicer place to live. Having desires is an important aspect of being human and can bring much joy. But at times, we may chase after these things thinking that they will bring lasting happiness when, in fact, they bring the opposite. When we cling to things that do not reflect our deeper values, we can lose that sense of meaning and purpose that is essential for happiness and wellbeing. Consider the following example:

For years, Jamie sought promotions in their company because they wanted status and recognition. They successfully climbed the ladder. Then, one day, Jamie realized they were in a position that no longer fit their skill set, and they were doing work they no longer found enjoyable and meaningful. Jamie realized that pursuing recognition and advancement above all else had led to unhappiness. With this insight, they requested a demotion to their former position, where they were able to thrive again. Jamie still had a desire for professional recognition, but it was no longer a compulsion; they understood that feeling a sense of joy and meaning in their work was what they needed.

Distinguishing wants from needs helps us to prioritize what we engage in. It also helps us to put less weight on the outcomes we pursue that are not necessary for our wellbeing. This does not mean we will stop pursuing our wants altogether; it simply means that we won't be as distressed if we don't achieve them. Distinguishing our wants from our needs in this way is self-compassion in action, helping us to put more energy toward the things we really need for lasting wellbeing, such as living by our core values.

> "What opposes our ability to accept our vulnerabilities voluntarily is the frustration that arises when one dreads adversities but encounters unwanted events and when one is particularly attached to pleasures but encounters obstacles to these desired goals. From these encounters arise frustrations and they in turn lead to anger or depression. Therefore, we should neither dread our adversities nor be attached to our pleasures."
>
> — SHANTIDEVA,
> THE COMPENDIUM
> OF TRAINING,
> 8TH CENTURY CE

Adversity as a Gateway to Empathy and Compassion

Teri was only 10, but she had already lived all over the world. She was moving, once again, to a new country and yet another new school. While she had done this many times before, this transition felt different. This was by far the smallest town she had lived in, and everything was foreign to her. She dressed differently from the other children in school and ate different food. Teri felt misunderstood and unwanted, every day feeling sadder and sadder. Then, she met Stephanie.

Stephanie had moved to this small town four years earlier and had been picked on when she first started at the school as well. Over time, her classmates got to know her, and friendships developed. When Teri joined the class, Stephanie remembered what she had gone through. Her memory of loneliness was so powerful that she couldn't stand by and let someone else feel as miserable as she had. One day at lunch, Stephanie got up from her usual table and went to sit with Teri, who was eating alone. That was the first of many lunches they had together, and they soon became close friends. While her memory of being isolated had always made Stephanie sad and uncomfortable, over time she began to look back on it with a new sense of gratitude. After all, it was that challenging experience that inspired her to help Teri, and she was glad that this experience allowed her to make a difference.

1. Think back to a time when you experienced a hard time and later met someone else going through a similar situation.

    ❀ How did your shared experience strengthen your understanding of their situation?

    ❀ How did this affect your feelings toward them?

    ❀ If you were able to offer support or help, how did that make you feel?

2. What does it feel like to look at your difficulty from this perspective? Reflect on any insights, feelings, or sensations that have come up.

3. What value would come from using our struggles to connect with and help others in the future? How might this shift how we relate to our own struggles?

▶ Takeaway

As we have explored, hardships can help make visible our deeper values—values that are often other-oriented. Just as importantly, these difficult moments can also help us to engage with, and act on, those other-oriented values. Research confirms that sharing similar experiences naturally unleashes empathy—our struggles provide a doorway to connecting with others similarly struggling.[52] That human connection not only feels good and enhances our sense of belonging, but it also provides understanding and insight into how we may act to help those around us. This knowledge offers an even deeper sense of purpose to our personal experience of challenges and heartache.

Making Self-Agency Visible

1. Review the list of self-compassion reappraisals below, which aligns with the list of Enduring Capabilities we have been strengthening in Modules 4 and 5. Then, think of a current situation you are going through that would benefit from one or more of these more holistic perspectives:

   ❀ I am not alone.

   ❀ I am not a failure.

   ❀ I am not a superhuman.

   ❀ I can find growth in challenges.

   ❀ I can connect to my values through my adversity.

   ❀ I can connect with others through our shared struggles.

   ❀ I can make a difference.

2. In what ways could these perspectives—as you are able to make them visible—foster a healthier and more positive outcome?

3. What does it feel like to see how you can positively impact your situation by shifting or broadening your perspectives?

4. How might greater awareness of your self-agency make a difference in your life over the long term?

▶ **Takeaway**

Throughout the first five modules of CBCT, we have been developing and strengthening inner skills—adding tools to our toolkit, so to speak. As we continue to strengthen those skills, we can carry them into our everyday lives, drawing on them to help us face real challenges. This expanded toolkit gives us self-agency, helping make visible what we can do when we feel stuck.

We will not be able to control all circumstances—we will never be able to cover the whole earth with leather—but we can always

*"Where could I possibly find the leather
To cover the whole surface of the earth?
But with leather just on the soles of my shoes,
It's the same as having covered the entire earth's surface."*

— SHANTIDEVA, *A GUIDE TO THE BODHISATTVA'S WAY OF LIFE*, 8TH CENTURY CE draw on our inner skills to help alleviate distress. This makes it easier to walk through even the rocky places of life. Just knowing that our Enduring Capabilities are available, and that they can make a real difference, can give us a sense of confidence and empowerment in the face of life's adversities.

Cognitive Reappraisal Strategy

Module 5 and the Emotion Timeline

In this module, we further examined distorted appraisals that may be taking a difficult situation and making it worse. We might see all of life's challenging events as 100 percent bad, or that there is nothing to be done about them, interpretations that shoot a "second arrow" of emotions like despair and hopelessness. Such emotions can then lead us to give up, retreat, or act in other harmful ways, as depicted in the diagram below.

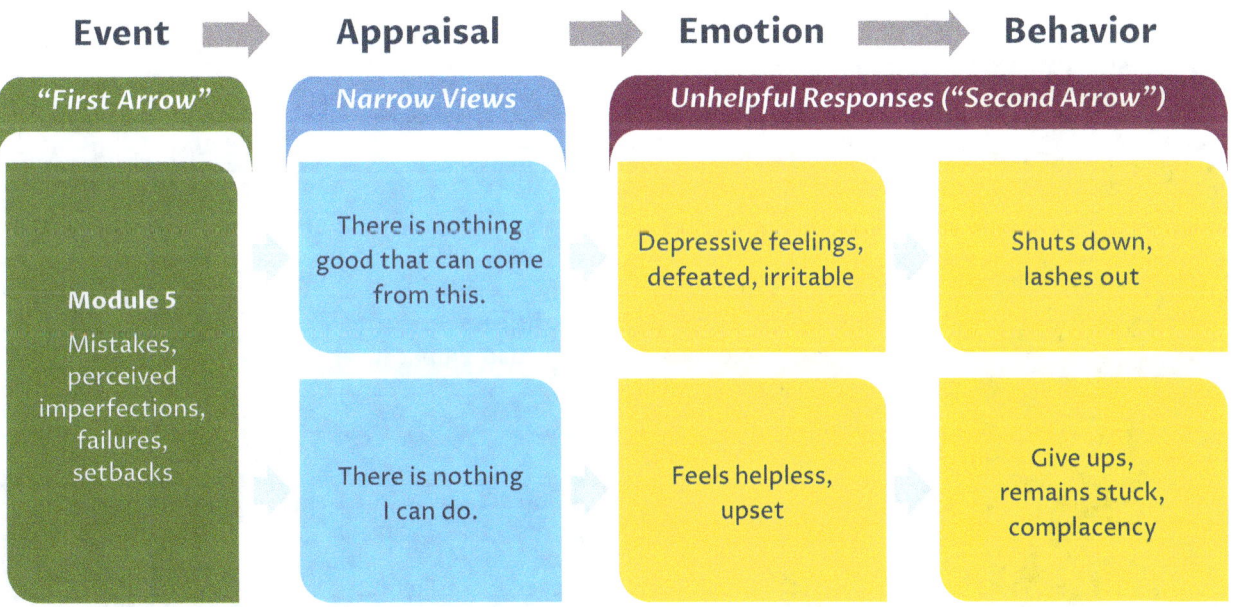

As we did in Module 4, we can transform our harmful emotional and behavioral responses through the process of cognitive reappraisal. This is not ignoring or turning away from what is really happening, but it means we see what is happening from a broader view. In other words, we familiarize ourselves with perspectives that lead to healthier responses, as depicted in the next diagram and captured in the four Enduring Capabilities of this module. We transform our responses by deepening the perspectives that (1) we can find meaning in vulnerabilities when we see that we can learn or grow from setbacks, (2) that they can help make our values clear and visible, and (3) that they help us connect to others with greater empathy and compassion. When we can find meaning in our vulnerabilities in these ways, we (4) strengthen responses of realistic hope and self-agency, the ability to stay focused on what we can do.

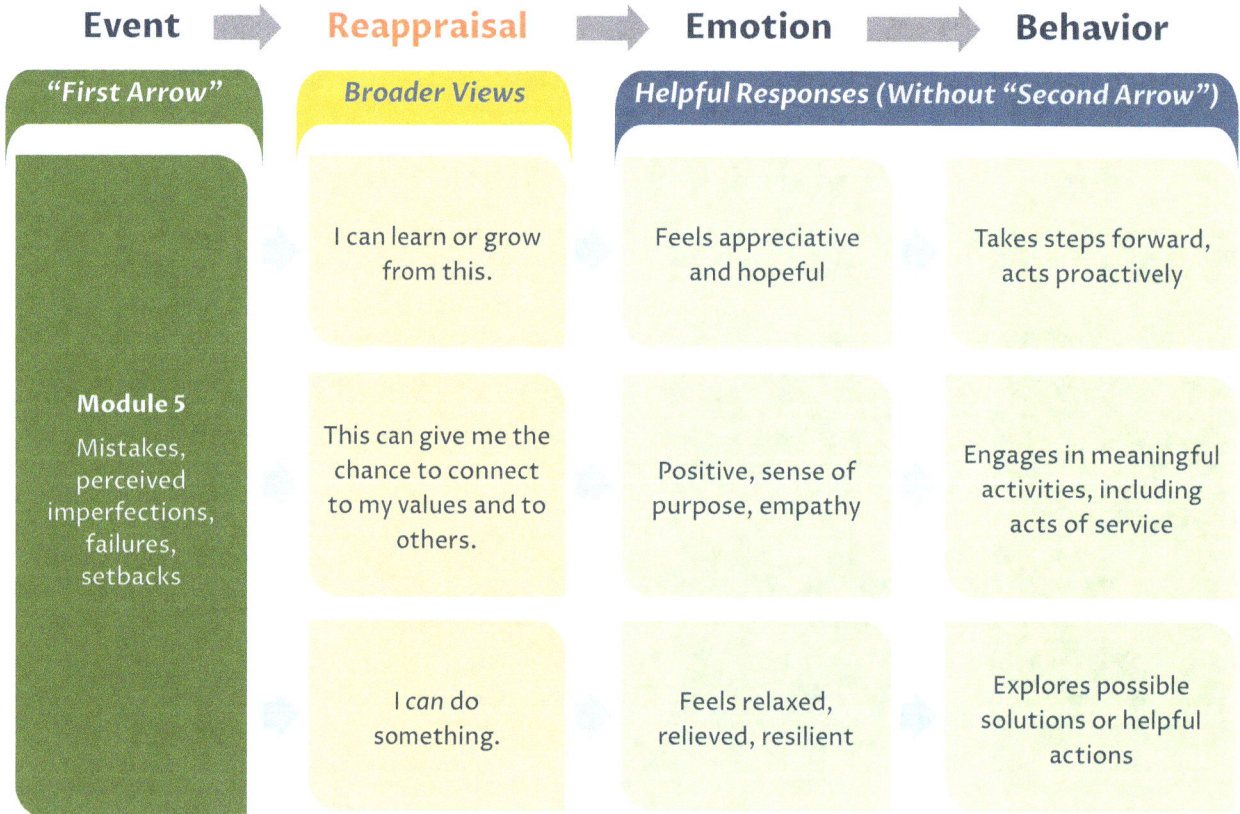

Event ➡ **Reappraisal** ➡ **Emotion** ➡ **Behavior**

"First Arrow"	Broader Views	Helpful Responses (Without "Second Arrow")	
Module 5 Mistakes, perceived imperfections, failures, setbacks	I can learn or grow from this.	Feels appreciative and hopeful	Takes steps forward, acts proactively
	This can give me the chance to connect to my values and to others.	Positive, sense of purpose, empathy	Engages in meaningful activities, including acts of service
	I *can* do something.	Feels relaxed, relieved, resilient	Explores possible solutions or helpful actions

Take a moment to **find a comfortable posture and connect with your body** and current feelings. If you notice tension in any part of the body, feel free to stretch or move.

Allow yourself to **settle into the present experience.** Take a few deep breaths if that is comfortable. Gently inhale, and, if you like, have the sense that nourishing air is infusing your entire being. As you breathe out, see if you can release tensions and worries to some degree to allow the body and mind to settle into an unfolding sense of calm or ease.

If settling is hard today, you may want to pause and spend a few moments with an earlier practice.

When ready, spend a few moments connecting to your **deep desire for wellbeing and freedom from harm.**

Despite this fundamental desire, at times, we may be overly harsh toward ourselves and unintentionally contribute to the distress we want to avoid.

Take some time to **reflect on how you tend to respond to yourself when things do not go well.** How do you respond to mistakes or perceived inadequacies? What emotions tend to arise in those moments?

Though setbacks and mistakes are natural, and resulting feelings of frustration are also natural, at times we may fan the flames of those distressing emotions to a self-defeating level. When that happens, the situation may seem 100 percent negative and unchangeable, that there is nothing we can do.

Take a moment to reflect: Is that really true? Can you think of a time when you failed at something but managed to pick yourself up again, and eventually got through it or even succeeded? **In what ways might your challenges have created valuable opportunities to learn or grow?** Reflect for a few moments on the knowledge you gained from going through those difficult experiences.

Nobody likes to have difficulties, but our most challenging moments often bring out the best in us, helping us to see what we really want and what we really value. Struggles can reveal our purpose in a way that ease might not.

Take a moment to examine your own challenges from this broader perspective. **Have any of your setbacks helped you move toward greater feelings of purpose or meaning?** Have your difficult moments ever provided an opportunity to **connect to or even help others going through a similar setback?** What does it feel like to view your challenges in this way?

We don't always have a choice or control over the situations that unfold around us, but **we can grow in our ability to choose how we view and respond to them.**

Consider: How does this possibility for growth shift your feelings about current challenges? See if this view allows you to move away from feelings of discouragement. If possible, allow yourself to **sit with growing feelings of confidence and courage**, seeing them unfold as an **empowering light at the center of the chest**. If you'd like, with each in-breath, you can let this light and all that it represents expand, filling and nourishing your whole being.

Finally, reflect on how helpful it is to be able to see the ups and downs of life from this broader perspective. How is the resulting sense of empowerment important for your own wellbeing and for healthy relationships with others?

Take a moment to dedicate your practice today to those you know to be in need of health and wellbeing and, as you are able, expand this dedication to include a widening circle of beings on this earth.

And conclude by setting an intention to extend the skills and insights from this practice into everyday life.

Bringing the Skills to Life

"If I cannot do great things, I can do small things in a great way."

— ATTRIBUTED TO MARTIN LUTHER KING, JR.

- **Engage your self-agency.** Catch yourself when you are feeling excessive anger, despair, or helplessness. Then, shift your focus to what you can do. Perhaps this involves finding something in the challenge from which you can learn for the future or finding a way to connect to your values or to others. Consider any small step you can take to make a repair or move forward.

- **Recall moments of growth.** Spend time reflecting on the moments in your life when you've learned or grown from the setbacks and challenges you've experienced, and write these in a journal. Try to make time to recall these moments, particularly when you're feeling bogged down by something not going so well in the present.

- **Connect to your core values daily.** Consider the following:

  ❋ Write down important values that you want to live by and put them in a place where you will frequently see them (e.g., Post-it note, computer wallpaper, etc.). Allow this to serve as a regular reminder to reflect on and connect with your values.

  ❋ Write down a list of your core values. Each morning, choose one that you think could use more attention and set small goals to engage with it. For example, if you choose kindness, set the goal to be kind and avoid being unkind all day. At the end of the day, review how this intention influenced your thoughts and behaviors. If you note missed opportunities (say, you recall a moment when your partner wanted to talk, but you stayed focused on your phone screen), set the intention to stay attuned to the value and live by it more fully the next day.

- **Use adversity for good.** If you are currently going through something challenging, or are still struggling with something difficult you've gone through in the past, consider how you can use your adverse experiences to contribute to the greater good of your community. Could this experience help you relate better to those who have also experienced such challenges? Allow this empathic understanding to strengthen your connection to those people and inspire you to help, or make a plan to help, even if in small ways.

Personal Reflections

" Before having this mindset, my life's difficulties always made me depressed. I was always complaining about the unfairness of life. However, when I realized that those experiences of facing setbacks made me more mature and made my life more interesting, it was easier for me to get rid of the negative feelings. Sometimes I would even feel grateful for the setbacks that I met. "

" I grew up as an athlete and viewed my active life and athletic nature as part of my identity. When I was pregnant, I experienced health complications that made me unable to engage in my active lifestyle. I was no longer able to do the simple things I once could and felt that part of my identity had been stripped away. I have since noticed a shift in my view of that situation—I no longer see it as so much of a loss but more as a situation that taught me so much and gave me the opportunity to grow and experience life in a new way. "

" One day, over the weeks I was taking my first CBCT course, I got into an argument with my partner. I caught myself during the fight getting wrapped up in trying to prove my point. I had just had this class on Module 5 where we spent a lot of time reflecting on what really matters to us and, in that class, one of the things that came to mind was a healthy relationship. That reflection helped me catch myself during the argument and realize that I was focusing on trying to be right when what I really cared about was having a healthy relationship. This shift has transformed the way I respond in these situations and has had such a positive impact on my relationship and my own feelings. "

Frequently Asked Questions

Is this module suggesting that there is always a "silver lining" or a "good side" to the challenges we experience?

While the module does focus on finding meaning in vulnerabilities, it does not mean that we can find a silver lining around every cloud in life. Some situations are just bad—we wish they never happened and hope they do not repeat themselves. But the question is this: When those situations occur, what do we do with them? How will they continue to impact us? How can we move forward? Taking the perspective that we may be able to find meaning in a difficult situation can help us to avoid getting stuck in all-encompassing hopelessness or rage. As Viktor Frankl, a psychiatrist and holocaust survivor, explains: Going through the horrors of the Holocaust is not something to be considered positively, but the ability to find meaning, purpose, and self-agency in the memory is something that many—including himself—attribute to their survival.

Do I need to abandon my pleasures in life?

While this module does aim to clarify the distinction between our wants and needs, it is not meant to suggest that pleasures don't matter or that we should avoid feeling good. In fact, having pleasure in life is directly linked to our wellbeing and is very important for our health and happiness. The key message here is understanding that temporary pleasures alone will not lead to lasting happiness, and that obsessions with those pleasures can cause harm on account of the devastating feelings that can result when we lose them.

Does self-compassion hinder the motivation to reach for and move toward goals?

No! Clarifying our purpose deepens the intrinsic motivation to keep working toward our goals. By understanding our values and how they shape our goals, we find all the more the motivation to accomplish them. Imagine you are going to nursing school because you want to be able to help the sick. By keeping this bigger purpose in mind, you'll find more motivation to keep going even when there are setbacks or distractions, like a troubling course or a difficult professor.

Conclusion

In this module, we explored finding meaning in our vulnerabilities as we reflected on the personal growth, the deeper connection to our values, and the greater empathy for others that can emerge from the challenges we face. With these insights, we considered the fact that we are not helpless, that there is always something we can do. We saw that as self-agency increases, so does our ability to respond to the challenges of life with greater resilience.

In the next module, we will turn our attention to others and begin to deepen and expand our sense of belonging. We will further deepen our reflection on our human condition. As we deepen this understanding through reflections on common humanity, we will strengthen our identification with others and expand our circle of concern.

Expanding Our
Circle of Concern

"When both myself and others
Are similar in that we wish to be happy,
What is so special about me
That I should strive for my happiness alone?
When both myself and others
Are similar in that we wish to avoid suffering,
What is so special about me
That I protect myself but not others?"

— SHANTIDEVA,
A GUIDE TO THE BODHISATTVA'S WAY OF LIFE, 8TH CENTURY CE

Module 6

Having attuned to our human condition, strengthened self-compassion, and fortified our personal resilience, we can now bring our attention to others by connecting on the basis of our common humanity and taking steps to expand our circle of concern.

We have a natural tendency to feel concern for those we feel close to, those with whom we identify and see as being like us. In this module, we cultivate the ability to identify with a widening group of individuals based on our shared human reality, thus promoting and extending feelings of connection. This increased connectivity is helpful for our own wellbeing, alleviating feelings of isolation, anger, and despair. And it contributes to the wellbeing of others, because our expanded sense of belonging urges us to act in ways that contribute to their flourishing.

ENDURING CAPABILITIES

6.1 Enhancing awareness of our unconscious biases, assumptions, and judgments of others

6.2 Connecting to others by making our similarities visible

6.3 Expanding our ingroup through awareness that everyone shares the fundamental desire to be well and to avoid harm

6.4 Increasing our capacity for acceptance, understanding, and forgiveness

6.5 Appreciating and respecting diversity and differences

Step In, Step Out

Nina arrived for her Module 6 class curious to see what was meant by "expanding our circle of concern." The instructor began by drawing a circle on the floor and asking participants to stand around it.

The instructor started: "Everyone who has a sister, please step into the circle." Nina has two sisters, so she stepped in. Looking around, she saw four others join her. They smiled at one another. Nina had never really given much thought to some of the people who stood in this little community, but now she felt a little connection on the basis of this commonality. The instructor then asked everyone to step out of the circle. The CBCT instructor proceeded, "Now, step in the circle if you love coffee." This time, more people stepped in, but not Nina. She prefers tea. The coffee drinkers stood together in the circle, smiling at each other with a new sort of shared recognition. Nina was surprised to feel a little left out.

Now, imagine yourself in this CBCT class receiving those instructions. Would you have stepped in or stayed out?

Step in if you . . .

have a sister

The instructor continued with more prompts. **Again, imagine yourself participating in the class and think about whether you would step in or stay out.**

Step in if you . . .

speak more than one language

play a musical instrument

belong to a religious group

With each prompt, new bonds emerged, and others dissolved. Then, the instructor asked the group to **step in if they have ever gotten angry**.

Nina suddenly felt a shift in the room. There was a slight pause in which nobody moved, then someone tentatively stepped into the circle. A few others followed. Finally, everyone moved into the circle. For the first time, no one was left out; awkward smiles were passed around in the now-crowded space.

For each of the remaining prompts, every individual in the class stepped in. **Take a moment to consider if you would have also stepped in when asked the following:**

have ever felt misunderstood.

have ever made a mistake and felt regret.

Step in if you . . .

have a strength
or a skill of any kind.

want to feel safe,
protected, and secure.

want to be happy and
would like to avoid suffering.

Upon stepping into the circle, participants were asked to look around and make eye contact with others. Nina felt slightly embarrassed and uncomfortable at first, but, looking at others, she realized: Despite their differences in upbringing, circumstances, and preferences, everyone in the class shared these basic human experiences, and the basic wish for wellbeing. Though she felt somewhat closer and identified with some more than others, recognizing what the whole class had in common expanded her sense of connection to everyone. Even as the circle dissolved and everyone took their seats for meditation, Nina felt a new sense of belonging with her CBCT classmates—every one of them.

Note:
Gatherings can often benefit from icebreakers. Consider trying this exercise with others at a social event. Then, offer the three reflection prompts above.

1. What did you notice from the Step In, Step Out activity (patterns, realizations, feelings, etc.)?

2. Describe any emotional shifts or perspectives that came up when everyone stepped into the circle.

3. Now, thinking back to moments from your own life, reflect on the following:

   ❋ Recall a time when you discovered something that you have in common with someone—perhaps that you are from the same town, or that you share a similar experience, interest, or belief. How did that shift your feelings toward them?

❀ Think of a time when you found out someone did *not* share the same interest, opinion, or experience as you—someone you saw as *different* from you—and describe how that influenced your feelings for them.

❀ Now, imagine you are back inside that circle with everyone because they, like you, want to be safe and well, and to avoid harm. And then imagine that this *different* person is also in the circle. How, if it all, would your views about or feelings for this person change as you stand in the circle together?

▶ **Takeaway**

This activity highlights the power of making our similarities visible. We can feel connected with others on the basis of simple preferences or shared experiences that open the door to identification. When we identify with someone, it is natural to feel closer to them. When we see that there is difference, on the other hand, this can lead to a sense of disconnection, indifference, or even negative feelings.

Since one of the main goals of compassion training is to expand our circle of concern, it is important that we find ways of connecting genuinely with a broader range of individuals. As humans, we naturally feel a connection with those we see as similar to us. While we have many differences with others, we can also identify with *anyone* on the basis of common humanity. We all share physical needs for food, water, air, and sleep. We share psychological needs for belonging, learning, and purpose. And beneath these needs, we share a profoundly simple goal that underlies our every emotion, thought, and action: the goal of flourishing, which pervades every aspect of life from the moment we are born. Each of us deeply values our own wellbeing, and we are committed to avoiding illness, loss, and setbacks that undermine that wellbeing. Bringing our attention to this

"Without exception, men and women of all ages, of all cultures, of all levels of education, and of all walks of economic life have emotions, are mindful of emotions of others, cultivate pastimes that manipulate their emotions, and govern their lives in no small part by the pursuit of one emotion, happiness, and the avoidance of unpleasant emotions."

— NEUROSCIENTIST ANTONIO DAMASIO, *THE FEELING OF WHAT HAPPENS*, 1999 deeper common humanity gives us the opportunity to identify and connect with an ever-widening group of individuals.

Key Elements of the Module

What does it feel like to connect with others, discover something we share, and develop a kinship or bond? How does it feel to belong? Belonging and connection are innate human desires; not only do we want these things, but we also rely on them for our survival and emotional wellbeing.

The realities we share as human beings, including our shared aspiration to be well and avoid harm, are the connective tissues that bind all of us together. We refer to this as our *common humanity.*

Seeing common humanity doesn't mean we ignore differences. Along with what we share, each of us is unique. But our uniqueness is itself something we all have in common—diversity is a core aspect of common humanity. That said, at times we may narrowly focus on our differences and lose sight of the shared reality that bonds us. Broadening our perspective and attuning to our common humanity can help us make that bond visible, protecting us from feelings of disconnection that lead to hurt and harm.

Ingroup bias, the tendency to favor individuals we identify with over those we do not, runs deep in human beings and can even be detected in babies.[53] Scientists propose that we evolved with this bias to bond together in communities, increasing our chances of survival. However, there is a tipping point when our bonding instincts can lead to local or global conflict with those we consider to be outside our community. This is even more likely, and harmful, when we view others as threatening or inferior just because they are different.

The "us and them" mentality is widespread. Dr. Mark Levine, a psychologist interested in how loyalty to a group might influence helping behaviors, explored this in the context of sports. His study on the interactions of rival Manchester United and Liverpool soccer club fans led to some astounding results.

Manchester United fans were asked to fill out a survey emphasizing their enthusiasm for their team specifically. After they finished, they were asked to walk to another building to continue

"Circle of concern" in this module refers to those we care about. When someone is in your circle of concern, their life trajectory, their ups and downs, and their wellbeing matter to you.

STAYING MINDFUL OF IMPORTANT DIFFERENCES

We are all vulnerable to life's challenges, but the challenges we experience vary in frequency and intensity depending on our circumstances. In some cases, differences are due to societal structures in which people are treated differently based on their identities. Reflecting on the things we share as humans does not mean we will ignore the important ways that some of us are treated unfairly. Rather, the shift toward seeing all others as *one of us* at a human level will naturally *strengthen* our sense of concern for their struggles.

Seeing that others too want to be well and avoid harm will make us more interested in their wellbeing, more curious and concerned about what they are up against, and more motivated to do something to help, even when our differences seem great.

Simultaneously recognizing both what we share and what makes us different allows for new alliances to be forged across the lines of power and status. We can then find creative solutions to support the equal right of each and every one of us to pursue and find happiness and flourishing.

the study. Along the way, they would encounter a stranger on the ground, pretending to be in great pain, as though they had just twisted an ankle.

If the "injured" person was wearing a Liverpool shirt or plain shirt, only around one-third of the Manchester United fans stopped to help. But if the "injured" person was wearing a Manchester United jersey, nearly every fan stopped to help.

Manchester United fans were then next asked to fill out a survey emphasizing their love for the sport of soccer overall, rather than just for their specific team. After filling out that survey, almost all Manchester United fans stopped for a fan of their own team, of course, but the surprise was that almost all stopped to help a Liverpool fan too. On the other hand, only about one-third stopped to help a person in a plain shirt.

This is a prime example of ingroup bias, yet all it took to expand the circle of concern was to redefine the ingroup. When the study participants thought only of their love for the Manchester United team, they were unlikely to help the opposing team or the neutral person. When they thought of their love of the sport overall, their ingroup expanded to include the fans of the opposing team. When we focus on our similarities, our circle of concern widens to include even those who, at the outset, may seem different from us.

In this module, we strive to approach all others with a greater sense of identification and kinship. By shifting our perspective to see all human beings as part of our ingroup, we can transform our bias into inclusion, promoting greater peace within ourselves and in our communities.

Seeing Humanity in Others

Content Warning: *The following true story includes descriptions of military violence.*

There are more than 30 armed conflicts happening in the world today. This is a true story from one of them.

A man lived in a small village with his wife, and their 6 children. One day, their 10-year-old daughter, went to play with her friends after school. While she was walking, a soldier—engaged in a confrontation nearby—shot a rubber bullet that hit his daughter directly in the head. The impact cracked her skull instantly. She fought hard for 2 days but did not survive.

Another man, who grew up on the other side of the conflict, lived nearby. One day he was at home with his wife when he heard news that a bombing happened in the city. Their 14-year-old daughter, had been walking in the direction of the now-destroyed area. They quickly rushed out in search of her, running from hospital to hospital. Eventually, they found his daughter in a morgue, a victim of the bombing.

Though practically neighbors, the two men grew up in different worlds. Born on different sides of the long conflict, they were taught to fear and even hate each other. Both of their families faced the worst experience imaginable: the loss of a child, during two separate incidents of violence near their home.

When telling their stories, they both spoke of having immediately felt grief and anger, feelings they couldn't seem to overcome. But then they reached a turning point. Eventually, they both, separately, realized they wanted to be part of the solution, to stop the cycle of violence and hatred that fueled such unbearable tragedy and pain. One explained, "We both lost our daughters and paid the highest price possible. Our blood is the same color, our pain is exactly the same pain, and the tears are just as bitter."

The two men met for the first time at a support group meeting. One shared, "I am ashamed to say . . . It was the first time in my life that I met [the people on the other side] as human beings. As people that carry the same burden as I do. That suffer the same way. I was completely shocked."

Standing together against violence and hatred, the two men became close friends. They now refer to each other as "brothers", something they admit could never have happened earlier in their lives.

The two men, connected through their vulnerability, their pain, their desire to flourish, and their dream of a more peaceful world, came to see the humanity in each other. Enemies transformed into friends. Separation transformed into connection. And hatred transformed into compassion.

Connecting through Our Shared Human Condition

"In today's world, there is too much division. Thinking of others in terms of 'us' and 'them' is too prevalent—and it leads to conflict. We constantly need to remind ourselves of the oneness of humanity. If we were to do that, there'd be no basis for hostility or bloodshed."

— THE DALAI LAMA, *DIALOGUE WITH YOUNG PEOPLE FROM SOUTHEAST ASIA*, 2020

Think for a moment about how we categorize people as we go about our lives. Most of us unconsciously see others in the following three categories: people I am close to, people I do not have strong feelings about (such as strangers), and people who bug me or whom I find difficult. These groups can seem fixed—a loved one will always be close to us; we will always be indifferent to a person who we do not know. But are these categories really so static?

Take a moment to pause and reflect: Has a stranger ever become a close friend? Or has a close friend ever become difficult, or dropped away from your life so that they become more like a stranger? Upon closer examination, we find that these categories are more subjective, fluid, and changeable. As we engage in this insight activity, keep in mind that even if someone is in one category today, it doesn't necessarily mean they will be there forever.

1. Think of three people, one from each of the three categories: (1) someone you feel close to, (2) someone you feel neutral about, and (3) someone you find slightly annoying or difficult. Consider the tips listed below.

   ❋ For those in the second category, it can be helpful to keep in mind that most people in the world will fall under this heading. Neutral does not mean we feel nothing for them but, rather, that we don't have a strong, obviously positive or negative feeling toward them.

   ❋ For the person in the third category, try not to pick someone who knocks you off-balance emotionally. As the purpose of this activity is to *begin* to see how we can expand our ingroup, it is better to bite off only what we can chew.

2. Beginning with the person you identified as close to you:

  ❀ Identify (or imagine) something that is going well for them.

    ✑ Consider how they might feel as they experience this.

    ✑ Consider how *you* feel as you think about or imagine them experiencing this.

  ❀ Then, identify something that is not going well for them. Take a moment to imagine this or write out the process.

    ✑ Consider how they might feel as they experience this.

    ✑ Consider how *you* feel as you think about or imagine them experiencing this.

3. Repeat Step 2 for the neutral and then for the difficult person.

  ❀ Reflect: How similar or different are your feelings for the ups and downs of these three individuals? Take a moment to write this out.

4. Now, reflect on your common humanity. In what ways do these individuals also have needs, goals, and dreams like yours? In what ways do they have vulnerabilities, limitations, and imperfections, as you do? How much do they share your deep desire to be well and avoid harm?

  ❀ As you reflect on your shared human condition, what shifts, if any, do you notice in your feelings for them and their ups and downs?

▶ **Takeaway**

In this activity, we begin to expand our circle of concern by making visible the reality that we are not alone in our human limitations

"Identification is the primary portal to empathy."

— FRANS DE WAAL,
AGE OF EMPATHY, 2009

and vulnerabilities. Even people we do not know well, or those whom we find annoying, share the basic desire to be safe and well, happy and included. If we can go into any interaction asking ourselves how we are alike, the dynamic can go from hostile or indifferent to connected.

The awareness of our common humanity can also help us see those closest to us more fully. The practice reduces our unrealistic expectations or idealization of those in our immediate ingroup and helps us to acknowledge when they do something wrong instead of turning a blind eye.

By relating to *all* others through the lens of common humanity, we soften our biases and foster healthier relationships—ones that have deep roots and are not easily swayed by surface level changes or differences.

HOW OTHERS EXPERIENCE OUR WARMTH

When we imagine our solar system, we see how the planets closest to the sun receive the most warmth and direct light. The farther away a planet is, the less it receives. Likewise, the closer people are to us, the more warm-heartedness they tend to receive. And that's okay! The goal of expanding our circle of concern is not to share the same degree of connection with everyone, but to begin to soften any barriers that may be blocking our warmth and light from reaching others. The sun does not share the same degree of warmth with each planet, but neither does it withhold its radiance from any of them.

Distinguishing Act from Actor

1. Recall and briefly describe a moment when you engaged your strengths or core values, or when you handled something well.

2. Now, think of a time when the opposite was true—when your actions didn't represent your best self. See if you can approach this reflection with self-compassion.

    ❀ Examples: offending someone by mistake, acting out of frustration or anger, neglecting to be there for someone in need, not following through on a promise.

    ❀ What would it feel like if someone saw only this action and judged you for it, without taking into account what led to the action, or the many other facets of yourself?

3. Now, recall or imagine a situation where you judged someone for an action they committed that you did not agree with, but later you had a shift in your view of and feelings for them when you learned more context about the situation or person.

    ❀ In what ways did the context shift your view or feelings for this person despite their action?

4. How might the ability to distinguish the act from the actor benefit your own life and the lives of others?

▶ **Takeaway**

It is only natural for us to feel an aversion toward those whose behaviors or attitudes we strongly disagree with. This aversion may spring from our deeper values. It can, however, become harmful when that aversion is directed at the person, instead of at the emotions or mindsets that fuel their harmful actions. When we reduce the person to being "bad," ignoring the many causes and conditions that led to the emotions and behavior, we feed our own feelings of anger or hatred. Such feelings can distance us from others and amplify our discomfort and distress.

Distinguishing the act from the actor allows us to gain a more complete understanding of a situation. An understanding that may even lead to forgiveness. Forgiveness, in this sense, does not mean supporting an action or saying that it is okay. Forgiveness here is based on seeing the humanity in others and softening the anger or resentment we hold for them, even as we choose to powerfully condemn or oppose their harmful actions. That being said, many of us have a difficult person or group we cannot imagine forgiving. If that is the case, we can focus on others for whom we see forgiveness as a possibility.

*"Just as a doctor is not agitated
With an enraged patient under the spell of harmful emotions,
A wise one sees the harmful emotions as the enemy,
Not the people who are under their spell."*

— ARYADEVA,
FOUR HUNDRED STANZAS,
2ND CENTURY CE

Appreciating Diversity

1. Call to mind a time when you were involved with a team, group, or community that benefited from diverse strengths or perspectives (e.g., when teammates with different skills worked together toward a shared goal).

2. Reflect on and describe that situation.

   ❁ What were the differences among the participants?

   ❁ What were the benefits that you saw in having diversity in the group? If helpful, consider what would have been lost if only a single viewpoint, strength, or approach had been present.

3. How might these perspectives influence how you view and engage with others moving forward, particularly when differences are present?

▶ Takeaway

Module 6 has focused mainly on all that we have in common with others. In this activity, we turned to something equally essential to grow compassion: appreciating our differences. If we only surround ourselves with those who share our views, experiences, skill sets, and backgrounds, we are more likely to fall prey to what psychologists call "confirmation bias."[54] When we get stuck in a narrow viewpoint that is never challenged, we lose the opportunity to learn from and connect with others. It is often this narrow focus that fuels conflict and stops progress. Being open to challenging our thinking and expanding our understanding is important for fostering possibility, innovation, cooperation, and respect.

Appreciating diversity can contribute to the growth and success of the groups we are a part of. In his book *The Big Sort*, author Bill Bishop examines this in the context of business. "[G]roupthink is powerful for rallying action around a single idea, but it is terrible when we need to brainstorm novel solutions. That, of course, is the challenge of every business today."[55] Bishop reports that successful institutions are ones that recognize a diversity of backgrounds and fields of study; he advocates for the interaction of people with different experience and knowledge, as this leads to new ideas, better ways of working, and breakthroughs.

While the primary approach for expanding our circle of concern is through identification, appreciating diversity also plays an important role. In this practice, we simultaneously hold two realities in our awareness: We are deeply connected at a fundamental human level, *and* we have differences that are real and valuable.

THE GOLDEN RULE IN WORLD RELIGIONS

ZOROASTRIANISM[57]
"That nature only is good when it shall not do unto another whatever is not good for its own self."

JUDAISM[58]
"What is hateful to you, do not do to your fellow human beings. That is the entire Law; all the rest is commentary."

CHRISTIANITY[60]
"Do unto others as you would have them do unto you."

ISLAM[56]
"No one of you is a believer until you desire for others what you desire for yourself."

BAHÁ'Í[61]
"Desire not for any one the things ye would not desire for yourselves."

BUDDHISM[62]
"Hurt not others with that which pains yourself."

HINDUISM[59]
"This is the sum of duty: do naught to others that which if done to thee would cause pain."

Cognitive Reappraisal Strategy

Module 6 and the Emotion Timeline

Consider once again the emotion timeline. The diagram below illustrates how our appraisals of an event, more than the event itself, can fuel how we feel and act. Let's see how this timeline might play out in the case of Module 6's appraisals and reappraisals.

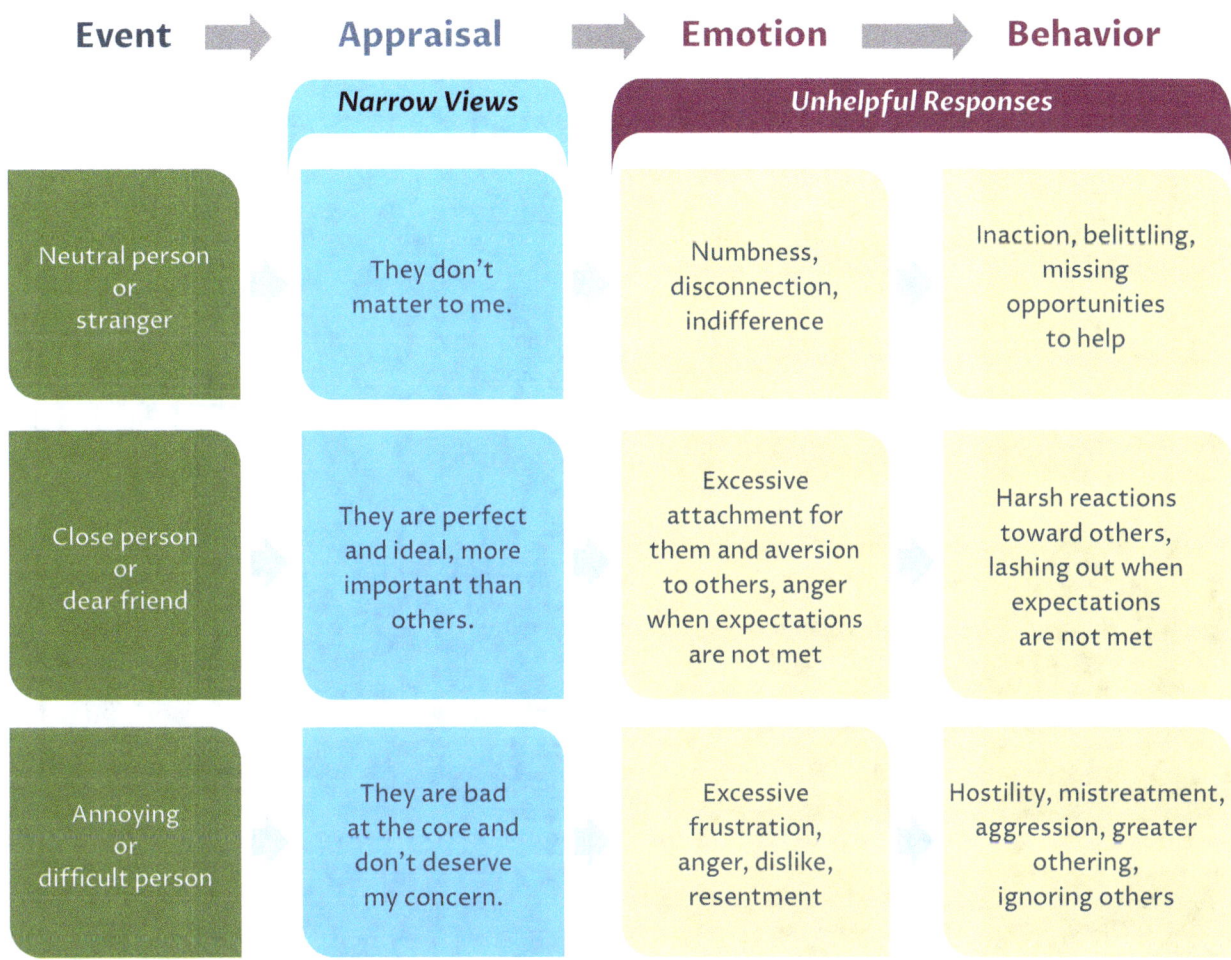

Event	Appraisal	Emotion	Behavior
	Narrow Views	**Unhelpful Responses**	
Neutral person or stranger	They don't matter to me.	Numbness, disconnection, indifference	Inaction, belittling, missing opportunities to help
Close person or dear friend	They are perfect and ideal, more important than others.	Excessive attachment for them and aversion to others, anger when expectations are not met	Harsh reactions toward others, lashing out when expectations are not met
Annoying or difficult person	They are bad at the core and don't deserve my concern.	Excessive frustration, anger, dislike, resentment	Hostility, mistreatment, aggression, greater othering, ignoring others

As we examined in the self-compassion modules, we may not be able to control the events, situations, or people around us, but we always have the capacity to shift our response. This includes our ability to change the way we relate to others. In this module, we take the opportunity to see how others are, in fact, like us, despite our differences. We examine how we can hold this understanding of our fundamental humanity while also appreciating and respecting differences. We, in turn, see those differences as opportunities to learn from and benefit each other. Deepening these perspectives then helps to alleviate distressing responses and foster greater connection, as depicted in the diagram below.

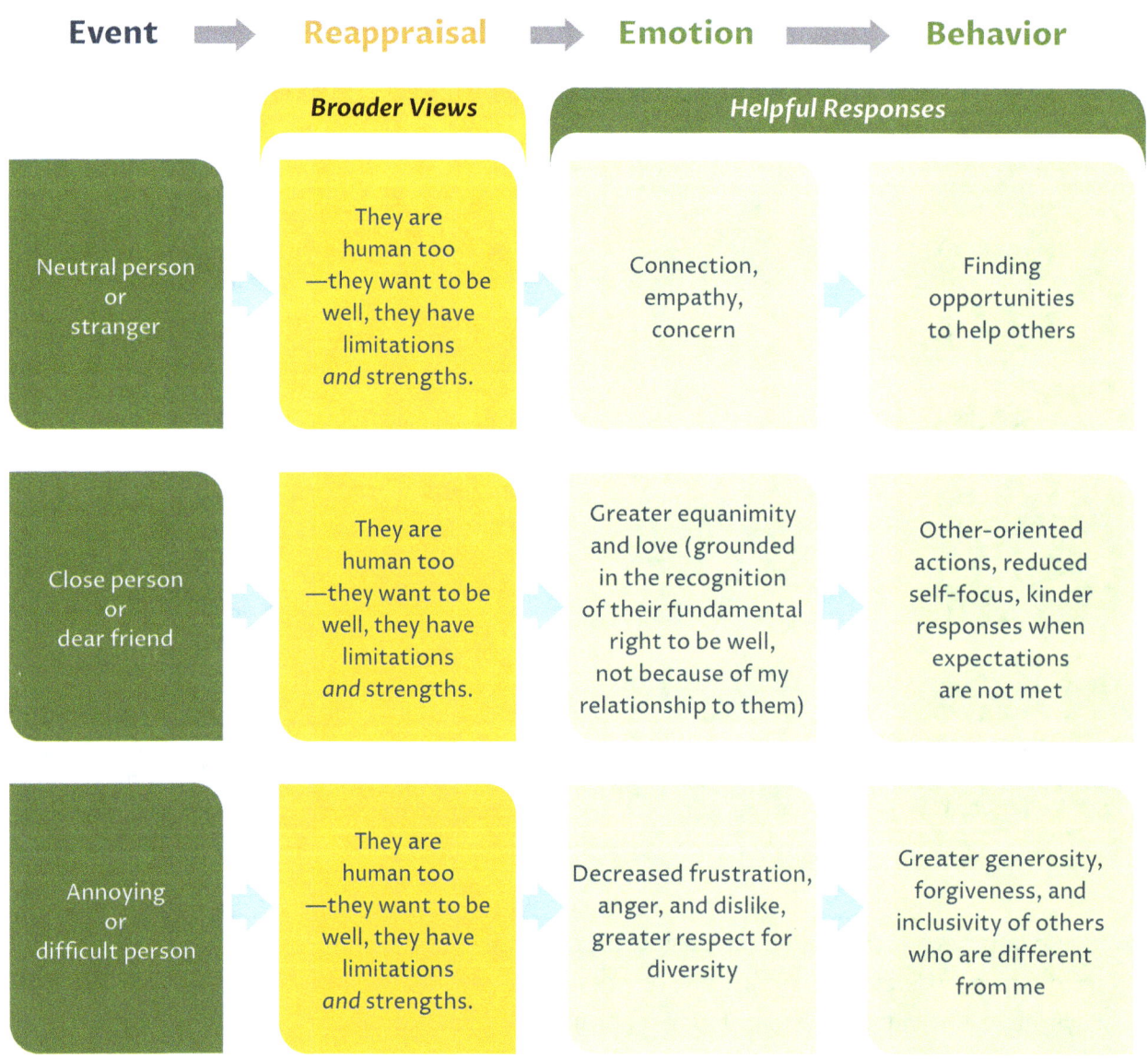

Take a moment to **find a comfortable posture and connect with your body** and current feelings. If you notice tension in any part of the body, feel free to stretch or move.

Allow yourself to **settle into the present experience**. Take a few deep breaths if that is comfortable. Gently inhale, and, if you like, have the sense that nourishing air is infusing your entire being. As you breathe out, see if you can release tensions and worries to some degree to allow the body and mind to settle into an unfolding sense of calm or ease.

If settling is hard today, you may want to pause and spend a few moments with an earlier practice.

When ready, **call to mind a person from each of the following three categories**: close ones, strangers, and those who annoy you.

- If it is an upsetting day, you can begin by just bringing to mind a close one. If you are feeling more comfortable, include a stranger. If you are feeling stronger, also bring to mind someone you find annoying or slightly difficult.

As you bring each person to mind, **attune to your feelings for them**. Are you happy when things go well for them? Do you feel concern when they are met with difficulty or setbacks?

It is natural to feel differently toward those who are in our inner circle and those who are not. But excessive bias exaggerates the divide between us and others, undermining our sense of community and feeding conflict.

Take a few moments to **recognize what you have in common** with the people you have called to mind: your shared human condition. Can you see that, as fellow human beings, they too must value being safe and having a meaningful life? Just like you, they too must desire to avoid harm and suffering of all kinds? Just like you, they too have limitations and vulnerabilities, along with their strengths?

As you begin to see your shared humanity more clearly, reflect: **Do you notice greater feelings of connection** with the people you called to mind? Do they feel like a part of your inner circle? Do you notice a greater concern for their ups and downs? If not, continue to reflect on what you have in common with them.

When ready, **expand your circle of concern**, gradually including more and more others in this reflection on our common humanity. Notice any accompanying feeling of connection or belonging and allow this to sink deeply into your heart and mind.

As you reflect on all that you share with others, also **keep in mind the many, real differences**. Reflect on the immense value of cultivating respect and collaboration among people with diverse backgrounds, talents, and perspectives.

Finally, reflect on how beneficial it would be if we could connect more easily with others, sustaining awareness of our common humanity. Might this sense of connection, as it deepens, promote greater inclusivity and respect?

Take a moment to dedicate your practice today to those you know to be in need of health and wellbeing and, as you are able, expand this dedication to include a widening circle of beings on this earth.

And **conclude by setting an intention** to extend the skills and insights from this practice into everyday life.

Bringing the Skills to Life

- **Expand your circle.** Catch yourself when you are irritated by people who seem fundamentally at odds with you, or when you feel indifferent toward people whom you don't know. Recall that these people also aspire to be well, though they too are vulnerable to life's setbacks. They too want to avoid harm, to find wellbeing, and to create a meaningful life. When you can apply this perspective, note how changing your view of the other person may change the way you relate to them. Consider any alterations in your own feelings as well. Perhaps these perspectives help you to come back to your ZOW in those frustrating moments and handle the situation with more clarity.

- **Create moments of connection.** Make a list of specific opportunities in your daily life to practice seeing how others are like you at a fundamental human level. Try to find a new opportunity every day.

  - This could be in the grocery store, where you take a moment to notice the people around you and consider each as human beings who want to be well and avoid harm.

  - This could be when you are stuck in traffic. Instead of getting bored or angry, try to practice connecting with others who are also stuck in the traffic, reflecting on their deep desire to be well and avoid harm.

- **See others as they are.** Try to notice moments when you may be idealizing others or setting expectations for them that are too high because of their closeness to you. In those moments, see if you can remind yourself that no one can be perfect in every situation, and that is okay.

Personal Reflections

I was doing my medical residency at a large, urban hospital, with lots of trauma and poverty. One semester—after I'd completed most of my CBCT classes—I was working with a patient who often came into the clinic, angry and complaining. In short, she was irritating. But thanks to CBCT, I was able to take a breath and remind myself, 'Just like me, she wants to avoid suffering and be happy.' That realization helped me see the patient in a new light and work with her to get the necessary tests and treatment she needed. By the end of the appointment, the patient's agitation was calmed, and she expressed her thanks and relief that I had helped her.

I am typically shy and introverted, but reflecting on what I share with others has allowed for both self-compassion and compassion for others to blossom. I used to be uncomfortable with strangers, but I now find myself more engaged with others, which has allowed for a better understanding and more warm-heartedness toward people— even those that are difficult. When my mind wants to judge others or fear them, I find it's easier to catch this old habit and replace it with a 'just like me' connection. Understanding our common humanity has allowed me to feel more connected with others and has enhanced my ability to care for them.

I am an attorney, and I have strong negative feelings toward members of a particular political party. The understanding that one's perspectives are shaped through many conditions has given me a small space to see the members of this party as human beings instead of 'evil beings.' I felt this more humanized view of my legal adversaries could possibly help me be a better attorney and let go of unnecessary feelings of anger. I was also able to go through a similar process with my mother, recognizing that my mother's difficult background was a strong influence in her life. Being able to empathize with my mother was a healing moment for our relationship.

Frequently Asked Questions

What if I find it disturbing to meditate on difficult people?

There is no need to focus on the most difficult person (or people) in this practice. If it's a stressful time, we may not want to work with all three categories of people but, instead, may want to focus only on a loved one. If we are feeling more comfortable, perhaps we can also focus on a stranger or distant acquaintance. If we are feeling solidly in our ZOW, we can focus on all three categories, including someone who annoys us or is giving us a hard time. Even in this case, however, start with someone less difficult. Perhaps this is someone who cut you off in traffic, a mechanic who did a poor job repairing your car, someone at home who leaves a mess that you end up having to deal with, or someone in your extended family whom you find annoying at holiday gatherings.

Many of us have been harmed by others, either directly or through neglect. This is an unfortunate reality. Before choosing to practice with a more challenging person, it is essential that your practice with the earlier modules is well-established, such that your mind and attention have gained some steadiness. Difficult memories or feelings may arise in this practice, so you should be especially comfortable with mentally engaging and disengaging your focus.

CBCT is meant to be practiced with gentleness, not to activate painful memories or cause distress. During practice with difficult people or issues, it is safer to "wade into the shallow end of the pond," dipping a toe in so that it will be easy to pull back to a place of comfort. Give yourself a break, and shift your focus away from that person or situation if strong unpleasant emotions occur. Gradually, as you gain confidence in your ability to disengage voluntarily from difficult memories or feelings, you'll be able to return to the practice with more confidence. And don't forget—you can always stop and return to earlier practices, or simply stop.

How do I set healthy boundaries in the face of someone else's wrong or harmful actions?

The CBCT principles and practices never encourage or expect us to condone, ignore, or forget harmful actions done to us or someone else. Compassion is, by definition, the urge to stop or prevent suffering. The practices are designed to increase this urgency and make us more likely to take action—even courageous action—to prevent injury or wrongdoing.

It is important to set healthy boundaries in any relationship. If someone in our lives is harmful, whether physically or emotionally, it makes sense to limit or stop interactions as best we can. CBCT is not insisting that anyone include people they don't want to include in their circle of concern. While the goal is to gently soften barriers and expand the circle of concern where we can, if for any reason we decide that we need to exclude certain people, that's fine.

If we feel comfortable trying it, CBCT offers a way to make visible the humanity we share with a difficult person while firmly maintaining the boundaries we need to protect ourselves. These boundaries may include physical distancing, taking steps to restrain someone's actions, or trying to hold them accountable for harm they have caused. In some cases, we may realize that if this difficult person were free from their suffering, they would not be causing the harm they are currently causing. Such reflections may allow us to soften our own difficult emotions, such as overpowering hatred or anxiety, while maintaining boundaries. Changing these aspects of our inner world does not at all require changing how we protect ourselves in the outer world.

Conclusion

In this module, we focused on making visible our common humanity, a basic fact of existence that too often goes unnoticed. We saw how identifying with others at a fundamental human level allows us to expand our circle of concern, soften excessive judgments, and let go of unrealistic expectations. We explored how connecting on the basis of common humanity can lead us to appreciate our diversity, helping us see that many of our differences can be valued and celebrated without causing separation and conflict.

Connection is essential for our survival as human beings and for the development of compassion. In the next module, we will build on the foundation of common humanity by reflecting on interdependence. This will allow us to further connect to others by deepening and expanding feelings of gratitude and tenderness.

Deepening Gratitude and Tenderness

"Gratitude helps us render another person his due. Since it keeps favors flowing, it is essential for a society based on reciprocity. Gratitude creates a warm feeling about the received benefits, which prompts us to repay them."

— FRANS DE WAAL,
THE BONOBO AND THE ATHEIST, 2013

Module 7

Having expanded our circle of concern through the recognition of our common humanity, we can now deepen our connection with others by making visible our interdependence and, in turn, promoting feelings of gratitude and tenderness.

It is natural for us to feel a sense of gratitude and tenderness toward those who contribute to our wellbeing. As we reflect on the many people on whom we rely daily, we expand this natural response. Seeing this interdependent reality allows us to shift the focus away from a narrow self-interest and cultivate a greater sense of connection and warmth for others. This warmth contributes to our own wellbeing and expands warm-hearted concern and compassion for others.

ENDURING CAPABILITIES

7.1 Seeing that we depend on others for our needs

7.2 Expanding feelings of gratitude and tenderness toward the many who benefit us, directly and indirectly, through the awareness of interdependence

7.3 Appreciating the benefits of other-oriented attitudes and seeing the drawbacks of excessive self-focus

Connecting to Feelings of Gratitude and Tenderness

1. Think of someone close to you who has clearly made a positive impact in your life.

2. Reflect on how they contributed to your wellbeing. Consider how this made a difference in your life.

3. What emotions and sensations arise as you think about this person? How do you feel about them now?

▶ **Takeaway**

We tend to naturally respond with gratitude and warmth when we see how others have benefited us. By making their contributions visible, we allow ourselves to connect to the nourishing feelings and sensations that positively impact our bodies and minds and deepen our connection to those individuals. When we look at those who made significant positive impacts on our lives, we naturally see our gratitude unfold along with a greater sense of closeness and, oftentimes, a desire to reciprocate that kindness. This response is deeply rooted in our biology, but often limited to those closest to us.

Key Elements of the Module

Have you ever felt alone in a room full of people? Researchers call this *perceived social isolation,*[63] based on the discovery that feeling alone is not the same as actually being alone. Just as we can feel lonely at a large gathering, we can also feel deeply connected to others when sitting by ourselves. Deepening gratitude and tenderness helps us move away from feelings of isolation and loneliness and toward belonging and connection.

Gratitude and warm-heartedness offer many benefits. They not only feel good, but they also orient us toward others and their needs. They bolster our natural kindness and encourage generosity,

motivating us to share what we have with others and to seek ways to fulfill their needs.

For those we feel close to, gratitude usually comes easy. It's often clear how much they contribute to our lives. But how do we expand gratitude beyond this inner circle? By attuning to our *interdependence*, we see that everyone is somehow part of the vast web that contributes to our wellbeing. When we expand our awareness to the many who benefit us every day, our sense of gratitude, connection, and warmth increases as well.

Interdependence is the reality that we rely on others to survive and thrive because, as social beings, we are deeply interconnected. As we make this reality visible, we will find there is no limit to how deeply we can connect with, and thus concern ourselves with, all beings on this planet. This understanding builds on our skills of identifying with others, opening our hearts to an ever more inclusive feeling of belonging. Like a gentle rain that nourishes a seed to grow into a gorgeous flower, tenderness is the essential ingredient that opens the heart to compassion.

Gratitude is the feeling of appreciation for someone or something that benefits us. Such appreciation toward others supports tenderness, a warm feeling of closeness or endearment.

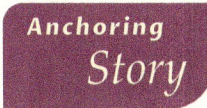

Anchoring
Story

Making the Shift toward Gratitude

Two co-workers, Beatrix and Carlos, just rubbed each other the wrong way. Their conversations were never comfortable; they were always competing whenever they were together. Carlos consistently felt undercut when Beatrix would question his ideas, while Beatrix felt silenced by Carlos in most interactions. Due to the tension in their relationship, they made it a point to avoid each other as much as possible.

After work one stormy winter evening, Carlos went to catch the train and realized it was out of service. All buses were delayed, and there were no taxis in sight. Not knowing what else to do, he began to walk in the direction of his home, knowing it would take hours.

It was dark, and freezing, and after a while, he started to doubt whether he could make it alone. His thoughts of uncertainty, worry, and slight panic were suddenly interrupted by a honking car horn. He turned around and saw Beatrix in her car. She pulled over and said, "Hop in, I can drive you home." Thanks to Beatrix, Carlos made it home safely. The next day, when Carlos saw Beatrix at work, he felt a new sense of warmth toward her and greeted her with a smile.

When we recognize that someone has done something kind for us, we, like Carlos, might feel tenderness develop, as well as an affection that arises because of our gratitude.

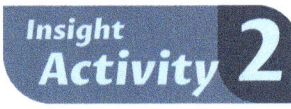

Seeing That We Depend on Others

1. Identify at least five of your core needs (physical, emotional, spiritual, social, professional, etc.). Then, reflect:

   ❀ What would happen if those needs were not met? How would that affect your life, and how would you feel?

   ❀ What role do others play in helping to fulfill these needs? If you can, identify at least one person who is crucial to each of the needs you listed.

2. Call to mind a skill or expertise you have that helps you to meet one of your needs and brings meaning to your life (e.g., abilities that help you succeed in your work, that benefit your family or community, or that allow you to engage in an activity that is important to your wellbeing).

   ❀ Now, see if you can identify individuals who have directly contributed to your having this skill or expertise (e.g., family members, friends, teachers, mentors, coaches, etc.). Try to list at least five, but you may think of many more.

3. As you make visible those who contribute to the fulfillment of your needs, what shifts do you notice in your feelings toward them?

▶ **Takeaway**

Our needs take many forms. Some are physical—the needs for food, water, and shelter, for example—and some are emotional— the need to feel safe or to feel empowered to act for our own wellbeing. Other needs are social, like the need to feel connected, included, and heard. The list of our needs is long, and in examining that list, we can see how other people are essential to having those needs met. As we look at the skills that help us to meet those needs, we see that even if our own hard work paved the way for us to gain those skills, others played important roles as well.

The awareness that other people are valuable to our lives has an impact on how we feel about and act toward them. Seeing how others are essential to our wellbeing not only enhances awareness of our connection, but also elicits feelings of gratitude and warmth for them.

MINDFULNESS OF INTERDEPENDENCE IN THE COVID-19 PANDEMIC

During the COVID-19 pandemic, schools closed across the globe. Parents and caregivers had to take on the role of "teacher" for children at home. As a result, thereafter teachers saw an outpouring of gratitude and appreciation from parents and caregivers everywhere.[64]

Why the sudden outpour of gratitude at this point in time? Why not before the pandemic, when students had been at schools with their teachers every week for years? The pandemic made visible what had previously been invisible: the reality that teachers have a tremendous impact on the lives of children and, in turn, on the lives of their caretakers. While this had always been a reality, the pandemic brought it to the forefront, which led to a greater sense of gratitude and appreciation for all that educators do.

Benefits of Gratitude

Of all the "positive" emotions in the field of positive psychology, gratitude was one of the first to be studied, and continues to be the *most* studied to date. Here is a sample of what the research shows:[65]

Psychological Benefits of Gratitude:

- Higher levels of positive emotions
- More alertness, aliveness, and awakeness
- More joy and pleasure
- More optimism and happiness

Social Benefits of Gratitude:

- More helpfulness, generosity, and compassion
- More forgiveness
- More outgoingness
- Less loneliness and feelings of isolation

Physical Benefits of Gratitude:

- Stronger immune system
- Less bothered by aches and pains
- Lower blood pressure
- More exercise and better health behaviors
- Longer sleep and feeling more refreshed upon waking

Web of Interdependence

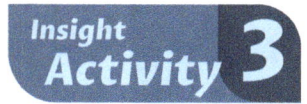
Insight **Activity 3**

1. Choose one human-made object that you value or need (e.g., a cell phone, pillow, sweater, bed, tea kettle, coffee maker, or something else you use every day).

2. Draw that object in the middle of a blank piece of paper, then chart the connections of people that helped make that object available to you.

   ❋ For guidance, consider the following example of a favorite sweater sent to someone by their grandmother:

1
GRANDMOTHER

3 SHOP
EMPLOYEES

100 SHOP BUILDERS   **1 TRUCK DRIVER**   **1000 TRUCK BUILDERS**

1000
SHEPHERDS   **100 YARN**
MAKERS   **10 CLOTHING**
MAKERS   **5 CLOTHING**
DESIGNERS

3. Count the number of individuals included in your drawing. Then, pause and consider if there is anyone missing. If so, add them! Be creative, and let your mind wander to include as many as you can imagine.

❀ Here are a few hints if you get stuck: What about trucks that transport your favorite item, or the people who made the trucks, or those who built the roads they use? What about the people who helped invent, manufacture, and sell them? What about all the people who grew food for all these other people to eat so they could do their jobs to get you this item?

4. If you identify any categories or groups of people involved in making the object available—such as truck drivers, factory workers, or farmers—estimate the total number of people that fall into that category, and put those numbers on your chart. Then, add up (or estimate if needed) the total number of people who made it possible for you to have your object, and write down that number on your paper.

❀ Does this number surprise you? Why or why not?

5. How could the awareness of the web of interdependence positively impact your wellbeing and your relationship to others?

▶ **Takeaway**

On this infinitely interconnected planet, there is not a moment that goes by without others contributing to our lives in some way. Our homes, having safe food to eat, clean water, jobs, roads, electricity, clothing—all of this is possible thanks to the efforts made by other human beings. And that doesn't even touch upon those who raised us! Consider the teachers, employers, colleagues, and friends who have supported us, as well as the family members who contribute to our daily needs, or the neighbors who keep an eye on things for us while we are away. If we can maintain awareness of how many people contribute to our wellbeing, we will more often be flooded with feelings of gratitude and warm-heartedness for them.

"And before you finish eating breakfast in the morning, you've depended on more than half the world. This is the way our universe is structured. It is its interrelated quality. We aren't going to have peace on earth until we recognize this basic fact of the interrelated structure of all reality."

— MARTIN LUTHER KING, JR.,
A CHRISTMAS SERMON ON PEACE, 1967

Reducing Narrow Self-Focus

For this insight activity, please read the short stories based on real situations and respond to the prompts that follow.

Story 1

Kenneth Lay, the head of the company Enron, managed his employees through fear of punishment. He had weekly meetings where he identified those who had not met goals and publicly shamed them. His hyper-focus on success at all costs led to a toxic work environment and encouraged behaviors that eventually resulted in the collapse of the company. His actions, fueled by self-interest, resulted in the mistreatment of his employees and eventually the loss of thousands of jobs. Though once a respected businessperson who shared his wealth through philanthropic ventures, Lay was revealed to have engaged in corruption to maintain Enron's appearance of success. He was convicted of 10 counts of securities fraud and died while awaiting sentencing. Despite being brilliant, hardworking, and creative—even kind and generous in some contexts—his excessive self-focus and craving for wealth or status was ultimately destructive to many of the lives he touched, including his own.[66]

1. Reflect on a situation where someone you know or have heard of was excessively self-focused and absorbed in themselves.

   ❃ In what ways did their self-focus manifest in their actions, behaviors, and decisions?

   ❃ How did those behaviors or actions affect their relationships with others?

   ❃ How did this affect the lives of those around them? How did it affect their own lives?

Story 2

Bob Chapman, the CEO of the international company Barry-Wehmiller, instituted a policy to encourage leaders to take a personal interest in the wellbeing of the workers. He retrained managers, helping them to let go of the mindset of seeing employees primarily as tools for production, and to embrace the mindset of seeing them as human beings. He had them reflect on the humanity of each employee, often reminding them that each person is someone's precious child and deserved to be treated as such. He encouraged leaders to approach their jobs as caregivers whose main objective was to support and trust each individual to become their best self at work. He created times at work for people to share experiences and learn about each others' personal lives, allowing for genuine connections to emerge. His strategy deemphasized both punishment and rewards, and emphasized relationships. Implementing this change had a tremendous positive impact on the workers, clients, and company at large. Soon after, this company, which had been headed toward bankruptcy, became a thriving business where many wanted to work.

2. Reflect on a time when someone you know or have heard of was very giving and other-oriented.

   ❀ In what ways did their other-oriented focus manifest in their actions, behaviors, and decisions?

   ❀ How did those behaviors or actions affect their relationships with others?

   ❀ How did this affect the lives of those around them? How did it affect their own lives?

3. In what ways can these stories and reflections positively influence your focus and actions? What concrete steps can you take toward increasing other-oriented thoughts, attitudes, or actions?

   ❀ Bear in mind that focusing on others does not mean

sacrificing our own wellbeing. Recall the insight from self-compassion: Taking good care of ourselves puts us in a better position to care for others. In other words, sometimes we need to put on our own oxygen mask first.

▶ Takeaway

While it is important to focus on ourselves and our needs to a certain extent, there are drawbacks when this becomes imbalanced. Studies have shown that excessive self-focus correlates with poorer health, greater unhappiness, and an increased risk of depression.[67] As David Brooks reflects in *The Second Mountain: The Quest for a Moral Life*, heightened self-interest is a timely, pressing issue:

> We live in a culture of hyper-individualism. There is always a tension between self and society, between the individual and the group. Over the past sixty years we have swung too far toward the self. The only way out is to rebalance, to build a culture that steers people toward relation, community, and commitment—the things we most deeply yearn for yet undermine with our hyper-individualistic way of life.[68]

In Module 6, we explored one way to shift our orientation toward others—by attuning to how they have the same desire to be happy that we do. When we see others' desire for wellbeing as equally important as our own, this puts their needs on our radar, naturally softening excessive self-focus. In this module, we continue to shift our focus to others by attuning to our social nature and making visible how deeply interconnected and interdependent we are.

Excessive self-focus undermines our happiness and wellbeing by placing our needs above all others'. When that happens, separation, disconnection, and isolation follow. Cultivating a more other-oriented focus promotes the connection that we need to thrive as social beings.

"Self-absorption in all its forms kills empathy, let alone compassion. When we focus on ourselves, our world contracts as our problems and preoccupations loom large. But when we focus on others, our world expands. Our own problems drift to the periphery of the mind and so seem smaller, and we increase our capacity for connection—or compassionate action."

— Daniel Goleman, *Social Intelligence: The New Science of Human Relationships*, 2006

Cognitive Reappraisal Strategy

Module 7 and the Emotion Timeline

Consider once again the emotion timeline. The diagram below illustrates how our appraisals of an event, more than the event itself, can fuel how we feel and act. Let's see how this timeline might play out in the case of Module 7's appraisals and reappraisals.

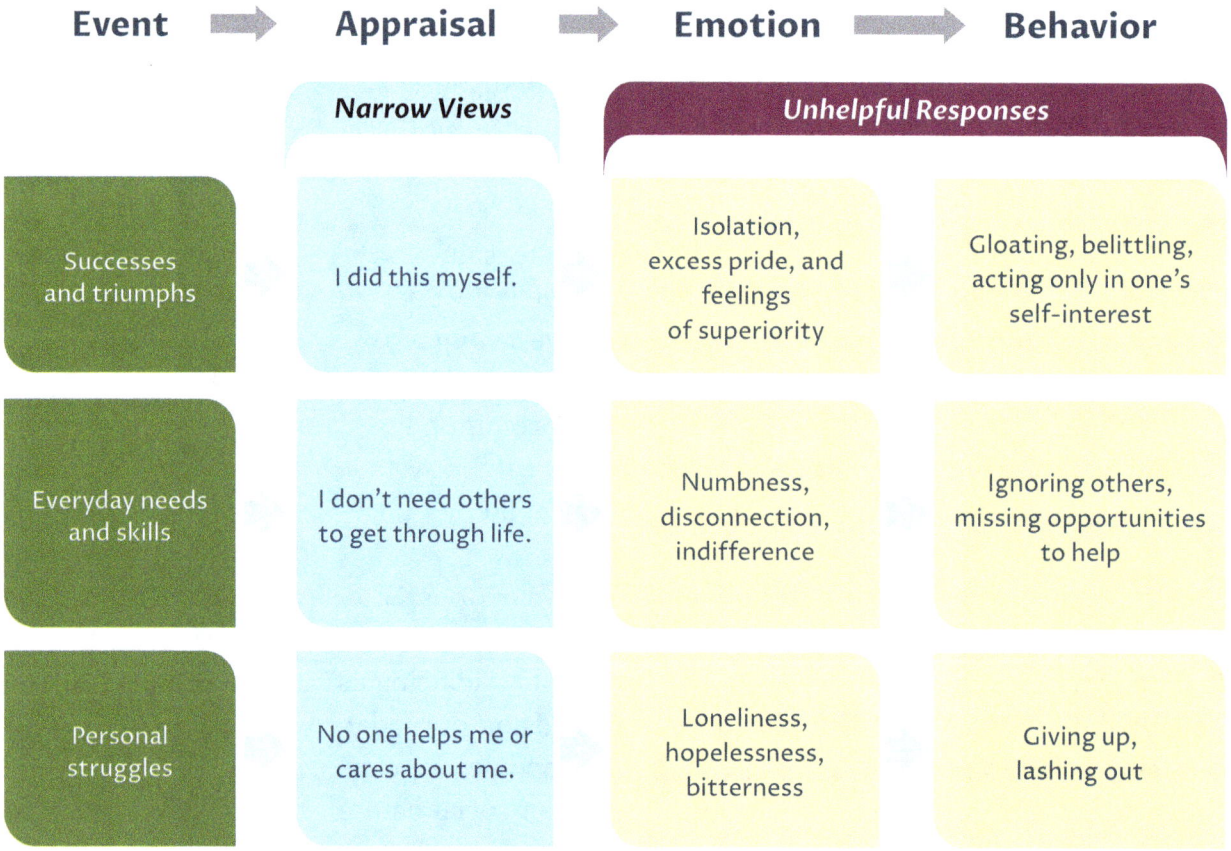

Event	Appraisal	Emotion	Behavior
	Narrow Views	*Unhelpful Responses*	
Successes and triumphs	I did this myself.	Isolation, excess pride, and feelings of superiority	Gloating, belittling, acting only in one's self-interest
Everyday needs and skills	I don't need others to get through life.	Numbness, disconnection, indifference	Ignoring others, missing opportunities to help
Personal struggles	No one helps me or cares about me.	Loneliness, hopelessness, bitterness	Giving up, lashing out

In this module, we work to expand our feelings of connection by recognizing that we depend on others for our fundamental needs. Without others, we cannot survive, much less thrive. As we *reappraise* the situation and make this reality more visible, we allow the natural reactions of gratitude, warmth, and connection to arise.

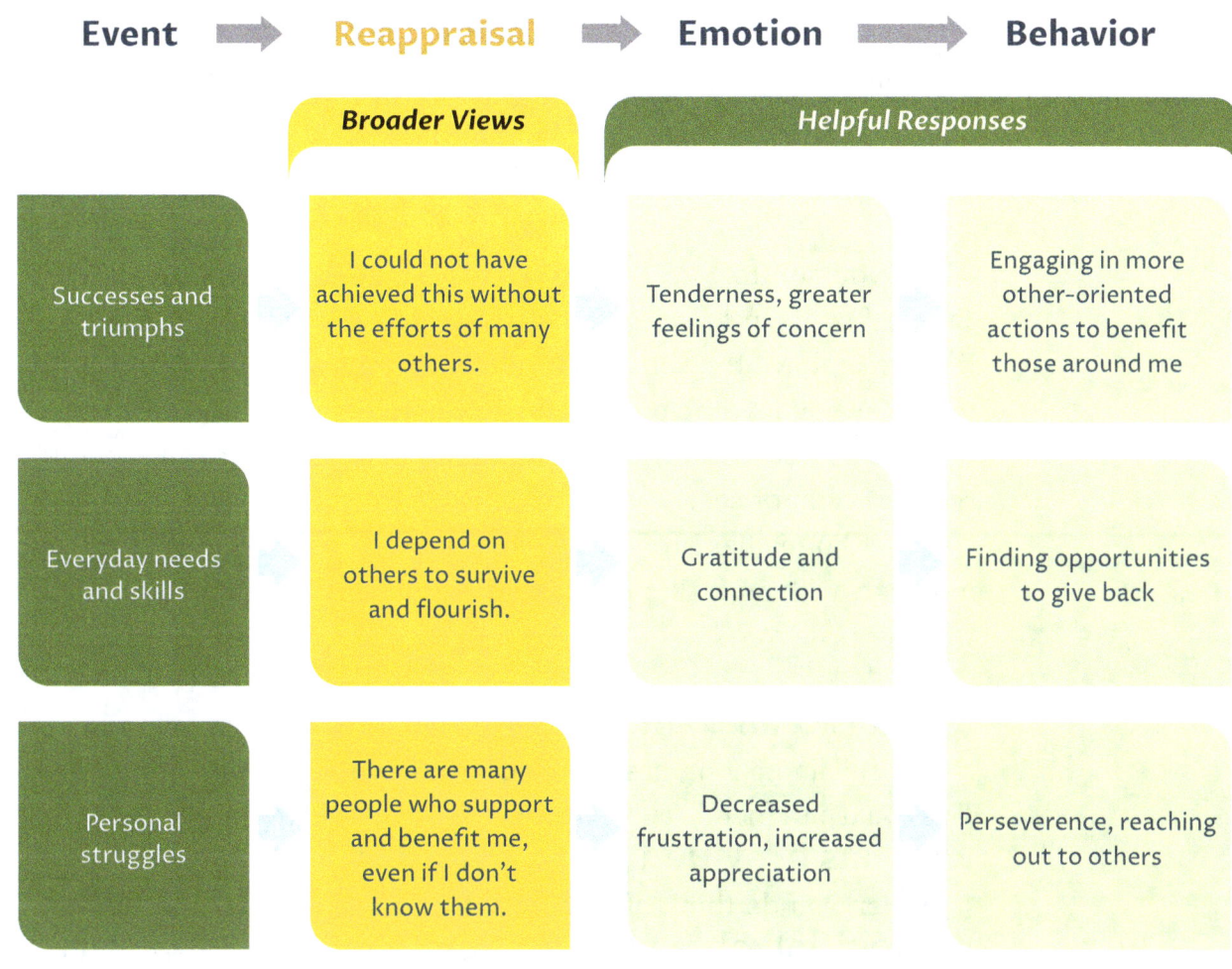

Event	→	Reappraisal	→	Emotion	→	Behavior
		Broader Views		**Helpful Responses**		
Successes and triumphs		I could not have achieved this without the efforts of many others.		Tenderness, greater feelings of concern		Engaging in more other-oriented actions to benefit those around me
Everyday needs and skills		I depend on others to survive and flourish.		Gratitude and connection		Finding opportunities to give back
Personal struggles		There are many people who support and benefit me, even if I don't know them.		Decreased frustration, increased appreciation		Perseverence, reaching out to others

Take a moment to **find a comfortable posture and connect with your body** and current feelings. If you notice tension in any part of the body, feel free to stretch or move.

Allow yourself to **settle into the present experience**. Take a few deep breaths if that is comfortable. Gently inhale, and, if you like, have the sense that nourishing air is infusing your entire being. As you breathe out, see if you can release tensions and worries to some degree to allow the body and mind to settle into an unfolding sense of calm or ease.

If settling is hard today, you may want to pause and spend a few moments with an earlier practice.

When ready, **call to mind** a person who, despite their own vulnerabilities and limitations, has attended to your physical or emotional needs. This could be a friend, family member, teacher, or caregiver, or **anyone who has provided you a kindness**, large or small.

When you do think of someone, take a few moments to **reflect on how valuable all their help has been** for your growth and wellbeing.

As you immerse yourself in this reflection, see if you notice an **emerging sense of warmth or tenderness** toward this person. If so, you may choose to simply sit with these feelings for a few moments, letting them sink deeply into your heart and mind.

As social beings, our lives are infinitely interwoven. Every resource, comfort, or skill that we enjoy is made possible by many others. Even something as simple as our breakfast, or any of the hundreds of things we depend on each day, connects us with countless others.

Take a few moments to expand your gratitude by making visible the many others who contribute to your life. **Bring to mind a skill that you cherish** and recall those who helped you gain this ability.

<hr>

You can **begin by recalling those who introduced you to the skill**, then those who helped you grow it or put it into practice. Then, gradually expand this awareness to include more and more people who make up your community of support.

<hr>

As you attune to the many who make up your web of support, reflect: Do you notice a shift in your feelings toward them? Perhaps an **expanding sense of gratitude or warmth**? If so, you can sit with these feelings for a few moments and let them soak in, infusing your whole being.

<hr>

Finally, explore how the growing awareness of your interdependence may increase tender feelings of connection with others. How might expanding warm-heartedness support your own wellbeing, as well as your ability to engage meaningfully with others, whether at home or across the world?

<hr>

Take a moment to dedicate your practice today to those you know to be in need of health and wellbeing and, as you are able, expand this dedication to include a widening circle of beings on this earth.

And **conclude by setting an intention** to extend the skills and insights from this practice into everyday life.

<hr>

Bringing the Skills to Life

↪ **Attune to our interdependence.** Catch yourself when you feel isolated or disconnected from others, and shift your mind to the awareness that your life depends on the kind efforts of many. Allow any resulting gratitude and warmth to deepen and grow.

↪ **Keep a positive events log.** To offset negativity bias, keep a log of all the positive things that have happened to you each day for one week. Each night, before going to bed, list at least five good things from the day. If you notice your mind tends to think of what went wrong that day, kindly acknowledge that and gently shift your focus back to what went right. Include even simple things that went well, simple pleasures that were available to you, or simple interactions that were pleasant and supportive. You can also reflect on what caused those good things to happen. Sometimes, we call this log a gratitude journal because it helps us bring to mind things that generate gratefulness and appreciation.

↪ **Make a gratitude visit.** Write a letter of gratitude to someone who has positively influenced your life but whom you have never really thanked, and send it or give it to them. If possible, do this in person, perhaps reading the letter to them.

Personal Reflections

❝ I've been going through a hard time and have been feeling overwhelmed. I lost both my parents, and things have been rough at home. But I've always been able to find solace in canoeing; it was the one joy in my life. One morning, after a storm, I went out to the backyard intending to spend some time paddling down the river I live on. I saw that, somehow, my canoe, which I spent a year saving money to buy, had come loose and smashed on some rocks down river. At that moment, I called to mind my lifelong best friend, someone with whom I could always find comfort and happiness, a refuge in the otherwise unrelenting storm. I was grateful for that friend's constant presence in my life. From there, I continued to think of my gratitude for others: my sister, brother, cousins with whom I am close, coworkers, and even strangers. It felt so much better to be filled with love and warmth and gratitude rather than anger and depression. And now I realize I have a tool to rely on when things get tough. Doing this meditation really helps. Even though the worst had happened—the loss of family, and the loss of my source of joy—it wasn't the end of everything. It was just another obstacle that I could handle with the help of my support system. Being conscious of gratitude and love, even in the worst times, can make life seem far more manageable. ❞

❝ Shifting from resentment to gratitude, I was able to soften toward my mother. Rather than keep the running list of what I hadn't received, I focused on what I did receive. I realized that it was my mother who taught me to read. As a journalist, remembering that, and focusing on how my mother had given me the gift that would determine my career, helped me drop the last of my resentment. Gratitude provided a spark of warmth and affection that infused the relationship with kindness and patience. ❞

Frequently Asked Questions

Why would I feel gratitude toward someone who did not intend to help me?

It feels great when someone goes out of their way to help us, whether it's a stranger holding a door open for us or a long-time friend providing a listening ear. Sometimes, we may think that these intentional acts of kindness are the only ones that deserve our gratitude. For instance, if someone delivers a package to our door because it is part of their job, we might think, "They don't deserve my gratitude; they are only doing this to get paid." But from a broader perspective, it does not make sense to withhold appreciation for someone who helps us—no matter their motivation.

Consider, for example, if we receive a package of life-saving medicine. We naturally feel gratitude for that medicine, but does the medicine intend to help us? Is the medicine thinking, "I hope this will make this person's life better"? When we think of it this way, we realize that the people who are helping us do not need to *intend* to help us in order to be appreciated. In fact, we come to understand that it's the *feeling* of appreciation for people (or medicine!) that feels good. Gratitude is a warm and positive feeling that spontaneously arises when we focus our attention on something that benefits us.

Our gratitude may not affect the other person at all, but it still helps us. As we grow in awareness of our interdependence, we realize we are supported by so many people we will never meet. We won't ever be able to thank everyone who deserves to be appreciated. Yet, we still benefit tremendously from holding them in our hearts with sustained appreciation and gratitude, reducing our feelings of loneliness, isolation, and disconnection, and—as we will see in the next module—laying the groundwork for a strengthened sense of compassion as well.

Is it realistic to feel affection toward everyone? For example, why would I want to have gratitude and feelings of tenderness toward those who cause harm to me or others?

CBCT provides us an opportunity to extend affection to include everyone, even difficult people. But please remember that this is not a requirement. Each of us is responsible for determining how far we extend our affection, and this decision should be made with common sense and personal experience. If we do not see a way to feel warmth for someone, that's fine. If we have a negative emotional response each time we think of a particular person, it is reasonable to leave them out of our meditation practice. While it is important to note that these categories can change over time, that does not mean we can force a shift.

If you do find yourself wishing you could have more affection for a difficult person, CBCT provides steps that can help move you in that direction. First, reflect on their humanity—they, too, want to be well and free from harm, and they also have vulnerabilities. They, too, have been shaped by circumstances beyond their choosing, and face the uncertainties of loss and mortality. From there, you can consider if there is anything you may have gained from having had them in your life. Have you learned anything from them? Have you depended on them for anything? Have you built any skills you value or formed valuable relationships because of them? Have you found meaning because of their impact on your life? Have you found strength or grown because of them? Often, with a little effort, we can find at least one good thing that has come from their presence in our lives, and we can find a bit of gratitude for that.

Shantideva, the eighth-century Indian philosopher often cited in the *lojong* tradition, wrote many verses on patience.[69] If we value patience, he asked, shouldn't we also value the opportunity to practice it? Without difficult people in our lives, how would we ever learn to practice patience? If everyone were nice to us all the time and never caused us problems, how would we ever discover our courage and strength? Another consideration is that our worst critics are often those who give us the honest feedback we need to help us learn about ourselves and see our shortcomings. Our friends, by contrast, might not see our flaws, might hold back from being honest, or might idealize or flatter us. In this way, we can see that even difficult people can sometimes benefit us greatly.

Please note: These reflections do not excuse or justify hurtful behavior, from ourselves or others. It's just that we may be surprised to find some good in even our most difficult relationships. As we explored in Module 5: Cultivating Self-Compassion: Part 2, challenges may help us in ways we do not expect.

What about the negative things that come from the web of interdependence? Aren't many of society's systems damaging and unfair to some groups of people?

As we begin to consider the web of interdependence, we might notice that the world it produces is not equally beneficial to everyone. For example, as we think about all the people who contributed to making our mobile phone, we can appreciate the big companies that invent and market the product, but also remain aware that they are possibly profiting off of underpaid workers—even child labor—working in hazardous conditions. Given this reality, we might ask: Is gratitude the proper response? What do we do with the justified frustration we feel at these abuses or toward the many inequities of our time?

It is important to remember that we are using awareness of interdependence as a tool to enhance our sense of connection to and warm feelings for others. If the reflection of interdependence actually makes visible the suffering of others, this too can be valuable in promoting our compassion, our wish to see them free from that suffering, and our desire to do something to help. This response to suffering, especially at the level of the system, will be a central focus of the next module.

Conclusion

In this module, we explored the reality of our interconnectedness and interdependence. We saw that, as social beings, the circle of those we depend on for our wellbeing is much greater than we may have realized. We focused on making this reality visible in order to foster a natural, other-oriented response of connection, gratitude, and tenderness. We also explored how valuable this other-oriented focus is for our flourishing, protecting us from the many drawbacks of excessive or narrow self-focus.

The warm-hearted connection we endeavored to foster in this module is at the heart of compassion. In the next and final module, we will attune to what others are up against and see how our tenderness strengthens the desire to relieve their suffering and motivates compassionate action.

Harnessing the Power of Compassion

"What you do makes a difference, and you have to decide what kind of difference you want to make."

— ATTRIBUTED TO DR. JANE GOODALL

Module 8

Having deepened our warm-heartedness for others through an awareness of both our common humanity and our interdependence, we can now attune to what others are up against and allow our compassion to grow and expand to a wider circle of beings.

Warm-heartedness lies at the root of love and compassion. It fuels our loving wish to see others endowed with health and wellbeing. When we become aware of their struggles, our tenderness for them fuels a desire to see them free from that suffering. Using discernment to more clearly see what others are up against allows our compassion to emerge for them and guides effective action.

ENDURING CAPABILITIES

8.1 Deepening awareness of the predicaments of those we hold with warm-heartedness

8.2 Engaging the wisdom of systems-thinking to guide our compassion toward effective action

8.3 Sustaining compassion in our hearts and through action

Tenderness, the Key to Compassion

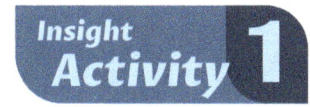

1. Reflect on or write down a list of three individuals you feel close to, but to varying degrees:

   ❀ Very close: Someone you are very close to, like a family member or best friend for whom you naturally feel tenderness.

   ❀ Fairly close: Someone you are close to, but who is not one of the closest people in your life. This could be a good friend (though not a "best friend").

   ❀ Somewhat close: Someone you like who is in one of your circles but is not a big part of your life. Perhaps this person is a teammate, neighbor, or community member.

2. Now, reflect on or write about what the person closest to you is struggling with at this time.

   ❀ Call to mind something manageable—say, an argument or a disappointment rather than a significant tragedy. As you bring this to mind, note your natural responses and describe the feelings that arise.

   ❀ If you aren't aware of a current struggle, recall something from the past or imagine something that they may be facing.

3. Repeat Step 2 for the other two people you identified.

4. What differences, if any, did you notice in your responses to each of the three individuals' predicaments?

▶ **Takeaway**

Compassion is a response to what others are up against, but being aware of their struggles is not all that is needed. A tender connection is also required. As we may have noticed in this exercise, the more tenderness we feel toward someone, the stronger our urge to relieve their suffering when we become aware of it.

As we expand our circle of concern, and with it our tender connections, we may become concerned that we will lose the strength of our connection with those closest to us. But as we explored in Module 6, this is not what actually happens. Just as the sun with its planets, we will naturally share more warmth with those closest to us. But that doesn't mean that we need to withhold warmth from those farther away. Our warmth can radiate in all directions, without blocks or barriers, and without being depleted.

Key Elements of the Module

Have you ever witnessed the struggles of others and found it overwhelming? Have you ever wanted to help, and were ready to do so, but couldn't see how to make a difference? Being aware of others' suffering is not easy. It can feel too heavy, too daunting, or just too much. Compassion gives us energy and patience to face suffering without feeling drained, burning out, or turning away. Unlike some other responses to suffering, compassion is rooted in a warm-hearted concern for others, a feeling that is nourishing and energizing.

Consider the definition of compassion that was introduced at the beginning of the book: *Compassion is the warm-hearted concern that unfolds when we witness the suffering of others and feel motivated to relieve it.*

This definition includes three crucial components:

1. A warm-hearted (tender, affectionate) connection

2. Recognition of what others are up against

3. The urge to do something to relieve their suffering

Compassion arises when we attune to the challenges or distress of others for whom we feel affection and concern. Just as striking a match on a matchbox gives rise to a flame, empathic awareness, coming together with affection, gives rise to genuine love and compassion.

As we cultivate compassion, it is important to distinguish it from some other common responses to suffering. Though the words compassion and empathy are used interchangeably by many, scientists have identified three types of empathy—only one of which is considered to be compassion.

- **Cognitive empathy:** Thinking about how others are feeling and intellectually understanding what the world looks like from their perspective. This is often referred to as "walking a mile in their shoes."

- **Empathic resonance:** Sharing the same feelings as another person. This comes from "mirroring" the feelings of the other or "resonating" with them. This is referred to as affective empathy or empathic contagion in emotion science.

- **Empathic concern:** Caring about the feelings or experiences of others in ways that motivate us to act on their behalf, to support their wellbeing, or to alleviate their distress. This is sometimes referred to as motivational empathy. In CBCT, this is what we mean when we use the word compassion.

Cognitive empathy and empathic resonance are important responses that can support compassion, but neither necessarily includes caring about the wellbeing of others. Empathic concern is the only type of empathy that is by nature other-oriented.

Harnessing the power of compassion requires wisdom. This means applying *discernment* alongside our compassion—using intelligence and critical thinking to help us more clearly see the causes of suffering and what we may do about them. Applying discernment requires us to turn once again to systems-thinking (introduced in Module 4: Cultivating Self-Compassion: Part 1, page 111), which is a way of investigating and understanding the many conditions that contribute to a given situation. This approach deepens our understanding of what we *can* do, even when facing complex or difficult problems, and helps us to navigate through feelings of anxiety or hopelessness and tap into steadiness and courage. As discernment opens us to a more complete understanding of what others are up against, it guides us toward effective action and can even ignite compassion more deeply than we felt it before. Compassion and discernment are like the two wings of a bird: The bird needs both to truly soar.

In this module, we strengthen wise compassion so that it can influence how we live each moment, infusing it into our interactions with others and sending ripples through our interconnected web of relationships. When we harness the power of compassion, we create change in ourselves, in our communities, and in the world.

UNPACKING EMPATHY

It may be surprising, but some types of empathy, when left alone, can lead to neglect for others or even greater harm to them or to ourselves. Consider, for example, if we experience *only* cognitive empathy when faced with someone's struggles. Without some amount of warm emotions, we may remain indifferent to their plight. We may even use cognitive empathy to manipulate or trick them, like a person who uses that knowledge of someone's struggles to undermine them further. But while cognitive empathy can be used for harm, it can also be used to inspire compassion. In fact, compassion relies on our ability to understand what others are up against. When this awareness is coupled with a tender connection, compassion naturally unfolds.

Furthermore, if we experience *only* empathic resonance, we may become overwhelmed by the experience of someone else's emotions. This is referred to as *empathic distress.* Such a reaction, if sustained, will be draining and potentially damaging. It can prevent us from being available for others as our nervous system moves into the mode of flight, fight, or freeze. Empathic resonance is not something we want to get rid of—it plays an important role in alerting us to others' feelings—but once we have noticed these emotions, it is important to make the shift toward empathic concern by tapping into our feelings of tenderness for the other and focusing on

"These [empathic] states inspire different actions. Easily distressed people avoid others' suffering, for instance, refusing volunteer opportunities that will put them in emotional situations. People who tend to feel concern are willing to engage in helping. In one study, people who experienced distress helped when it was their only option but stayed away when they could. People who experienced concern helped even when given the option not to."

— Jamil Zaki,
The War for Kindness: Building Empathy in a Fractured World, 2019

what they are up against. This helps us recall that their situation is not our situation, that their emotions are not our emotions, and yet we can stay fully present and connected. This allows the response of empathic concern (that is, compassion) to grow. In this way, we shift our focus away from the pain we have taken on and toward the other person and their needs. While it may take time, making this shift is crucial to harness the full power of compassion.

In sum, we are not turning away from empathy! With practice, we are learning to recognize and channel cognitive empathy and empathic resonance to feed our compassion. In strengthening these skills, we sustain our own wellbeing and our capacity to be there for others.

Can I Give
Him My Eyes?

Content Warning: The following true story includes descriptions of military violence.

Richard Moore was a young boy living in Derry, Northern Ireland, during a time known as "the Troubles", a period of violent conflict in Northern Ireland that started in the late 1960s and lasted for over 30 years. The 6 counties of Northern Ireland were, at that time, part of the United Kingdom, while the remaining 26 counties belonged to the Republic of Ireland. Intense conflict arose within these counties between the Unionist community, who wanted Northern Ireland to remain part of the United Kingdom, and the Nationalist community, who wanted Northern Ireland to join the Republic. The population was polarized. The streets, patrolled daily by the British Army, were full of violence.

On May 4, 1972, 10-year-old Richard was racing along the bottom of the school soccer pitch with his friends after school. A British soldier fired a rubber bullet in the direction of the children, and this bullet struck Richard on the bridge of the nose. Richard spent 2 weeks in the hospital, where doctors feared that he was going to die. Although he survived, Richard's parents were told he'd be blind for the rest of his life. Immediately upon hearing this, Richard's father turned to the doctor and asked, "Can I give him my eyes?"

Supported by his loving family, young Richard grew up to be a successful business-man in his community. He started Children in Crossfire, a charity to help kids across the world whose lives have been disrupted by war. At age 44, Richard reached out to Charles Innes, the British soldier who had shot him decades earlier, to express forgiveness. When they met, the two discovered that they have many things in common, and they became friends. They now travel together to spread the message of forgiveness and compassion. Hearing Richard's story, the Dalai Lama was moved to call him "my hero." Richard named his autobiography after his father's plea: *Can I Give Him My Eyes*?

Two elements work together to magnify compassion. The more warm-heartedness we feel toward someone and the greater our awareness of their predicament, the stronger our desire is to do something, even when the cost is high. In the moment Richard's father offered up his own eyes, his focus wasn't on his own distress, but on the concern that he had for his dear son. These endearing feelings, combined with the awareness that his son would face enormous challenges going through life without sight, led to his deep urge to do anything to help, even if that meant giving up his own eyes. This is a tale of extraordinary compassion in an extraordinary situation, but we can learn from it to make sense of our own feelings of compassion and how they manifest in our day-to-day lives.

What Are They Up Against?

1. Think of an individual or a group that you care about that is going through a difficult time. Describe the challenge they are facing and how it is affecting their wellbeing.

2. Apply systems-thinking to examine the causes of their challenge:

   ❋ What factors are directly and indirectly contributing to their challenge?

      ⤙ External factors: circumstances, environment, people, systems, etc.

      ⤙ Internal factors: habits, perspectives, reactions, etc.

   Consider the example of a child who is struggling in school:

      ⤙ *External factors: school environment, peers, education system, etc.*

      ⤙ *Internal factors: habit of binge-watching videos, low self-compassion, social anxiety, etc.*

   ❋ Take it a step further: What contributed to the factors you listed above?

      ⤙ If they have a habit that is contributing to their suffering, where did that habit come from?

3. Pause and reflect: What feelings arise toward this person or group as you deepen your understanding of what they are up against?

4. What benefits may come from deepening awareness of the challenges faced by those we hold with warm-heartedness?

▶ **Takeaway**

Becoming aware of others' struggles can sometimes happen spontaneously, as it did with Richard's father when he found out that his son would never see again. In other cases, this awareness requires greater effort. Taking the time to examine what others are up against using discernment and, more specifically, systems-thinking is an important step for deepening our compassionate response. With a deeper awareness and understanding of what others are experiencing, we can naturally enhance feelings of tenderness for those we care about. This increases our drive to act.

Holding more people in our ever-widening circle of concern with empathic awareness and tenderness can even lead us to seek changes at a societal or global level. For example, if we become aware that people are struggling with food insecurity systemically, we might develop the drive to change the system that we see prolonging or magnifying their suffering.

The Most Pressing Concern in Your Community, Society, or World

Insight **Activity 3**

When we consider how we might make a positive difference in the wider world, it can seem overwhelming: "Where do I start? What issues do I tackle? There are so many of them and only one of me." A sense of helplessness or hopelessness can easily creep in. Let's take this one step at a time and see if we can take a broader perspective. This will allow us to uncover our leverage point, the place from which we can take action and make the most difference.

1. Think of a few issues that you care about and pick one that feels most pressing to you.

   ❀ Examples: the mental health crisis, increasing violence or war, global warming, political polarization, injustice, the loneliness epidemic, food or employment insecurity, etc.

   ❀ Feel free to pick an issue that feels closer to home, impacting someone you know.

2. With this in mind, write a few words describing what positive outcome you hope to see in relation to this issue (e.g., improved mental health, less violence, healthier climate, etc.).

3. Make it personal. Write down a list of individuals or groups that you know are or will be most impacted by this issue. Then, describe how their lives would improve if this positive outcome could be accomplished.

4. Write down the positive outcome you've identified in the center of a piece of paper and, from there, draw or write the major factors that would contribute to this goal. Map as many layers of direct and indirect causes as you can, from global to local, from actions to attitudes that contribute to the situation.

5. As you map out these multiple contributing factors, note where you might be able to make a difference and describe *how* you would make that difference. Consider your strengths, connections, resources, and circumstances, and how those might help you find a leverage point.

6. Write down one to two sentences clearly articulating one step—big or small—that you could take to have a positive impact.

❉ Imagine taking this step. How does that feel? Note and describe any difference between how you felt when you began thinking about the larger issue and how you feel now.

▶ Takeaway

Systems-thinking guides discernment in several important ways that support compassion. Not only does the deepened awareness of an issue inspire a greater drive to help, but it also helps us find ways to take effective action and make a difference where we are able. As we examine the complexity of any issue, we uncover different layers that we may impact.

We will find that acting from compassion looks different for each of us. Our acts of kindness will depend on many factors, like our abilities, roles, and context. In a hospital, a patient with heart disease may receive an examination from a doctor, pain management from a nurse, and counseling from a mental health clinician. Each of these caring acts can be motivated by compassion and contribute to the healing of the patient, but the actions are quite different. Each actor relies on personal knowledge and resources to know how they can best serve.

Sometimes the only thing we can think to do is hold others with our compassionate wish, but this too can be powerful. When we are with those who are suffering, our warm-hearted presence can itself be a source of comfort and nurturance. And as we sustain our compassionate wish, we remain on alert, ready to act as soon as we see how we can make a difference.

Systems-thinking also helps us to face obstacles with perseverance. Consider instances where our best efforts fail due to circumstances outside of our control, or when we simply make a mistake, or when we see that the change we seek will take time. We can persevere in these situations, moving past the common roadblocks of hopelessness and frustration, by recalling that many factors of any situation are outside our full control. As we explored in Module 4: Cultivating Self-Compassion: Part 1, this understanding helps us to relieve excessive self-criticism, protects against feelings of helplessness, and lets us focus on our next best move. It inspires us to keep working toward our goal and to examine alternative ways to achieve it, meeting setbacks with resilience.

> *"We are visitors on this planet. We are here for 90 or 100 years at the very most. During that period, we must try to do something good, something useful, with our lives. If you contribute to other people's happiness, you will find the true goal, the true meaning of life."*
>
> — THE DALAI LAMA, *MY TIBET*, 1995

EVEN A SMALL ACT CAN MAKE A DIFFERENCE

One day, a man was walking along the beach when he noticed a boy picking things up and gently throwing them into the ocean. Approaching the boy, he asked, "Young man, what are you doing?" The boy replied, "Throwing starfish back into the ocean. The surf is up, and the tide is going out. If I don't throw them back, they'll die." The man laughed to himself and said, "Do you realize there are miles of beach and hundreds of starfish? You can't make any difference." After listening politely, the boy bent down, picked up another starfish, and threw it into the surf. Then, smiling at the man, he said, "I made a difference to that one."[70]

Creating a Ripple Effect

1. Take a few moments to recall small acts of kindness or compassion you received that made a difference in your life (e.g., helped you to grow, resolve a challenge you were experiencing, etc.).

2. Pick one of these acts and describe the details of it and the benefit(s) it led to.

3. In what ways did this impact your life or the lives of others? In what ways did or could this lead to even greater impacts elsewhere?

   ❇ Challenge yourself to continue thinking of impacts beyond what initially comes to mind. Consider even large-scale changes that could result.

4. What feelings or sensations arise as you reflect on the positive outcomes of receiving this small act of kindness?

5. How might this reflection affect how you think, feel, or act, moving forward? Reflect or write about any other insights or takeaways that came up from this reflection.

▶ Takeaway

It can be hard to remember that even a small act can have broad ripple effects over time, especially when we are faced with big challenges without a clear path forward. We won't always see the ripples that our actions make, but reminding ourselves that even something small can have a big impact inspires hope and motivates us to engage more compassionately in the world.

Each of us, acting compassionately, will help to relieve suffering in our own way; consider a teacher who educates the young, a friend who listens well, a nurse who cares for a patient, a campaigner who advocates for safety or justice, a journalist who tells the stories of the unheard, a neighbor who tends to a lonely elder.

"No kind action ever stops with itself. One kind action leads to another. Good example is followed. A single act of kindness throws out roots in all directions, and the roots spring up and make new trees. The greatest work that kindness does to others is that it makes them kind themselves."

— AMELIA EARHART

Even the largest ocean is simply a collection of many small drops of water, accumulated one by one. Embodying a systems-thinking perspective makes visible our role in addressing even the largest problems that face humanity, empowering us to engage our compassion.

The Power of a Sustained Warm-Hearted Wish

There are several benefits to sustaining the warm-hearted wish to see others free from suffering.

The wish can lead to actions that help others.

By sustaining the compassionate wish and growing the urge to make a difference, even when there is no apparent "fix" or solution, we are primed and ready to act if and when we do see a way.

"Life's most persistent and urgent question is: 'What are you doing for others?'"

— Martin Luther King, Jr., *The Strength to Love*, 1963

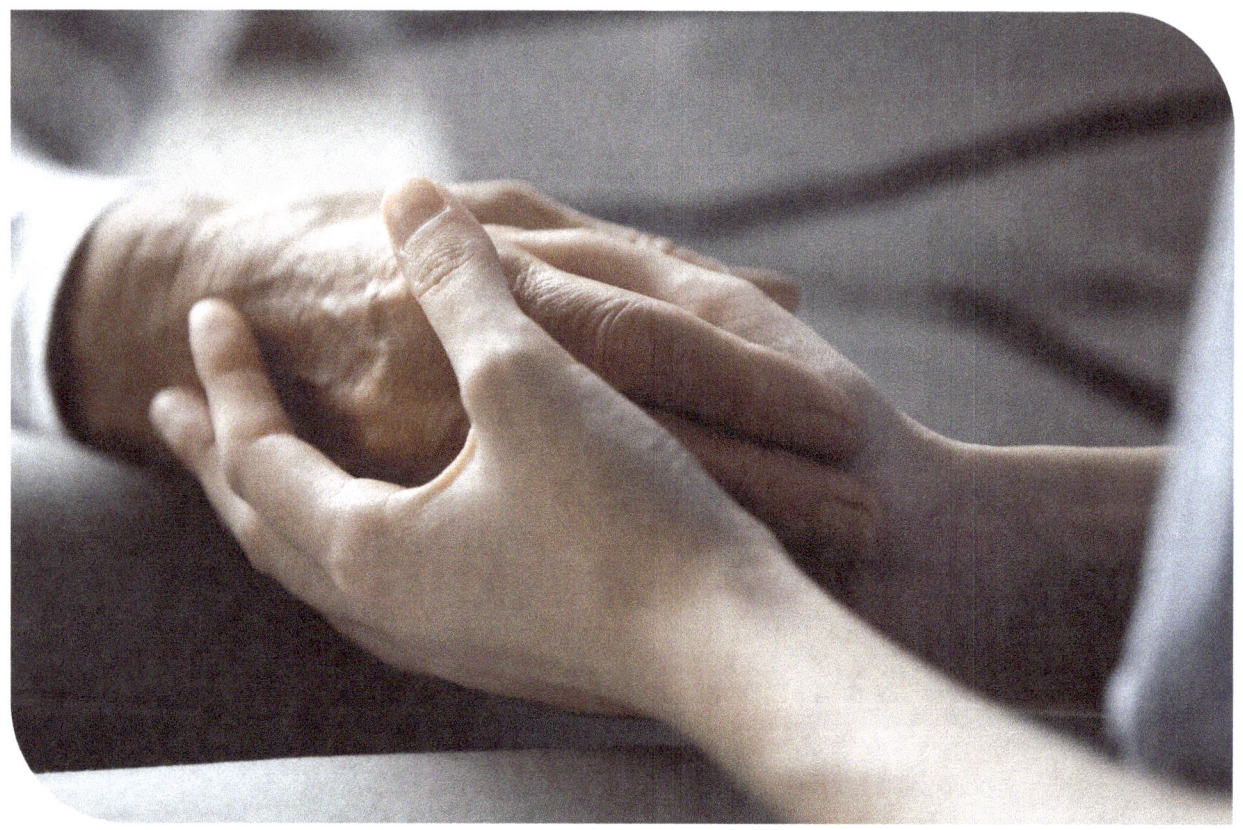

This will not happen if we have turned away or withdrawn our attention.

The wish, in and of itself, strengthens and sustains meaningful relationships.

Sometimes we wonder: Why would it matter if we sustain the compassionate wish if there is no immediate way to help? But simply holding onto that wish can make a profound difference in our relationships. Our compassionate presence can become their "nurturing moment," providing the comfort or strength they need to make it through a tough situation or that they can fall back on in times of hardship. This could be the best gift they ever receive.

Even if the wish doesn't help others immediately, it is still beneficial to our own wellbeing.

Research confirms how much compassion contributes to our sense of wellbeing and to our finding meaning in life. Studies suggest that the more compassion we have for others, the happier we are.[71] Our health is better and we live longer.[72] We likely experience more pleasure.[73] Our relationships improve as we impact the lives of others for the better.[74] Why would compassion make such a difference? Why would researchers conclude that compassion is "an antidote to burnout"?[75]

As compassion is rooted in warm-heartedness, it fills us with feelings of connection associated with pleasure, safety, and calm. Feeling connected to others also combats the feelings of isolation that can deteriorate our mental health and even decrease our life span.[76] Expansive compassion also gives meaning and purpose to our lives, which can carry us through when the going gets rough. Thus, the person who embodies compassion is truly the first to benefit.

Intentionally revisiting the inclusive and warm wish for all others to be well reinforces love and compassion, making them stable and sustainable. We become more able to face difficulties with strength and courage. We become more focused on creative, effective, and realistic solutions to problems, thus lowering our chances of despair or burnout. Compassion and love keep us motivated, even when confronted with setbacks. They help us to remain present and to find the most skillful ways to serve others during our short time on this planet.

The aspiration to embody inclusive compassion is ambitious, and it may overwhelm us if we forget to bring self-compassion along. These lines from *Pirkei Avot,* an ancient Jewish text on ethics, beautifully express the tension of remaining realistic and kind to ourselves as we aspire to a universal mission: "You are not obligated to finish the work, but neither are you allowed to abandon it."[77]

Take a moment to **find a comfortable posture** and **connect with your body** and current feelings. If you notice tension in any part of the body, feel free to stretch or move.

⁓

Allow yourself to **settle into the present experience**. Take a few deep breaths if that is comfortable. Gently inhale, and, if you like, have the sense that nourishing air is infusing your entire being. As you breathe out, see if you can release tensions and worries to some degree to allow the body and mind to settle into an unfolding sense of calm or ease.

If settling is hard today, you may want to pause and spend a few moments with an earlier practice.

⁓

When ready, take a few moments to **get in touch with any feelings of tenderness you may have for others**, by calling to mind all that you have in common with them, as well as the ways that you have benefited from them, both directly and indirectly.

⁓

You may begin by focusing on your loved ones and, when you feel ready, **gradually expanding this awareness** to include strangers, and perhaps even some of those whose values or behaviors you disagree with.

⁓

For those you connect to with growing tenderness, **reflect on what they are up against**. What challenges? What struggles do they face? How are they vulnerable to life's ups and downs?

⁓

As you reflect on others' challenges or struggles, note your feelings. Do you feel a **compassionate urge to be of help**? If so, you may choose to sit with this for a few moments, letting it soak into your whole being. You can **imagine this urge as a pearl of light at the center of the chest**—with each in-breath, you can see this warm light grow, and, with each out-breath, send this light out toward those in your expanding circle of concern, relieving their suffering and nourishing them with health and wellbeing.

To strengthen this urge, you may also **repeat these phrases**: "May you be free from suffering and the causes of suffering. May you have happiness and the causes of happiness."

Finally, take a moment to notice any shifts in your feelings as you connect to others with a deepened sense of love and compassion. Imagine how this ability, as it grows, could enhance your own wellbeing and your relationships with others and the whole world.

Take a moment to dedicate your practice today to those you know to be in need of health and wellbeing and, as you are able, expand this dedication to include a widening circle of beings on this earth.

And **conclude by setting an intention** to extend the skills and insights from this practice into everyday life.

Bringing the Skills to Life

You can also visit www.kindspring. org to find 21-day kindness challenges that can support your family or organization in its effort to engage in small acts of kindness. At this site, you can also order a free set of "smile cards" that can be left behind when you do an anonymous act of kindness, encouraging the recipient to "pay it forward."

- **Apply discernment.** Catch yourself when you are feeling overwhelmed or indifferent in the face of others' suffering. Connect to your tender feelings for them, as well as your desire to see them flourish. With a settled body and mind, consider the causes and conditions contributing to what they are up against, then see if you can discern something you can do, even if that is simply sustaining a compassionate wish for them.

- **Perform small acts of kindness.** Brainstorm three small acts of kindness—that you could take this week—that might lessen the suffering of another person. Reflect on them or write them down. Commit to doing at least one. When you have completed the act, write about how it went, how it felt, and whether you would consider doing more.

- **Connect with your motivation.** When you face an ethical dilemma, perhaps one in which you are being forced to choose between two important values or principles, consider this step-by-step discernment process that the Dalai Lama describes in *Beyond Religion, Ethics for a Whole World:*

"In my own case, when called upon to make a difficult decision, I always start by checking my motivation. Do I truly have others' well-being at heart? Am I under the sway of disturbing emotions, such as anger, impatience, or hostility? Having determined that my motivation is sound, I then look carefully at the situation in context. What are the underlying causes and conditions that have given rise to it? What choices do I have? What are their likely outcomes? And which course of action, on balance, is most likely to yield the greatest long-term benefit for others? Making decisions in this way, I find, means they are not the cause of any regret later on."

Personal Reflections

" I volunteered to support a student who had experienced severe burns and was undergoing reconstruction, but I was apprehensive about my ability to manage and self-regulate through the experiences of debridement and her pain. I needed to be able to assist with dressing changes and care, as well as emotional and spiritual support. I drew upon CBCT practice intensively and, during one particularly difficult moment, found that the practice helped me sense into the strength and courage and resource of compassion—deeply into my heart—and the ability to stay present and grounded and provide care. The boundlessness and strength of compassion was very real and accessible in that difficult circumstance, and I recognized that it arose from CBCT practice. I'm still very grateful! It gave me confidence in compassion that is also a resource. "

" CBCT practices have been very helpful. For the past couple of years, I have been looking at ways that I can be of service to people who are nearing the end of life. CBCT helps me to confront and be present with suffering in a constructive way. I am reminded that there is always something that I can do. Maybe not directly, but I can always be with the suffering and be with the person who suffers. I can always offer a compassionate heart. I have also found that, by looking at suffering directly and not turning away, I am able to find the joy that is present in almost every situation. In this way, I find that I am more able to 'weather' the suffering that is all around me. "

" I saw a patient the other day that was in a terrible mood after she had to wait all day to see me in the clinic. When I walked to her, before I could even open my mouth to say anything, she laid into me and started yelling. I had actually done a mini–CBCT meditation before the clinic, so I suppose I was more attuned to what she may have been experiencing, and how she may also have just been afraid, because she had a newly diagnosed life-threatening condition. Instead of yelling back, I took a deep breath and apologized for keeping her waiting and asked that she stay since she waited so long so that we could take care of her problems and help make her feel better. Not easy when you are stressed and being yelled at for trying to help someone . . . on a busy day. The follow up: She came back on Friday and I did the procedure. As I was leaning over her to take the ECG leads off her, she reached up and hugged me tight, and said, 'Thank you so much for everything you've done, I'm lucky you are my doctor.' And we both kind of teared up a little. "

Frequently Asked Questions

Why practice the earlier modules with the stabilizing and analytical practices? Why not just skip straight to the final step, wishing others to be well and free from distress and harm?

As we have mentioned, cultivating compassion can be compared to cultivating a garden. If we want a flourishing garden, we don't just say we want it and expect it to appear. The same is true for compassion. By strengthening the skills and further embodying the understandings of the earlier modules, we cultivate the conditions for compassion to naturally arise.

There is always room to continue developing our compassion, and we do so by leaning on the earlier practices. For example, if the suffering of others pushes us out of the ZOW, we can return to the stabilizing practices to re-center so that we don't shut down. If we are struggling to extend compassion to someone who is difficult, we can dive deeper into the reflection on our common humanity or return to self-compassion. The more we return to and deepen the perspectives from the analytical modules, the more they become the lens through which we see others and the world; the more embodied they become. Compassion, then, won't require as much effort because our embodied understanding will naturally lead to more compassionate feelings and responses. It is the familiarization process of returning to and sustaining the earlier practices that continues to strengthen our compassion.

See pages 10–13 for more information on CBCT's cognitive theory of change and the importance of moving through the three levels of understanding to eventually reach an embodied level.

Why do we visualize a light in our chest for this practice? Does this have anything to do with the Tibetan Buddhist practice called *tonglen*?

In Tibetan Buddhism, *tonglen* is an advanced practice known as giving-and-taking. In *tonglen*, on the in-breath, the practitioner imagines they are taking on all the darkest challenges and problems of others. Then, on the out-breath, they send others all of their own light, wellbeing, and happiness, giving them all the goodness they have. CBCT does not recommend this practice for beginners, as it can be destabilizing to invite the illness, loss, and distress of others into one's body and mind without significant preparation.

Instead, CBCT draws from another practice from the Tibetan tradition, one in which the concluding practice uses the in-breath to visualize a strengthening light of compassion growing in one's body. The out-breath then sends this source of wellbeing out to others as we imagine them filled with that healing light. This practice can be very powerful, aiding us to embody compassion after we have learned and practiced the full sequence of modules.

At times, this practice may feel imaginary or "fake," or else we may feel like we are merely going through the motions. But with practice, this final step will be felt more often at a personal level. Of course, this visualization is not an end in itself; instead, it builds on all the prior modules, ingraining the desire to help others and to remain mentally prepared to do so in all moments of our lives. As the compassionate urge becomes deeply established, we will naturally and spontaneously do what we can to help others.

Is there a difference between love and being overly attached?

Compassion and love can be seen as "two sides of the same coin," or two aspects of the same emotion. But this is only true when we are talking about a particular meaning of the word "love." A better phrase for this may be "altruistic love," a type of love focused entirely on the warm-hearted wish to see others flourish.

In English, the term "love" is used in many other ways, however. We often say things like, "I love to play football," or, "I love ice cream." This meaning of love is sometimes called *attachment*, meaning we are focused on what the object of our love can do for us, not on what we can do for it. If something can bring us pleasure, status, money, etc., we may say that we "love" it or that we have "fallen in love" with it (or with him or her).

Our relationships with people typically involve both types of love, altruistic love and attachment. According to Indo-Tibetan Buddhist psychology, these two emotions are mixed like milk and water; in other words, they are very difficult to separate. And yet, it is helpful to understand and notice when we are relating to our close friends, romantic partners, or family with one or the other. If we are primarily thinking about what will be good for them, then this is altruistic love. If we are thinking mainly of how much they do for us, then this is likely attachment.

Romantic relationships often have a heavy dose of attachment, as we begin to imagine that this other person is the main source of our happiness. We may even tell ourselves that we could not be happy without them. This state may feel as if it is focused on the other, but it is actually focused on our own wants and happiness. This is not to say that attachment is bad. It is very human, and CBCT's approach does not expect us to set aside or transcend these natural ways of relating to each other. There is nothing wrong with finding joy in our relationships and taking pleasure in the good that we receive from others. However, it is also helpful to remember that this is not the same as wishing that another will flourish and wanting them to be free from their difficulties and struggles.

While reflecting on types of love, it may help to consider a type of love that gets mixed up with altruism, which we may call "pathological altruism."[78] In this state, we make look like we are very caring on the surface, but underneath our focus is actually on our own reputation, status, or control. We may find, after some self-reflection, that we frequently serve or give to others so that we will be liked or accepted, or so we can feel in control of others' happiness. These are common human tendencies, and we should not judge ourselves harshly if we find that we have them. But by understanding our motivations more clearly, we can practice shifting our focus to sustain a more genuine altruistic motivation.

Conclusion

In this module, we attuned to the struggles of those we hold with warm-heartedness and allowed our compassion to unfold for a widening group of people. We explored the need to couple compassion with discernment, engaging in the wisdom of systems-thinking to guide us toward effective action. We worked on connecting to a feeling of empowerment as we reminded ourselves that our actions matter, whether large or small, and that each one of us can contribute to making a better world.

We saw how deepening our understanding of compassion's value can feed our motivation to sustain it in our hearts and through our actions. Then, we explored how compassion can influence the way we interact with and engage with those nearest to us, and how it can contribute to our communities and to the world. We also began to see that the work of compassion training does not end here.

In the concluding chapter, we will take a step back to look at the steps we have taken together and all we have accomplished so far. We will also explore the question: What's next? How do we keep working with the CBCT skills, perspectives, and practices? Where will our journey take us? While there is no single path to follow, we can each find ways to continue our efforts, strengthen our inner capabilities, and bring compassion into being.

What's Next?

*"Our world needs a compassion
revolution, and we need it now."*

— THE DALAI LAMA,
LETTER TO THE COMPASSION CENTER, 2019

On this journey, you've watered the seeds of compassion. You've uncovered this innate quality within you and your capacity to expand it. You've cultivated the conditions for growing compassion as you strengthened each enduring capability. Some of these skills and insights may still feel challenging, while others may feel like established strengths. No matter where you find yourself on the journey, we hope you've also seen that it is worth it to keep going, continuing to uncover meaning and finding more connection and joy along the way.

EIGHT MODULES OF CBCT

Module 1: Connecting to a Moment of Nurturance

Module 2: Developing Stable and Clear Attention

Module 3: Enhancing Self-Awareness

Module 4: Cultivating Self-Compassion: Part 1

Module 5: Cultivating Self-Compassion: Part 2

Module 6: Expanding Our Circle of Concern

Module 7: Deepening Gratitude and Tenderness

Module 8: Harnessing the Power of Compassion

Review of the CBCT Journey

We began in Module 1 with a nurturing moment to set the foundation for compassion training. By connecting to the felt sense and value of nurturance, we were able to establish a state of safety and calm, as well as a genuine motivation to expand compassion to others—both of which are essential for this journey. In Modules 2 and 3, we refined our skills of attention and self-awareness, beginning to see our mental patterns more clearly.

We also strengthened our resilience, as we learned how to catch emotional sparks before they turn into fires. Having practiced refraining from automatic judgment and entanglement with our mental experiences, we then turned to analytical meditation to transform habits that we find do not serve us well.

In Modules 4 and 5, we focused on how we respond in the face of our setbacks. We worked to alleviate any harmful reactions of excessive self-criticism, shame, or feelings of helplessness by making visible our human condition and finding meaning in our vulnerabilities. We were able to strengthen our resilience and self-agency, reinforcing habits of self-compassion.

Our attention then turned toward our relationships with others. In Modules 6 and 7, we attuned to our common humanity and interdependence, strengthening our sense of connection to others and feelings of tenderness for them. And finally, in Module 8, we made visible what others are up against. The warm-heartedness we cultivated coupled with an awareness of others' struggles led to the natural response of compassion—a deep wish to see them free from their suffering.

So, here we are—not at the end of a journey so much as at the beginning. If we have experienced any benefits from these practices or insights, we can let those benefits guide our intention to continue our practice. There is much more to learn from studying compassion and the conditions that give rise to it—not just book learning, but learning that comes from applying this knowledge in our own lives.

As we move forward, it is important to balance inspiration with realistic expectations. It is okay if we do not feel compassion for the whole world, or if we do not feel compassion all the time. That is only human. We can remind ourselves that increasing compassion into any aspect of our lives, no matter how small, has the potential to benefit ourselves, our community, and beyond.

Continuing to Bring the Skills to Life

Compassion is not just for big life decisions, like where to work, what to study, or who to befriend. Anything we do presents an opportunity to put CBCT skills and perspectives into practice.

For most of us, our existing roles, jobs, and routines give ample opportunities for compassion practice each day—nourishing others with the food we cook, soothing others with a listening ear, or inspiring others with the music we make. We can always find new opportunities to act with compassion, even in small ways. Perhaps we might go out of our way to connect with someone, to greet them with a kind gesture or word. Otherwise, we might reach out to an old friend or check in with lonely neighbor; choose to listen to others more instead of speaking first; offer to take on a task at home that someone else usually does; conclude an email with an extra note of encouragement or thanks; donate to an organization or public figure that is doing work we admire; let strangers go ahead of us whether we are walking, driving, or riding a bike; share a sincere thanks for something we normally take for granted; or engage in a five-minute settling practice before a meeting or conversation in order to be more present and able to meaningfully connect. There are so many opportunities to harness the power of compassion in our lives, and the more we engage it, the more it grows.

Continuing the Formal Practice

Compassion is something we can also continue to train and strengthen through formal practice. Setting time aside to meditate allows us to move toward greater embodiment of compassion. Research has shown that with greater practice comes greater benefit; discipline plays an important role in this process and may take some extra effort at first. Consider the following steps to build a strong and sustained practice:

- **Form a daily practice and build it over time.** Make the practice a habit. Start small and gradually expand it. Research has found that progress and commitment is sustained by taking small steps forward.

- **Attend a meditation retreat.** Having extended periods to practice every so often is important for further deepening and refining our skills.

- **Find opportunities to practice in community.** This gives us the chance to connect with and feel supported by others who are also working toward the shared goal of expanding compassion.

Many compassion practitioners find that community is the most empowering and energizing resource in one's journey to compassion. Sharing the journey with others can help us to learn and grow, and can inspire and sustain a regular formal practice. It can be found in many places, not only in a class or retreat. We might consider joining or starting a group in our social circles, whether they are faith-based, neighborhood, political, or other. The right community will help when we hit low points or setbacks, which are natural, in this process. Community can help us find joy in the journey and motivate us to stay with it.

Exploring Different Approaches

Now that we have become familiar with all eight modules, how do we know which practice to do next and in which order to do them? The good news is that, now knowing the basics, we can choose an approach that suits our situation.

We may lean on the linear progression of CBCT, repeatedly cycling through the formal practices in order. Or we may identify specific CBCT skills that we want to strengthen and focus on those for a while—for example, spending a few weeks on Module 3's approach to enhancing self-awareness. If we go this route and the effort is getting frustrating, we can recall that the skills of each module are supported by skills from prior modules. So if we are feeling stuck in Module 3, perhaps having a hard time allowing thoughts and emotions to come and go without becoming entangled, we can spend more time in Module 2, refining the skills of focused attention. Having stabilized our attention, whether it takes a few minutes in one session or multiple sessions over a few weeks, we can then return to Module 3.

This same approach can apply to any of the modules. If expanding our circle of concern (Module 6) is proving challenging, and it is hard to relate to others with a sense of common humanity, it may help to spend more time in the self-compassion modules (Modules 4 and 5). If facing others' suffering and holding them with compassion (Module 8) feels like an impossible and overwhelming task, it may help to stay with the earlier suite of modules focusing on resilience (Modules 1–5) to gain confidence in our ability to manage bigger emotions that arise when we turn toward bigger struggles. For moments when it all seems too difficult, we can lean into self-compassion by reminding ourselves that no one "gets it right" every time. And if at any moment, in any of the modules, we feel insecure, unsteady, or out of our ZOW, we can return to Module 1 and the nurturing moment.

There is a compelling logic to the way CBCT is sequenced. But the truth is that CBCT does not only work in this linear way, from one module to the next. Sometimes it may be more helpful to do one of the later modules first. For example, as we gain more skill with the later modules, we might find it useful to deepen self-compassion (Modules 4) to release ourselves from an active episode of self-shaming *before* engaging more with the work of training attention (Module 2). Or, at times, expanding compassion (Modules 6–8) will feel powerful and meaningful, even when self-compassion feels way out of reach. That is all fine; the process will look different for each of us. As we decide what we need, keep in mind that each module is there to create a condition required for compassion. Even if we are spending more time with earlier practices that seem "self-focused," we are still cultivating compassion in the broader context. The more regulated we are, the more we are able to act compassionately with others.

In sum, it is fine to "bounce around" to different practices depending on what we need. And as we navigate all the many options for CBCT practice, and perhaps learn from a variety of teachers, it is important to stay open to messages from our own bodies, minds, and emotions. In the long run, we find that those messages will guide us best. No matter where we feel that we are in our journey, we are each beginning where we are. We are finding the process that works for us.

Setting Intentions

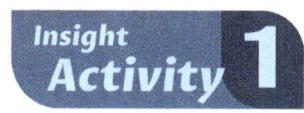

As with anything important that we want to continue to foster, compassion training will be easier with a clear intention and a plan. When you think back over the Enduring Capabilities of the eight modules, how will you commit to developing them? How will you keep up your practice? How will you integrate them into your life, and how will you approach compassionate engagement in the world?

If you intend to maintain the skills and insights of CBCT in your life, here is an exercise to help. Set aside 15–30 minutes to do some reflective writing, asking yourself the following:

1. What are the most important skills or insights I have encountered while exploring CBCT?

   ❀ If helpful, refer to the Enduring Capabilities list in the Appendix (page 237).

2. What are some ways that I could keep these skills or insights alive in my life, going forward? Name a few situations, relationships, or places in which they could be applied.

3. How can I see my current roles and/or work in life as a way of expressing compassion? Are there things I already do that activate my compassion? Are there opportunities within my current situation that would allow for more compassion to manifest?

4. What realistic commitments am I willing to make, starting today, to sustain momentum in the direction I have imagined?

▶ **Takeaway**

Each one of us plays a crucial role in bringing compassion into our lives, our communities, our social structures, and the world. We each make a difference as we continue to deepen our commitment,

Note:

This reflection is wonderful to do as a contemplative conversation, perhaps with a friend who would be willing to simply listen to you while you talk. Or, if the other person has also been studying CBCT, you could take turns, setting a timer for five or so minutes for each of you to freely share and see where your thoughts take you. Pauses are fine. The listener can simply hold the space with focused attention and compassion.

strengthen our inner skills, act with wisdom, and move toward a greater embodiment of compassion. On this journey, we—as individuals and as a community—are sending ripples of compassion spreading far and wide. Those ripples have impact, whether or not we witness them. Imagine the systemic changes that would be enjoyed by the world's children, and their children, and so on, if more individuals harness the power of compassion! A global shift toward compassion would drive our collective effort to extend the causes of happiness and wellbeing to all.

Conclusion

We conclude this book with a promise and an invitation from the Emory Compassion Center: We pledge that we will continue to create, improve, and share quality compassion education for as long as it is needed. We will continue to engage in scientific research to strengthen the worldwide understanding of compassion and the potential for its cultivation, and we will serve as a crossroads for making connections and sharing knowledge in this emerging field. We invite you to join hands with us and the many others who see an urgent need for a compassion revolution. Let us step toward this reality together.

Appendix
CBCT Enduring Capabilities

Module 1: Connecting to a Moment of Nurturance

1.1 Attuning to one's sensations and feelings

1.2 Accessing moments of nurturance to activate feelings of safety and comfort

1.3 Valuing being nurtured as a way to increase motivation to provide nurturance to others

Module 2: Developing Stable and Clear Attention

2.1 Enhancing the ability to sustain attention on our chosen task, object, or experience

2.2 Increasing the ability to notice unhelpful impulses, emotions, and distractions

2.3 Strengthening our ability to disengage and redirect the attention where we want it to be

Module 3: Enhancing Self-Awareness

3.1 Enhancing awareness of the patterns of thoughts and emotions in our inner life

3.2 Strengthening the ability to distinguish reality from our projections

3.3 Deepening the understanding that thoughts and emotions are fluid and changing, not fixed or solid

3.4 Increasing the gap between impulse and behavior, allowing greater choice and flexibility in our responses

Module 4: Cultivating Self-Compassion: Part 1

4.1 Sustaining awareness that we are not alone in having setbacks and limitations

4.2 Maintaining the broader perspective that, while we may have limitations and challenges, we also have strengths and opportunities

4.3 Applying a systems-thinking perspective to setbacks, understanding that there are many contributing factors to any outcome that are not all within our control

Module 5: Cultivating Self-Compassion: Part 2

5.1 Sustaining the awareness that we can grow and learn from our mistakes, failures, and setbacks

5.2 Using adversity as a way to clarify our core values and purpose

5.3 Enhancing sensitivity and compassion for others who share our experiences of vulnerability

5.4 Strengthening self-agency and fostering confidence in our ability to alleviate our distress

Module 6: Expanding Our Circle of Concern

6.1 Enhancing awareness of our unconscious biases, assumptions, and judgments of others

6.2 Connecting to others by making our similarities visible

6.3 Expanding our ingroup through awareness that everyone shares the fundamental desire to be well and to avoid harm

6.4 Increasing our capacity for acceptance, understanding, and forgiveness

6.5 Appreciating and respecting diversity and differences

Module 7: Deepening Gratitude and Tenderness

7.1 Seeing that we depend on others for our needs

7.2 Expanding feelings of gratitude and tenderness toward the many who benefit us, directly and indirectly, through the awareness of interdependence

7.3 Appreciating the benefits of other-oriented attitudes and seeing the drawbacks of excessive self-focus

Module 8: Harnessing the Power of Compassion

8.1 Deepening awareness of the predicaments of those we hold with warm-heartedness

8.2 Engaging the wisdom of systems-thinking to guide our compassion toward effective action

8.3 Sustaining compassion in our hearts and through action

Acknowledgments

I t would be impossible to list all the names of the many who have contributed meaningfully to the development and proliferation of the CBCT program and, in recent years, to the creation of this book, *Training Compassion: The Official Guide to CBCT©*. The authors offer our sincere gratitude to CBCT's wide community of practitioners, supporters, and constructive critics. We hope that our collective effort will contribute some amount to humanity's understanding of compassion and compassion training, ultimately leading to a kinder and more ethical world for all.

We are deeply indebted to Tangerine Ink, led by Amy Hertz and including Mark Magill and Larissa Silva McDonnell, MA for their invaluable and fundamental contributions to the writing, structure, style, and editing of the guide. We also appreciate the expert line editing and proofreading of the final draft by Ariel Liberman, JD, LLM, SJD.

We would like to acknowledge the valuable guidance we received from the book's expert advisory council, a group of dedicated and long-time CBCT instructors who gathered in Atlanta to launch this project in March 2019. Along with the developer of CBCT, Lobsang Tenzin Negi, PhD, the committee consisted of psychologists, scientists, and educators. These included Marcia Ash, MPH; Carol Beck, MFA; Penny Clements; Sally Dodds, PhD; Samuel Fernandez-Carriba, PhD; Edgar González-Hernández, PhD; Timothy Harrison, MArch; Michelle Liberman, MSc; Brendan Ozawa-de Silva, PhD; and Marcelo "Bento" Soares, PhD. This group brainstormed options for the guide that shaped its initial

CBCT Guide Advisory Council in 2019

structure and format. They also contributed to and reviewed early drafts. We want to thank all these members for their invaluable effort and early guidance. Of this group, we acknowledge a special debt to Sally Dodds, PhD, psychologist and CBCT researcher, who edited the text of early drafts and provided valuable ideas and input on the structure of the opening chapters. We also appreciate the expert line editing and proofreading of the final draft by Ariel Liberman and the multiple comprehensive and precise reviews by Alice Goddard.

We would also like to express our gratitude to the expert working groups who tailored the CBCT program to the business, healthcare, mental health, and education sectors (for more information about the tailored versions, visit www.compassion.emory.edu), and who offered constructive feedback and substantial improvements to this guide. Thank you to Melanie Anderson, LCSW, Dianne Andree, EdS, MEd, George Brooks, JD, Ann McKay Bryson, Ellen Coggeshall, MD, Ryder Delaloye, EdD, William J. Eley, MD, MPH, Janice Gates, Kalie Giovanni, LCSW, Charles Lane, MD, Kirstie Papworth, MSc, Adam Silberman, MD, and Eamonn Walsh, LCSW. We are grateful for the partnership of Hillside, a psychiatric residential treatment facility here in Atlanta. Through our continued efforts, children, youth, and staff have been able to benefit from receiving CBCT. Our collaborative efforts have resulted in new insights as to how CBCT can be impactful to individuals with mental health needs.

We recognize that, while CBCT's principles are meant to be universal, each author's perspective is, in some ways, limited by their culture. Thus, we are grateful for the extensive contributions by the members of the International Cross-Cultural Review Committee: Corina Aguilar-Raab, PhD, from Germany; Neha Bhatia, MCom, from India; Edgar González Hernández, PhD, from Mexico; Memoona Hasnain, MD, from the United States and Pakistan; Maya Jenkins, MEd, from the United States; Flávia C. Kolchraiber, PhD, from Brazil; Reshma Piramal, MSc, from India; and Ofer Yifrach, PhD, from Israel. This group of diverse and talented CBCT instructors reviewed every page in the interest of generating a more meaningful and accessible program for many individuals from multiple backgrounds—cultures, religions, professions, nationalities, ethnicities, genders, races, religions, and ages.

We are very grateful to Pollyanna Casmar, PhD, and Ariel Lang, PhD, psychologists at University of California San Diego, with whom we collaborated in 2015–16 to create CBCT-Veteran. This project, which continues to flourish, is a clinical intervention with its own manual for teaching CBCT to veterans in support of their recovery from clinically diagnosed PTSD. That collaborative effort helped inform the design of The CBCT Guide.

We express our deep gratitude to director of the Trauma Resource Institute, Elaine Miller-Karas, LCSW, for supporting the CBCT program and generously permitting the use and adaptation of important materials on trauma and resiliency, in particular the Zone of Resiliency (or Wellbeing) that is featured in the Overview and Module 1.

Training Compassion: The Official Guide for CBCT© has also benefited from our longtime collaboration with a teacher residency program in the Atlanta Public Schools and Georgia State University, the Collaborative and Reflection to Enhance Atlanta Teacher Effectiveness (CREATE). CREATE offered CBCT in a suite of successful efforts to promote teacher excellence in the context of social and racial disparities. The dialogues with and insights from those teachers, in particular Rosalynne Duff, Ayodele Harrison, MS, Elizabeth Hearn, EdS, MS, and Maya Jenkins, MEd, have shaped the presentation of the CBCT material herein. We would especially like to thank the members of a focus group of CBCT instructors who shared lessons from their years of experience tailoring the program to meet the needs of primarily Black teachers in under-resourced schools. Their insights and guidance helped make the material more inclusive and accessible to marginalized groups. The members of this focus group included Tanya Frierson, MEd, Anthony Lobban, Dumaka Moultrie, MEd, Penny Clements, and Maya Jenkins, MEd.

We want to acknowledge the valuable insights that have come from our partnership with Spiritual Health at Emory Healthcare through the co-creation of Compassion-Centered Spiritual Health

(CCSH™), a training program for hospital chaplains and related professionals. In particular, we thank Maureen Shelton, MDiv, and George Grant, PhD, who have shared their faith in the value of compassion training across all religious traditions, as well as their generative wisdom about how to communicate spiritual ideas and practices skillfully in a multicultural world.

We thank Michael Rohani at Design for Books for his flexibility, insight, and talent to be able to take the complex material and organize it visually for comprehension, flow, and ease of reference.

We send much warm-hearted appreciation to the numerous certified CBCT instructors who have brought CBCT to a wide range of populations across the United States and to many countries—including Brazil, Canada, Chile, England, Germany, India, Israel, Italy, Mexico, Mongolia, Peru, South Africa, South Korea, and Taiwan—and the many who have implemented CBCT in their own communities and organizations, all while generously sharing stories of their experience with us along with valuable insights about how CBCT is received in context. So many of you have provided feedback that has shaped the material in this book, in large and small ways, and we trust you will see your fingerprints here and there.

We would like to express much gratitude to Emory University for their steadfast support of the CBCT program and the Center for Contemplative Science and Compassion-Based Ethics, formerly known as the Emory–Tibet Partnership. A special thanks to Dean Robert Paul, former dean of Emory College, and Gary Hauk, PhD, former Vice President and Deputy to the President of Emory University, whose guidance was instrumental in founding the program. We are also deeply indebted to Charles Raison, PhD, who, together with Lobsang Tenzin Negi, PhD, launched the initial research studies on CBCT, along with co-investigators Thaddeus Pace, PhD, Terri Sivilli, and many volunteers who supported this early work. Though too numerous to mention, we extend our gratitude to the many other scientists who have carried out research with diverse populations in the years since. We also thank our friends and partners at the School of Medicine, where CBCT has been offered to students, faculty, and staff since 2015.

We offer a deep thanks to each and every member of the Center's staff who has contributed to the success of the CBCT program, with special thanks due to Zipporah Slaughter, senior program coordinator for CBCT; Hannah Smith, senior program coordinator for CBCT's Compassion Shift projects; Penny Clements, lead facilitator of teacher certification; and Brooke D. Lavelle, PhD, early facilitator of teacher certification.

We are deeply grateful for all the work that was relied upon in the development of CBCT. The program would not be possible without the efforts of numerous researchers in the fields of emotion science, neuroscience, biology, social science, and psychology who have pioneered the study of "positive" emotions, especially compassion, and all those who have contributed to the contemplative knowledge from the *lojong* tradition.

His Holiness the Dalai Lama and Lobsang Tenzin Negi at Emory University in 1998, inaugurating the Emory Compassion Center.

We would like to recognize the Compassion Shift initiative's founding benefactors, the Rob and Melani Walton Foundation and the Gaden Phodrang Foundation of the Dalai Lama. It is through their generous seed funding that we can embark on the ambitious journey to advance a global culture of compassion. We would also like to acknowledge the support of many other donors who have contributed to the Compassion Shift and CBCT programs, with a special thanks to the Adelphia Fund, Alessia Bulgari, Lucile Hamlin, the Krueger Foundation, Lexi and Robert Potamkin, Marco Spinner, and Joni Winston, without whom CBCT would not have the depth and reach that it does today.

Finally, we express much appreciation to His Holiness the Dalai Lama, whose vision to educate the heart and the mind, as well as to advocate for the importance of compassion in the world today, has been an ongoing inspiration for the Emory Compassion Center. His vision is expressed forcefully and eloquently in his talks and writings, which lay the foundation for a universal approach to compassion-based ethics grounded in science and reason. He has frequently called for the development of educational programs, such as CBCT and SEE Learning, that promote compassion and can be implemented across the world.

Notes

1   De Waal, F. B. M. (2009).

2   Begley, S. (2007).

3   Personal Reflections are offered through the Guide from past CBCT participants (with their permission). Some details have been altered to protect privacy.

4   Pace, T. W. W. et al. (2009); Pace, T. W. W. et al. (2010).

5   Mayo Clinic (2021).

6   Pace, T. W. W. et al. (2009); Pace, T. W. W. et al. (2013); Pace, T. W. W. et al. (2012); Reddy, S. et al. (2013); Titanji, B. K. et al. (2022).

7   Mascaro, J. et al. (2016); Lang, A. J. et al. (2017).

8   Mascaro, J. et al. (2016).

9   Lang, A. J. et al. (2017).

10 Reddy, S. et al. (2013).

11 Mascaro, J. et al. (2016); Desbordes, G. et al. (2012).

12 Mascaro, J. et al. (2012).

13 Titanji, B. K. et al. (2022); Gonzalez-Hernandez, E. et al. (2018); Sun, S. et al. (2019).

14 The Greater Good Science Center at UC Berkeley (2023); Pace, T. W. W. et al. (2009); Gilbert, P. et al. (2011).

15 Keltner, D. (2009).

16 Moodie, C. A. et al. (2020).

17 Siegel, D. J., & McNamara, S. (2008).

18 Ash, M., et al. (2021).

19 Goleman, D., & Senge, P. M. (2014).

20 Miller-Karas, E. (2015).

21 List adapted from https://peoria.medicine.uic.edu/wp-content/uploads/sites/8/2020/10/Resiliency-Building-Help-Now-Activities.pdf.

22 Lang, A.J. et al. (2017); Lang, A.J. et al. (2019).

23 Mascaro, J. et al. (2016); Aguilar-Raab, C. et al. (2018).

24 LoParo, D. et al. (2018).

25 Dodds, S. E. et al. (2015); Gonzalez-Hernandez, E. et al. (2018).

26 Beckes, L., & Coan, J. A. (2011).

27 Öner, S., & Gülgöz, S. (2018).

28 Ochsner, K. N., & Gross, J. J. (2008).

29 Klineberg, S. L., & Hertz, A. (2020).

30 Klimecki, O. M. et al. (2013).

31 Rowe, A. C. et al. (2020).

32 Moodie, C. A. et al. (2020).

33 Moodie, C. A. et al. (2020).

34 Lama, D., & Ekman, P. (2009).

35 Siegel, D. (2009).

36 Vaish, A. et al. (2008).

37 Ekman, P. (2007).

38 Terry, M. L., & Leary, M. R. (2011).

39 Moodie, C. A. et al. (2020).

40 This story comes from the ancient Buddhist tradition.

41 Niemiec, R. M. (2018).

42 Adapted from https://www.viacharacter.org/character-strengths.

43 Proyer, R. T. et al. (2015).

44 Niemiec, R. M. & McGrath, R. E. (2019).

45 Dahm, K. A. et al. (2015).

46 Neff, K. D., & Dahm, K. A. (2015).

47 Zhang, J. W., & Chen, S. (2016).

48 Ferlazzo, L. (2011).

49 Yousafzai, M. (2014).

50 Dahl, C. J. et al. (2020).

51 Shantideva, A., & Batchelor, S. (1992).

52 Hodges, S. D. et al. (2010)

53 Bloom, P. (2013).

54 Healy, P. (2016).

55 Bishop, B., & Cushing, R. G. (2009).

56 Riyad as-Salihin 236.

57 Dadisten-I-dinik 94,5.

58 Elder Hillel in Babylonian Talmud, Shabbat 31a.

59 Mahabharata 5:1517.

60 Gospel of Matthew 7:12.

61 Bahá'u'lláh, *Gleanings from the Writings of Bahá'u'lláh*, p. 127.

62 The Buddha, Udânavarga 5:18, trans. 1883:27.

63 Bhatti, A. B., & Haq, A. (2017).

64 Queen's University Belfast (2020).

65 Emmons, R. A. (2007).

66 De Waal, F. B. M. (2009).

67 Kowalski, R. M. (1996).

68 Brooks, D. (2020).

69 Shantideva (2006).

70 Eiseley, L. C. (1985).

71 Dunn, E. W. et al. (2008); Aknin, L. B. et al. (2012).

72 Black, W., & Living, R. (2004); Lum, T.Y., & Lightfoot, E. (2005).

73 Moll, J. et al. (2006).

74 Trzeciak, S., & Mazzarelli, A. (2019).

75 Trzeciak, S., & Mazzarelli, A. (2019).

76 Holt-Lunstad, J. et al. (2015).

77 Pirkei Avot 2:21

78 Halifax, J. (2018).

Glossary

adverse childhood experiences (ACES)   a set of potentially traumatic events that occur in childhood or adolescence. If left unaddressed, these may have a negative impact on long-term wellbeing in adulthood.

adversity   difficulties, obstacles, or challenges to flourishing or being in a healthy state, whether physical or psychological, and whether at an individual or collective level.

affective   pertaining to emotion or feeling, sometimes contrasted with cognitive.

affective empathy   sharing or mirroring the emotions of others in response to being in the presence of their emotions, typically at an automatic or unconscious level.

aha moment   the moment of realizing for oneself the relevance and importance of a truth that one previously did not understand or understood only superficially as received knowledge. See also: personalized insight, reappraisal.

appraisal   an evaluation of a situation (often as positive or negative), which can lead to an emotional response, especially if there is a high investment in the situation. See also: reappraisal.

attention   the mental process of focusing on or being aware of something; focus. In SEE Learning, this involves learning to attend especially to one's own inner states, to the presence of others, and to wider systems.

attention deployment   placing one's focus deliberately on a chosen object; one of the three cognitive strategies for regulating emotions.

attention training   structured methods for learning to attend to one's feelings, thoughts, and impulses with stability and clarity.

awareness   perceiving or knowing something external or internal to oneself. In CBCT and SEE Learning, awareness refers to first-person recognition and understanding of thoughts, sensations, and emotions on the personal level; coming to perceive and understand the emotions and needs of others on the social level; and recognizing interdependence and common humanity on the systems level.

basic human values   ethical principles that are found in all human societies that derive from common sense, common experience, and science, such as fairness, compassion, self-discipline, gratitude, generosity, and forgiveness.

behavior   how a person acts in their physical actions or speech.

bigger picture   a fuller or more complete view of an event or situation that includes multiple perspectives and is not limited to a single or narrow viewpoint.

body sensations   perception of the signals and information provided by the parts of the body through the nervous system. This can include the five basic senses (taste, touch, sight, sound, smell) and interoception. In CBCT and SEE Learning, discussion of body sensations is often focused on the senses of touch and interoception when exploring the practices of grounding and tracking. This is because those sensations are most strongly associated with emotions and awareness of emotions.

burnout   a state characterized by emotional and physical exhaustion, depersonalization, and perceived lack of efficacy, typically associated with prolonged experience of a difficult work environment.

CBCT   Cognitively Based Compassion Training; training developed at the Emory University Center for Contemplative Science and Compassion-Based Ethics that offers a method for adults to cultivate greater compassion, resilience, and wellbeing.

circle of concern   a group of individuals we care about. When someone is in our circle of concern, their life trajectory, their ups and downs, and their wellbeing matter to us.

cognition   the conscious and unconscious mental processes involved in thinking, perceiving, and reasoning. Examples include paying attention to something, learning something new, making decisions, processing language, sensing and perceiving stimuli, solving problems, and using memory. In some contexts, the term may refer more narrowly to processes of thinking, reasoning, and analysis.

cognitive   of or related to cognition.

cognitive empathy   taking the point of view of another person so that one is aware of their inner perspective and feelings; this is not the same as, nor does it require, mirroring or sharing those feelings. See also: affective empathy.

cognitive reappraisal   see reappraisal.

common humanity   the principle that all people share important similarities and are equal at a fundamental human level, alongside the reality that individuals and groups have unique identities. Similarities include: being born, growing, aging, and dying; wishing to have wellbeing and to avoid distress, loss, and heartache; having a body and emotions; requiring the help of others to grow and survive; and being vulnerable to forces beyond one's own control such as illness, natural disasters, genetic and epigenetic predispositions, societal structures, and cultural influences.

compassion   the warm-hearted concern, arising from witnessing the struggles or challenges of others, that wishes to see those struggles and challenges alleviated.

compassion fatigue   see empathic fatigue.

compassion-based ethics   an approach to ethics where basic human values such as compassion are derived from common sense, common experience, and science, rather than from a belief system or from a particular faith or religious tradition. This form of ethics—forcefully advocated by the Dalai Lama in many of his books and talks, often using the term "secular ethics"—aims to be compatible with individuals across cultures, nationalities, and faiths.

constructive   beneficial to oneself or to others; not harmful (often used in CBCT and SEE Learning to describe emotions and behaviors).

constructive perspectives   views that, because they align more with the full reality of a situation, are more likely to support the physical and psychological wellbeing of oneself and of others, and less likely to lead to harm.

contemplative practice   reflections and activities, including but not limited to meditation, that support the cultivation of basic human values, attention, introspection, balancing the body, wisdom, and other inner qualities conducive to wellbeing. In CBCT and SEE Learning, contemplative practices are always secular (non-religious) and are offered as an important technique for personalizing the content and embodying the understandings.

content knowledge   information that can be known and understood at an intellectual level, even before there is a strong feeling of its relevance to one's personal life or day-to-day experience. See also: personalized insight, aha moment.

critical insight   a personal recognition of something as true for oneself, whether this happens gradually or through a sudden realization (an *aha* moment). Repeated revisitation to and familiarization with a critical insight over time can lead to embodied understanding.

critical thinking analyzing, investigating, and questioning something for one-self using the best of one's resources. This is a central activity of CBCT and SEE Learning and can involve looking at a situation from multiple perspectives, journaling, meditating, collecting and considering available information, conversing and debating with others, and many other methods.

CRM® Community Resiliency Model; a program of six skills developed and offered by the Trauma Resource Institute aimed at helping individuals and communities re-set the natural balance of the nervous system.

dereification relating to the contents of the mind (thoughts, memories, feelings, etc.) as mental activities that are changing and fluid while retaining awareness that these mental contents are distinct from the more solid or permanent objects or events that they often reflect or represent.

destructive leading to harm to oneself or others, leading away from what is beneficial. In CBCT and SEE Learning, the term "destructive emotions" is sometimes used to describe harmful emotions and resulting behaviors.

discernment the capacity to analyze and judge accurately what is beneficial and what is harmful, especially in the bigger picture.

distraction an event or experience that pulls one's attention away from one's intended object of focus.

dysregulated a state in which the autonomic nervous system is out of balance, either favoring sympathetic or parasympathetic arousal, or swinging between the two in unhelpful ways, which can generate unwanted or harmful emotional states. Dysregulation can result after stress or trauma, but also from illness, diet, or environmental factors, and can make us more easily bumped out of the Zone of Wellbeing.

embodied understanding knowledge that has been internalized such that the learner's understanding is not temporary but has become a new disposition, a natural part of who they are and how they respond to their environment. Of the three levels of understanding in the pedagogical model of CBCT and SEE Learning, this is the deepest. However, embodied understanding can itself be deepened continuously.

emotion an affective state, such as anger, fear, sadness, or joy, that arises in one's mental life in response to perceiving and appraising an event. Typically, emotions include a motivation to act (or refrain from action) and are stronger the more one sees the event as salient to one's wellbeing. Emotions typically occur alongside related body sensations, though body sensations are typically localized in the body, while emotions invoke mental states like judgment and motivation and tend to want to prompt an action, even if that action is to retreat or to freeze.

emotion timeline a simplified diagram of the typical path of an unfolding emotional experience, from event to appraisal to emotion to behavior.

emotional hygiene behaviors designed to shape one's emotional life to promote long-term health and happiness (the same way as one promotes good physical health through practicing physical hygiene).

emotional intelligence the capacity to be aware of, understand, regulate, and express one's emotions, as well as being aware of and sensitive to the emotions of others.

empathic concern understanding the situation of another person (or people) and being concerned for their wellbeing. Empathic concern is naturally other-oriented, and in CBCT and SEE Learning, empathic concern means the same thing as compassion, though the term is typically used to denote a milder form. For a stronger form, please see engaged compassion.

empathic distress feeling overwhelmed or disturbed by the suffering of another person in a way that makes one self-oriented. Unlike empathic concern, which tends to prompt action to help others for their own sake, empathic distress is primarily concerned with alleviating one's own distress, and leads toward exhaustion and burnout.

empathic fatigue a state of emotional numbing that can arise from empathic distress; sometimes (confusingly) referred to as compassion fatigue.

empathy a broad term referring to the human (and more generally, mammalian) ability to understand and resonate with another being's emotions, experiences, needs, and perspectives. Empathy can be divided into roughly three types with distinct characteristics: affective empathy, cognitive empathy, and empathic concern.

empowering psychologically strengthening, leading to greater self-agency.

enduring capability a skill or type of knowledge that one can continue to return to, reflect upon, and more deeply embody throughout one's entire life. The learning objectives of CBCT and SEE Learning are summarized in a set of Enduring Capabilities.

engaged compassion a deep desire to see others gain freedom from their distress and struggles. Engaged compassion grows from viewing them with genuine warm-heartedness and a full awareness of what they are up against.

equity fairness and impartiality applied at both individual and systemic levels; an equity perspective seeks ways for every person to succeed to their greatest potential regardless of circumstances beyond their control.

ethical   having the quality of leading to one's own and others' long-term benefit and wellbeing, in a manner consistent with basic human values. This definition of ethics is sometimes called secular ethics, as it is intended to be meaningful for those who follow a religious tradition as well as those who do not.

ethical engagement   action that is intended to lead to one's own and others' long-term benefits and that does not violate basic human values (such as not harming or compromising the wellbeing of oneself or others).

ethics   moral principles or values that can help guide one's thoughts and actions for one's own and others' benefit.

familiarization   the process of deepening perspectives so that they become personalized and eventually embodied.

feeling   an emotion or physical sensation. In CBCT and SEE Learning, feeling is typically used as a broader term that includes both emotions and sensations.

flourishing   wellbeing of a person, community, or environment; the ever-deepening realization of one's potential.

forgiveness   seeing others' humanity and softening the anger or resentment we hold for them, even if we choose to powerfully condemn or oppose their harmful actions.

formal practice   deliberate mental exercises aimed at strengthening a particular skill or insight. Commonly referred to as meditation.

gratitude   an emotional response that comes from deeply recognizing and appreciating the ways one has received benefits from others. Gratitude is often accompanied by warm feelings toward those who have benefited oneself, as well as a wish to repay their kindness or pay it forward to others.

grounding   stabilizing the mind and nervous system by placing one's attention on the physical contact of one's body to an object, surface, or another part of one's body. Grounding is a key resilience skill in SEE Learning and CBCT and is always taught in conjunction with tracking.

growth mindset   the view that one's abilities and skills are not fixed but can be cultivated and improved based on effort.

harmful emotions   emotions that have the tendency to cause harm to oneself or others if they become too strong or are not transformed or managed in a productive way.

heedfulness   being cautious and careful about things that could cause problems for oneself or others. In CBCT and SEE Learning, this is used in particular to refer to being heedful of one's own mental and physical activities, such as the arising of destructive emotions.

Help Now! strategies   techniques for bringing the body's autonomic nervous system into a more regulated state when one is bumped out of, or about to be bumped out of, one's Zone of Wellbeing.

high zone   a state of hyper-arousal in the body and mind where one may feel anxiety, fear, anger, frustration, helplessness, or stress, and where one does not feel in control. In this state, one is not in the Zone of Wellbeing.

identification   perceiving others as similar to oneself based on shared characteristics, goals, activities, preferences, background, etc., typically accompanied by increased feelings of connection.

impermanence   the principle that things (including experiences and emotions) are not static, but are rather in a continual state of flux and change that unfolds due to the nature of cause and effect.

informal practice   ways in which we deliberately engage the skills and insights of CBCT and SEE Learning in our daily lives.

innate capacity   a biologically natural ability that one is born with the ability to develop, given the necessary circumstances.

insight activity   an activity designed to bring about personalized insight and/or embodied understanding of an Enduring Capability of CBCT or SEE Learning.

interconnectedness   the bond that exists between people based on common humanity and interdependence.

interdependence   the principle that objects and events arise from a multiplicity of other causes and conditions; therefore, people and events can be dependent on each other even across long distances or periods of time. This principle promotes an understanding that our lives do not exist in a vacuum and that there is an inherent relationship between ourselves and broader society. Interdependence is a key characteristic of systems, especially human societal systems, where one part of a system can impact several other parts through chains of causal relations.

interpersonal awareness   the ability to recognize our inherently social nature and attend to the presence of others and the roles they play in our lives.

lojong   "mind-training" tradition of Indo-Tibetan Buddhism with a focus on cultivating unbiased compassion.

love   the wish for another person to flourish and have the long-term causes of wellbeing. Genuine love is other-oriented, and not focused on what the other person can do for oneself. Love (wishing happiness for another) is the constant companion to compassion (wishing that another be free of suffering).

low zone   a state of hypo-arousal in the body and mind in which one may feel lethargic, sad, depressed, lonely, uninterested in activities, or lacking enthusiasm for life. When one is stuck in the low zone, one is not in the Zone of Wellbeing. However, one can use various strategies, such as resourcing, grounding, and Help Now! Strategies, to return to the Zone of Wellbeing.

map of the mind   a conceptual model of the mind and its mental states that can be used to help better navigate one's emotions and experiences. The map of the mind can at first be based on information presented by others, but over time it will gain complexity, subtlety, and usefulness as it is built on personal experience, observation, and critical thinking.

meta-awareness   awareness of awareness; being aware that thoughts, emotions, etc., are arising in one's mind and that one can notice and observe them.

mindful dialogue   a protocol for reflection and sharing in which one person asks a series of questions and listens attentively to another person, without comment or interruption, switching roles after a set period.

mindfulness   retaining something in one's mind and not forgetting it, getting distracted, or losing sight of it. Can be cultivated through attention training. Note that CBCT's and SEE Learning's definition of mindfulness differs from some popular definitions of mindfulness as non-judgmental present-moment awareness. See CBCT Module 3 for further explanation.

mindset   a fixed or habitual way of seeing the events of one's life.

monitoring awareness   the capacity and mental process of repeatedly observing and checking in on the activities of one's mind. This is important for noting dullness or distraction when cultivating attention, or for noticing destructive emotions as they arise so that they can be addressed, i.e., putting out a spark before it becomes a forest fire.

narrow views or perspectives   views that are out of alignment with reality, including biases, prejudices, false assumptions, misconceptions, unrealistic or exaggerated expectations, and projections.

needs   things that all human beings require in order to have wellbeing and to flourish, such as safety, sleep, nourishment, and healthy relationships.

negativity bias   noticing and recalling negative events more than positive events.

nurturing   supportive, kind, and protective. Noun form: nurturance.

nurturing moment   a recalled moment of feeling safe and secure (or safer and more secure), perhaps due to receiving support, kindness, or protection. Can be imaginary.

parasympathetic nervous system (PNS)   the part of the autonomic nervous system that relaxes body systems, such as breathing and heart rate, and activates systems like digestion. Sometimes referred to the "rest and digest" system in contrast to the "fight or flight" sympathetic nervous system.

perceived social isolation   a perceived state of being disconnected from others.

personalized insight   an insight into the nature of reality based on seeing the relevance to one's own lived experience. A felt sense of a truth that is deeper than a mere abstract or conceptual understanding.

perspective   how one views oneself, a situation, or others.

projection   a distorted interpretation of an event or situation; projections are often shaped by prior conditioning, which generates biases, assumptions, self-centeredness, or exaggerated expectations. CBCT and SEE Learning use this broader definition rather than the narrower one that is common in psychotherapy (a view or opinion about oneself that is unconsciously placed onto another person).

reappraisal   a shift from having one perspective on a situation or event to having a different perspective on that same situation or event.

received knowledge   knowledge based on instruction from others (such as teachers or books) or experiential learning, but before the knowledge has led to personalized insight; see content knowledge.

reciprocity   mutuality and fairness in exchanges between individuals or groups in which all parties act to benefit the others.

reflective practice   activities in which learners direct attention toward their inner experience in a sustained and structured way in order to develop deeper personal understanding and to gain familiarity and internalize desired skills or insights.

regulation of the nervous system   a healthy (homeostatic) balance between the two main arms of the autonomic nervous system—sympathetic and parasympathetic.

resilience   the ability to respond in a productive way to challenges, stress, threats, and unexpected surprises, which might otherwise destabilize a person or group. Resilience can be promoted at an individual level, an interpersonal level (within a group or community), a structural level (policies and institutions), and a cultural level (values, beliefs, and practices).

resilience-informed pedagogy a strengths-based approach to learning that recognizes that everyone has some level of resilience that has allowed them to survive in the face of life's stressors and traumas, and which can be strengthened further with knowledge and practice. CBCT and SEE Learning are based on resilience-based pedagogy.

resilient zone see Zone of Wellbeing.

resource any remembered or imagined event, person, place, object, or activity that one associates with greater safety, security, or wellbeing. See also: nurturing moment.

resourcing bringing a resource—such as a nurturing moment—to mind vividly so that the body responds with a greater sense of wellbeing. Resourcing works most reliably when combined with the tracking of sensations in the body.

restraint holding back from doing things that may harm oneself or others.

secular ethics a non-sectarian approach to universal ethics, based on common sense, common experience, and science, that can be acceptable to people of any or no religious faith. Secular ethics is the approach SEE Learning takes to ethics in education.

SEE Learning Social, Emotional and Ethical Learning; a program of the Emory University Center for Contemplative Science and Compassion-Based Ethics that provides a school-based curriculum for kids and young adults to cultivate greater compassion, resilience, and wellbeing.

self-agency the ability to intentionally direct one's thoughts and behavioral responses, no matter the situation.

self-awareness awareness of sensations, images, feelings, and thoughts, the patterns of our minds, and the impermanent and subjective nature of our mental experiences.

self-compassion an inner fortitude that fosters an enduring attitude of kindness toward the self, especially in the face of life's adversities, and a commitment to identify and alleviate the underlying causes of one's suffering.

self-distancing a cognitive strategy for regulating emotions in which one observes one's own mental activity without becoming entangled in it, neither repressing it nor inviting more. By allowing mental activity to arise and pass of its own accord, one can pause the automatic fanning of the flames of any emotional sparks that arise, thus reducing reactivity and allowing for more choice in one's response. Other terms for self-distancing are open monitoring and resting the mind in its natural state.

self-regulation   the ability to navigate one's emotions, nervous system, and behaviors to sustain an emotional balance that promotes wellbeing and minimizes causing harm to oneself or others.

sensation   see body sensations.

shift and stay   redirecting attention from a stimulus or sensation that is unpleasant toward one that is less unpleasant (shifting), and then keeping one's attention there for a few moments to reset or re-regulate the nervous system (staying). For example, redirecting attention from a part of the body that is painful to another part that is in less pain; or redirecting attention from a thought or worry to something that is less distressing, such as a resource, an external sensation like sights or sounds, or a part of the body in contact with an object.

social intelligence   the ability to be aware of others and relate to them in a positive and productive way; the ability to understand human interactions on individual and collective levels.

stress   physical or emotional strain or tension resulting from adverse or very demanding circumstances. Mild to moderate acute stress is part of everyday life, but because severe and chronic stress are damaging to physical and emotional health, CBCT and SEE Learning offer resilience strategies to combat stress on individual and systemic levels.

subjectivity   the way an individual perceives and interprets the world; first-person perspective.

sympathetic nervous system (SNS)   the part of the autonomic nervous system that prepares the body for activity and danger, changing muscle tone and heart rate and turning off the body's systems that help it relax and rest. The SNS is called the body's fight or flight system, although it is activated by ordinary daily activities like waking up, standing, and breathing. Excessive stress from trauma or prolonged threat can overtax the SNS, resulting in dysregulation of the autonomic nervous system.

systems thinking   the ability to understand, model, and analyze how objects and events share complex networks of causality with other objects and events, following the principle of interdependence.

tenderness   a warm feeling of closeness or endearment. Sometimes referred to as warm-heartedness.

tracking   bringing conscious awareness to inner sensations in the body as they unfold. This ability to "read" sensations in the body, using interoception, leads to the cultivation of body literacy: understanding the signals of our nervous system and how they relate to our emotions and wellbeing. This helps us remain in, expand, or go deeper into our resilient zone.

trauma   a natural response to a stressful or threatening event (or series of events) that overwhelms the person's nervous system and undermines its sense of safety, leading to lasting but not necessarily permanent impacts on the body and mind. CBCT and SEE Learning take the resilience-informed approach that adversity is not destiny, and people can learn to build upon their natural resilience to trauma and adversity to cultivate greater wellbeing.

trauma-informed   guided by an understanding of how stress and trauma impact individuals' and communities' emotional and physical life, learning, and wellbeing. CBCT and SEE Learning rely on trauma-informed peda-gogy, which includes creating an educational environment that supports a sense of belonging and promotes individual and collective resilience.

triple focus   three broad areas that require attention in order create greater flourishing: the inner (personal) domain, the other (interpersonal) domain, and the outer (systems level) domain. This term was coined by Daniel Goleman and Peter Senge.

values   what an individual or society esteems and deems most important; principles that underlie and orient an individual's or a society's actions and aspirations.

warm-hearted   see tenderness.

wellbeing   a state of being happy, healthy, and satisfied.

zone of wellbeing (ZOW)   a state of wellbeing and balanced regulation of the body and mind. In this state, a person feels in control of their actions, is able to assimilate new information or perspectives, and is able to make decisions and take actions that are constructive. If not in the Zone of Wellbeing, one does not feel in control of one's behavior and cannot easily take in new information, and one's decisions and actions are more likely to be harmful or destructive. Also known as the resilient zone or OK Zone. See also: low zone, high zone.

Bibliography

Aguilar-Raab, C., Jarczok, M., Warth, M., Stoffel, M., Winter, F., Tieck, M., Berg, J., Negi, L., Harrison, T., Pace, T., & Ditzen, B. (2018). Enhancing social interaction in depression (SIDE study): Protocol of a randomized controlled trial on the effects of a cognitively based compassion training (CBCT) for couples. *BMJ Open*, 8(9)., e020448. https://doi.org/10.1136/bmjopen-2017-020448

Aknin, L. B., Hamlin, J. K., & Dunn, E. W. (2012). Giving leads to happiness in young children. *PLoS ONE*, 7(6), e39211. https://doi.org/10.1371/journal.pone.0039211

Ash, M., Harrison, T., Pinto, M., DiClemente, R., & Negi, L. T. (2021). A model for cognitively-based compassion training: Theoretical underpinnings and proposed mechanisms. *Social Theory & Health*, 19(1), 43–67. https://doi.org/10.1057/s41285-019-00124-x

Beckes, L., & Coan, J. A. (2011). Social baseline theory: The role of social proximity in emotion and economy of action: Social baseline theory. *Social and Personality Psychology Compass*, 5(12), 976–988. https://doi.org/10.1111/j.1751-9004.2011.00400

Begley, S. (2007). *Train Your Mind, Change Your Brain: How a New Science Reveals Our Extraordinary Potential to Transform Ourselves*. New York: Ballantine Books.

Bhatti, A. B., & Haq, A. (2017). The pathophysiology of perceived social isolation: Effects on health and mortality. *Cureus*, 9(1), e994. https://doi.org/10.7759/cureus.994

Bishop, B., & Cushing, R. G. (2009). *The Big Sort: Why the Clustering of Like-Minded America Is Tearing Us Apart*. Boston: Houghton Mifflin Harcourt.

Black, W., & Living, R. (2004). Volunteerism as an occupation and its relationship to health and wellbeing. *British Journal of Occupational Therapy*, 67(12), 526–532. https://doi.org/10.1177/030802260406701202

Bloom, P. (2013). *Just Babies: The Origins of Good and Evil* (First edition). New York: Crown Publishers.

Brooks, D. (2020). *The Second Mountain: The Quest for a Moral Life.* New York: Random House.

Dahl, C. J., Wilson-Mendenhall, C. D., & Davidson, R. J. (2020). The plasticity of well-being: A training-based framework for the cultivation of human flourishing. *Proceedings of the National Academy of Sciences,* 117(51), 32197–32206. https://doi.org/10.1073/pnas.2014859117

Dahm, K. A., Meyer, E. C., Neff, K. D., Kimbrel, N. A., Gulliver, S. B., & Morissette, S. B. (2015). Mindfulness, self-compassion, posttraumatic stress disorder symptoms, and functional disability in U. S. Iraq and Afghanistan war veterans: Self-compassion and mindfulness in U. S. war veterans. *Journal of Traumatic Stress,* 28(5), 460–464. https://doi.org/10.1002/jts.22045

De Waal, F. B. M. (2009). *The Age of Empathy: Nature's Lessons for a Kinder Society* (First paperback edition). New York: Three Rivers Press.

Desbordes, G., Negi, L. T., Pace, T. W., Wallace, B. A., Raison, C. L., & Schwartz. E. L. (2012). Effects of mindful-attention and compassion meditation training on amygdala response to emotional stimuli in an ordinary, non-meditative state. *Frontiers in Human Neuroscience,* 6, 292. https://doi.org/10.3389/fnhum.2012.00292

Dodds, S. E., Pace, T. W. W., Bell, M. L., Fiero, M., Negi, L. T., Raison, C. L., & Weihs, K. L. (2015). Feasibility of Cognitively-Based Compassion Training (CBCT) for breast cancer survivors: a randomized, wait list controlled pilot study. *Support Care Cancer,* 23(12), 3599–3608. https://doi.org/10.1007/s00520-015-2888-1

Dunn, E. W., Aknin, L. B., & Norton, M. I. (2008). Spending money on others promotes happiness. *Science,* 319(5870), 1687–1688. https://doi.org/10.1126/science.1150952

Earhart, A. (2017, August 21). Quotes by Amelia Earhart. https://www.ameliaearhart.com/quotes/

Eiseley, L. C. (1985). *The Unexpected Universe.* New York: Harcourt Brace Jovanovich.

Ekman, P. (2007). *Emotions Revealed: Recognizing Faces and Feelings to Improve Communication and Emotional Life* (Second edition). New York: Owl Books.

Emmons, R. A. (2007). *Thanks! How the New Science of Gratitude Can Make You Happier.* Boston: Houghton Mifflin Harcourt.

Ferlazzo, L. (2011, June 11). What is the accurate Edison quote on learning from failure? Larry Ferlazzo's Websites of the Day. https://larryferlazzo.edublogs.org/2011/06/11/what-is-the-accurate-edison-quote-on-learning-from-failure/

Gilbert, P., McEwan, K., Matos, M., & Rivis, A. (2011). Fears of compassion: Development of three self-report measures. *Psychology and Psychotherapy: Theory, Research and Practice,* 84(3), 239–255. https://doi.org/10.1348/147608310x526511

Goleman, D., & Senge, P. M. (2014). *The Triple Focus: A New Approach to Education* (First edition). Florence, MA: More Than Sound.

Gonzalez-Hernandez, E., Romero, R., Campos, D., Burychka, D., Diego-Pedro, R., Baños, R., Negi, L., & Cebolla, A. (2018). Cognitively-Based Compassion Training (CBCT) in breast cancer survivors: A randomized clinical trial study. *Integrative Cancer Therapies*, 17(3), 684–696. https://doi.org/10.1177/1534735418772095

Graham, A. (2022, November 18). Tis the season for an attitude of gratitude. *Las Cruces Sun News*. https://www.lcsun-news.com/story/life/2022/11/18/maintaining-balance-tis-the-season-for-an-attitude-of-gratitude/69653974007/

The Greater Good Science Center at UC Berkeley. (2023). The science of a meaningful life. https://greatergood.berkeley.edu/

Halifax, J. (2018). *Standing at the Edge: Finding Freedom Where Fear and Courage Meet*. New York: Flatiron Books.

Healy, P. (2016, August 18). Confirmation bias: How it affects your organization. HBS Online Business Insights Blog. https://online.hbs.edu/blog/post/confirmation-bias-how-it-affects-your-organization-and-how-to-overcome-it

Hodges, S. D., Kiel, K. J., Kramer, A. D. I., Veach, D., & Villanueva, B. R. (2010). Giving birth to empathy: The effects of similar experience on empathic accuracy, empathic concern, and perceived empathy. *Personality and Social Psychology Bulletin*, 36(3), 398–409. https://doi.org/10.1177/0146167209350326

Holt-Lunstad, J., Smith, T. B., Baker, M., Harris, T., & Stephenson, D. (2015). Loneliness and social isolation as risk factors for mortality: A meta-analytic review. *Perspectives on Psychological Science*, 10(2), 227–237. https://doi.org/10.1177/1745691614568352

Keltner, D. (2009). *Born to Be Good: The Science of a Meaningful Life* (First edition). New York: W.W. Norton & Co.

Klimecki, O. M., Leiberg, S., Lamm, C., & Singer, T. (2013). Functional neural plasticity and associated changes in positive affect after compassion training. *Cerebral Cortex*, 23(7), 1552–1561. https://doi.org/10.1093/cercor/bhs142

Klineberg, S. L., & Hertz, A. (2020). *Prophetic City: Houston on the Cusp of a Changing America* (First hardcover edition). New York: Avid Reader Press.

Kowalski, R. M. (1996). Complaints and complaining: Functions, antecedents, and consequences. *Psychological Bulletin*, 119(2), 179–196. https://doi.org/10.1037/0033-2909.119.2.179

Lama, D., & Ekman, P. (2009). *Emotional Awareness: Overcoming the Obstacles to Psychological Balance and Compassion*. New York: Henry Holt & Co.

Lang, A. J., Casmar, P., Hurst, S., Harrison, T., Golshan, S., Good, R., Essex, M., & Negi, L. (2017). Compassion meditation for veterans with posttraumatic stress disorder (PTSD): A nonrandomized study. *Mindfulness*, 11(1), 63–74. https://doi.org/10.1007/s12671-017-0866-z

Lang, A. J., Malaktaris, A. L., Casmar, P., Baca, S. A., Golshan, S., Harrison, T., & Negi, L. (2019). Compassion meditation for posttraumatic stress disorder in veterans: A randomized proof of concept study. *Journal of Traumatic Stress*, 32(2), 299–309. https://doi.org/10.1002/jts.22397

LoParo, D., Mack, S. A., Patterson, B., Negi, L. T., & Kaslow, N. J. (2018). The efficacy of Cognitively-Based Compassion Training for African American suicide attempters. *Mindfulness*, 9(6), 1941–1954. https://doi.org/10.1007/s12671-018-0940-1

Lum, T. Y., & Lightfoot, E. (2005). The effects of volunteering on the physical and mental health of older people. *Research on Aging*, 27(1), 31–55. https://doi.org/10.1177/0164027504271349

Marcus, Y et al. Mascaro, J., Rilling, J., Negi, L. T., & Raison, C. (2012). Compassion meditation enhances empathic accuracy and related neural activity. *Social Cognitive and Affective Neuroscience*, 8(1), 48–55. https://doi.org/10.1093/scan/nss095

Mascaro, J. S., Kelley, S., Darcher, A., Negi, L. T., Worthman, C., Miller, A., & Raison, C. (2016). Meditation buffers medical student compassion from the deleterious effects of depression. *Journal of Positive Psychology*, 13(2), 133–142. https://doi.org/10.1080/17439760.2016.1233348

Mayo Clinic. (2021, July 8). Chronic stress puts your health at risk. https://www.mayoclinic.org/healthy-lifestyle/stress-management/in-depth/stress/art-20046037

Miller-Karas, E. (2015). *Building Resilience to Trauma: The Trauma and Community Resiliency Models*. New York: Routledge.

Moll, J., Krueger, F., Zahn, R., Pardini, M., De Oliveira-Souza, R., & Grafman, J. (2006). Human fronto–mesolimbic networks guide decisions about charitable donation. *Proceedings of the National Academy of Sciences*, 103(42), 15623–15628. https://doi.org/10.1073/pnas.0604475103

Moodie, C. A., Suri, G., Goerlitz, D. S., Mateen, M. A., Sheppes, G., McRae, K., Lakhan-Pal, S., Thiruchselvam, R., & Gross, J. J. (2020). The neural bases of cognitive emotion regulation: The roles of strategy and intensity. *Cognitive, Affective, & Behavioral Neuroscience*, 20(2), 387–407. https://doi.org/10.3758/s13415-020-00775-8

Neff, K. D., & Dahm, K. A. (2015). Self-compassion: What it is, what it does, and how it relates to mindfulness. In B. D. Ostafin, M. D. Robinson, & B. P. Meier (Eds.), *Handbook of Mindfulness and Self-Regulation* (pp. 121–137). New York: Springer. https://doi.org/10.1007/978-1-4939-2263-5_10

Niemiec, R. M. (2018). *Character Strengths Interventions: A Field Guide for Practitioners*. Göttingen: Hogrefe Publishing.

Niemiec, R. M., & McGrath, R. E. (2019). *The Power of Character Strengths:*

Appreciate and Ignite Your Positive Personality. Cincinnati: VIA Institute on Character.

Ochsner, K. N., & Gross, J. J. (2008). Cognitive emotion regulation: Insights from social cognitive and affective neuroscience. *Current Directions in Psychological Science*, 17(2), 153–158. https://doi.org/10.1111/j.1467-8721.2008.00566.x

Öner, S., & Gülgöz, S. (2018). Autobiographical remembering regulates emotions: A functional perspective. *Memory*, 26(1), 15–28. https://doi.org/10.1080/09658211.2017.1316510

Pace, T. W. W., Negi, L. T., Adame, D. D., Cole, S. P., Sivilli, T. I., Brown, T. D., Issa, M. J., & Raison, C. L. (2009). Effect of compassion meditation on neuroendocrine, innate immune and behavioral responses to psychosocial stress. *Psychoneuroendocrinology*, 34(1), 87–98. https://doi.org/10.1016/j.psyneuen.2008.08.011

Pace, T. W. W., Negi, L. T., Dodson-Lavelle, B., Ozawa-de Silva, B., Reddy, S. D., Cole, S. P., Danese, A., Craighead, L. W., & Raison, C. L. (2013). Engagement with Cognitively-Based Compassion Training is associated with reduced salivary C-reactive protein from before to after training in foster care program adolescents. *Psychoneuroendocrinology*, 38(2), 294–299. https://doi.org/10.1016/j.psyneuen.2012.05.019

Pace, T., Negi, L., Donaldson-Lavelle, B., Ozawa-de Silva, B., Reddy, S., Cole, S., Craighead, L., & Raison, C. (2012). Cognitively-Based Compassion Training reduces peripheral inflammation in adolescents in foster care with high rates of early life adversity. *BMC Complementary and Alternative Medicine*, 12(Suppl 1), 175. https://doi.org/10.1186%2F1472-6882-12-S1-P175

Pace, T. W. W., Negi, L. T., Sivilli, T. I., Issa, M. J., Cole, S. P., Adame, D. D., & Raison, C. L. (2010). Innate immune, neuroendocrine and behavioral responses to psychosocial stress do not predict subsequent compassion meditation practice time. *Psychoneuroendocrinology*, 35(2), 310–315. https://doi.org/10.1016/j.psyneuen.2009.06.008

Proyer, R. T., Gander, F., Wellenzohn, S., & Ruch, W. (2015). Strengths-based positive psychology interventions: a randomized placebo-controlled online trial on long-term effects for a signature strengths- vs. a lesser strengths-intervention. *Frontiers in Psychology*, 6, 456. https://doi.org/10.3389/fpsyg.2015.00456

Queens University Belfast. (2020, April 27). Coronavirus and the new appreciation of teachers. https://www.qub.ac.uk/coronavirus/analysis-commentary/coronavirus-new-appreciation-of-teachers/

Reddy, S., Negi, L., Dodson-Lavelle, B., Ozawa-de Silva, B., Pace, T., Cole, S., Raison, C., & Craighead, L. (2013). Cognitive-based compassion training: A promising prevention strategy for at-risk adolescents. *Journal of Child and Family Studies*, 22(2), 219–230. http://dx.doi.org/10.1007/s10826-012-9571-7

Rowe, A. C., Gold, E. R., & Carnelley, K. B. (2020). The effectiveness of attachment security priming in improving positive affect and reducing negative affect: A systematic review. *International Journal of Environmental Research and Public Health*, 17(3), 968. https://doi.org/10.3390/ijerph17030968

Shantideva. (2006). Chapter 6: Patience. In *The Way of the Bodhisattva: A Translation of the Bodhicharyāvatāra* (Second edition, revised). Boulder, CO: Shambhala.

Shantideva, A., & Batchelor, S. (1992). Library of Tibetan Works and Archives.

Siegel, D. (2009). *Mindsight: The New Science of Personal Transformation*. New York: Bantam Books.

Siegel, D. J., & McNamara, S. (2008). *The Neurobiology of "We": How Relationships, the Mind, and the Brain Interact to Shape Who We Are* (Unabridged). Louisville, CO: Sounds True.

Sun, S., Pickover, A. M., Goldberg, S. B., Bhimji, J., Nguyen, J. K., Evans, A. E., Patterson, B., & Kaslow, N. J. (2019). For whom does Cognitively Based Compassion Training (CBCT) work? An analysis of predictors and moderators among African American suicide attempters. *Mindfulness*, 10(11), 2327–2340. https://doi.org/10.1007/s12671-019-01207-6

Terry, M. L., & Leary, M. R. (2011). Self-compassion, self-regulation, and health. *Self and Identity*, 10(3), 352–362. https://doi.org/10.1080/15298868.2011.558404

Titanji, B. K., Tejani, M., Farber, E. W., Mehta, C. C., Pace, T. W., Meagley, K., Gavegnano, C., Harrison, T., Kokubun, C. W., Negi, S. D., Schinazi, R. F., & Marconi, V. C. (2022). Cognitively Based Compassion Training for HIV immune nonresponders—An attention-placebo randomized controlled trial. *Journal of Acquired Immune Deficiency Syndromes*, 89(3), 340–348. https://doi.org/10.1097/QAI.0000000000002874

Trzeciak, S., & Mazzarelli, A. (2019). *Compassionomics: The Revolutionary Scientific Evidence That Caring Makes a Difference*. Pensacola, FL: Studer Group.

Vaish, A., Grossmann, T., & Woodward, A. (2008). Not all emotions are created equal: The negativity bias in social-emotional development. *Psychological Bulletin*, 134(3), 383–403. https://doi.org/10.1037/0033-2909.134.3.383

Yousafzai, M. (2014). Malala's story. Malala Fund. https://malala.org/malalas-story

Zhang, J. W., & Chen, S. (2016). Self-compassion promotes personal improvement from regret experiences via acceptance. *Personality and Social Psychology Bulletin*, 42(2), 244–258. https://doi.org/10.1177/0146167215623271

ABOUT THE AUTHOR

Lobsang Tenzin Negi, PhD is the founding director of the Center for Contemplative Science and Compassion-Based Ethics (Emory Compassion Center) and a professor in the Department of Religion at Emory University. Dr. Negi's research brings his deep knowledge of Indo-Tibetan Buddhist and contemporary scientific perspectives together to study the relationship between emotions and wellbeing. A former Tibetan Buddhist monk for 27 years, Dr. Negi received his Geshe Lharampa degree after completing his studies at Drepung Loseling Monastery and then earned his doctorate at Emory University. He is also the founder and spiritual director of Drepung Loseling Monastery in Atlanta, United States. As Executive Director of the Emory Compassion Center, he directs the higher education programming, the CBCT® program, the Emory-Tibet Science Initiative, which integrates modern science and contemplative monastic education, and SEE Learning® (Social, Emotional and Ethical Learning), a K-12 educational framework and curriculum.

Guided by the vision of a compassion and ethical world for all, the **Emory Compassion Center** promotes human flourishing by developing educational programs, facilitating dialogue, and engaging in research.

The **Compassion Shift**® is an initiative of the center to advance a global culture of compassion through two educational programs – CBCT® for adults and SEE Learning® for children. This initiative aims to expand and make these innovative research-based programs accessible to people across the globe and especially to those working in the critical areas of education, business, healthcare, and mental health.

Learning And Practicing CBCT With Others

Launched in 2025, **Compassion U**™ is the digital learning platform designed to make CBCT available worldwide. Compassion U delivers compassion training courses through cutting-edge e-learning experiences coupled with live sessions facilitated by certified teachers. Tailored versions of the course are also available for those in specialized professions, including education, healthcare, business and leadership, and mental health. All courses provide the full CBCT experience and any of them can serve as the first step for those interested in applying to Emory's CBCT Teacher Certification program. Compassion U provides a free compassion community for connecting with others and a free overview of the basic course.

COMPASSIONU.APP

www.ingramcontent.com/pod-product-compliance
Lightning Source LLC
Chambersburg PA
CBHW081530120626
46550CB00009B/2668